Mobilizing Music in Wartime British Film

THE OXFORD MUSIC / MEDIA SERIES

Daniel Goldmark, Series Editor

Tuning In: American Narrative Television Music
Ron Rodman

Special Sound: The Creation and Legacy of the BBC Radiophonic Workshop
Louis Niebur

Seeing Through Music: Gender and Modernism in Classic Hollywood Film Scores
Peter Franklin

An Eye for Music: Popular Music and the Audiovisual Surreal
John Richardson

Playing Along: Digital Games, YouTube, and Virtual Performance
Kiri Miller

Sounding the Gallery: Video and the Rise of Art-Music
Holly Rogers

Composing for the Red Screen: Prokofiev and Soviet Film
Kevin Bartig

Saying It with Songs: Popular Music and the Coming of Sound to Hollywood Cinema
Katherine Spring

We'll Meet Again: Musical Design in the Films of Stanley Kubrick
Kate McQuiston

Occult Aesthetics: Synchronization in Sound Film
K. J. Donnelly

Sound Play: Video Games and the Musical Imagination
William Cheng

Sounding American: Hollywood, Opera, and Jazz
Jennifer Fleeger

Mismatched Women: The Siren's Song Through the Machine
Jennifer Fleeger

Robert Altman's Soundtracks: Film, Music and Sound from M*A*S*H *to* A Prairie Home Companion
Gayle Sherwood Magee

Back to the Fifties: Nostalgia, Hollywood Film, and Popular Music of the Seventies and Eighties
Michael D. Dwyer

The Early Film Music of Dmitry Shostakovich
Joan Titus

Making Music in Selznick's Hollywood
Nathan Platte

Hearing Haneke: The Sound Tracks of a Radical Auteur
Elsie Walker

Unlimited Replays: Video Games and Classical Music
William Gibbons

Hollywood Harmony: Musical Wonder and the Sound of Cinema
Frank Lehman

French Musical Culture and the Coming of Sound Cinema
Hannah Lewis

Theories of the Soundtrack
James Buhler

Through the Looking Glass: John Cage and Avant-Garde Film
Richard H. Brown

Cinesonidos: Film Music and National Identity During Mexico's Época de Oro
Jacqueline Avila

Sound Design Is the New Score: Theory, Aesthetics, and Erotics of the Integrated Soundtrack
Danijela Kulezic-Wilson

Rock Star/Movie Star: Power and Performance in Cinematic Rock Stardom
Landon Palmer

The Presence of the Past: Temporal Experience and the New Hollywood Soundtrack
Daniel Bishop

Metafilm Music in Jean-Luc Godard's Cinema
Michael Baumgartner

Acoustic Profiles: A Sound Ecology of the Cinema
Randolph Jordan

Four Ways of Hearing Video Game Music
Michiel Kamp

Defining Cinema: Rouben Mamoulian and Hollywood Film Style, 1929–1957
Michael Slowik

Mobilizing Music in Wartime British Film
Heather Wiebe

Mobilizing Music in Wartime British Film

HEATHER WIEBE

OXFORD
UNIVERSITY PRESS

Oxford University Press is a department of the University of Oxford. It furthers the University's objective of excellence in research, scholarship, and education by publishing worldwide. Oxford is a registered trade mark of Oxford University Press in the UK and certain other countries.

Published in the United States of America by Oxford University Press
198 Madison Avenue, New York, NY 10016, United States of America.

CIP data is on file at the Library of Congress

ISBN 978-0-19-763172-0 (pbk.)
ISBN 978-0-19-763171-3 (hbk.)

DOI: 10.1093/oso/9780197631713.001.0001

Paperback printed by Marquis Book Printing, Canada
Hardback printed by Bridgeport National Bindery, Inc., United States of America

Contents

Figures

Acknowledgments

This project has been with me for a long time, in its various forms. It started as a set of side projects, and it was only with some trepidation that I finally decided it needed to be a book, which then, of course, took much longer than expected. The book was mostly drafted by 2020, but living in London as it shut down that year suddenly changed my relationship to the material, making it much more immediate in various ways and causing me to rethink a number of assumptions about what World War Two London might have felt like. My wartime subjects were also good companions, populating an empty cityscape—as when I realized that David Lean used to live in the forbidding Thames-side building I'd been walking past every day—and giving me something to think about besides the never-ending quest for a Sainsbury's delivery slot. In some ways, it's hard to let them go.

A book with as long and halting a gestation as this incurs many debts—so many that I can't possibly recognize them all here. But I want to begin where the project did, with intellectual debts. David Rosen introduced me to *Listen to Britain* in a wonderful talk given at a Stanford film music conference in the early 2000s; the work of Peter Franklin and Ivan Raykoff, which I encountered around the same time, also had a formative influence on this project. In the later stages of writing, discovering Kent Puckett's work on wartime British film (thanks to Kate Guthrie) injected much-needed new life into my thinking.

This book has seen me through many institutional contexts, but it is mainly a product of my time at King's College London (2013–2022) and is deeply indebted to my wonderful colleagues and students there. Roger Parker has read and commented on more instantiations of these chapters over the years than I care to remember. I'm sure I would have given up on this project a long time ago without his support and encouragement. I'm grateful to Martin Stokes, Matthew Head, Andy Fry, Ditlev Rindom, Gavin Williams, Kate Guthrie, Harriet Boyd Bennett, Sue Daniels, and Giles Masters for their engagement and helpful thoughts at crucial moments. I have also taught some of this material to undergraduate and master's students at King's, and their thoughts and observations over the years have informed my thinking in myriad ways.

Sarah Collins facilitated a trip to the University of Western Australia, to visit the Eileen Joyce Collection at its Callaway Centre Archive—a trip that ended up being one of the most enjoyable and memorable stages of this project, thanks to Sarah. I'm also indebted to librarians and archivists at BFI Special Collections and the National Archives of the UK, and most recently at the University of Notre Dame. I'm grateful for feedback from my anonymous readers at Oxford University Press, and also to Norm Hirschy, for his support and immense patience throughout this process. At Notre Dame, new colleagues also provided helpful feedback in the final stages of editing, as (further afield) did Maria Fuchs and David Gutkin. Matthew MacLellan came to the rescue with his careful and attentive indexing.

This book would never have been written without the support of a Research Fellowship from The Leverhulme Trust, which allowed me a year of leave. I'm also grateful to King's for financial support for research, especially a grant from the College of Arts and Humanities that enabled my trip to Australia. A final brief research trip and the indexing of this book were both supported by grants from the Institute for Scholarship in the Liberal Arts, College of Arts and Letters, University of Notre Dame. I also want to thank Taylor & Francis for permission to reuse some of the material in Chapter 1, which is derived in part from an article published in *Sound Studies*.[1]

Finally, I'd like to acknowledge some institutions that gave me space to think and write when that was hard to find, especially the Royal Foundation of St. Katherine in Limehouse and the Whitechapel public library (or "Idea Store," as it's called), where it was always (or at least usually) more inspiring than distracting to work alongside students studying for exams, tutors patiently explaining the basics of resume writing, adults taking introductory computing classes, and fellow lost souls toiling away on their own solitary projects. My neighbors at Trinity Green (especially the inspiring Joy and Paul) provided an invaluable community. Most of all, I'm grateful to my family in Canada for their abiding support, and to Arman Schwartz, for always believing I had something to say with this strange little book.

[1] Heather Wiebe, "Morale as Sonic Force: *Listen to Britain* and Total War," *Sound Studies* 7, no. 1 (2021): 24–41, http://www.tandfonline.com/10.1080/20551940.2019.1649230.

Introduction

The 1941 film *Dangerous Moonlight* opens with a kind of musical cure. The great Polish pianist Stefan Radetzky, injured while flying in combat, is in a London hospital. Amid the sounds of bombing—the film was both made and set during the Blitz—he mechanically bangs out clusters on his piano, all memory and identity gone. His doctor observes, "If we could get him better, I should feel that we'd *done* something for the world, something for . . . well you know what I mean."[1] Before joining the Royal Air Force's new Polish squadrons, Radetzky had toured incessantly, performing his Rachmaninoff-style *Warsaw Concerto* to raise funds for the war effort. Now he is rendered useless, another casualty. But music will come to the rescue, reanimating him and restoring him to the world. When he suddenly begins to play his concerto once more, his memory flooding back, his doctor comments hopefully, "Perhaps that music will bring back a lot of things."

Radetzky is one of many pianists who show up in wartime British films, beleaguered but playing on. In these films' frequent recourse to art music and musicians, they call on some familiar tropes, casting music as spiritual sustenance and consolation in wartime or as building morale and solidarity. As this episode suggests, though, these films also probe a more elaborate set of concerns with music's efficacy, with its power to *do* things in the world. In *Dangerous Moonlight*, music is something that can be mobilized for war. At the same time, it stands for what survives war and stands apart from it. The tension between these two positions is key to this book.

In *Mobilizing Music*, I trace a preoccupation with art music and total war that animates 1940s British films, from documentary shorts and colonial propaganda to melodrama and "woman's pictures." Despite their generic differences, these films engaged in an elaborate dialogue with each other and with British musical culture, drawing on the same musicians, institutions, and trends and

[1] *Dangerous Moonlight*, dir. Brian Desmond Hurst, RKO Radio Pictures, 1941 (Odeon Entertainment, 2010, DVD).

Mobilizing Music in Wartime British Film. Heather Wiebe, Oxford University Press. © Oxford University Press 2024.
DOI: 10.1093/oso/9780197631713.003.0001

feeding back into concert culture itself. (The fact that the British film industry, unlike Hollywood, was based in the same city as its music industry resulted in a peculiar intimacy between film and performance culture, and a distinctive realism in cinematic representation of musical life.) In prestige films such as *Brief Encounter* and *The Red Shoes* but also in largely forgotten ephemera, music is persistently given a central role in the action, to the extent that it becomes an agent itself. These films are driven by questions around the efficacy of art music, not just in the conventional sense of uplift or morale-building, but also as a sonic force acting on bodies, minds, and materials—as a resource to be mobilized or demobilized. Their elaborations of these questions are in some ways specific to World War Two Britain, but they also provide an illuminating perspective on the efficacy of music more broadly, and on more contemporary pressures on the arts to be useful and productive.

In their concerns with music and wartime life away from the battlefront, these films also offer insight into the affective experience of war—not just as violence and trauma, but also as everyday boredom and melancholy, as loneliness, helplessness, and disappointment. To mobilize art music (especially the Late Romanticism at issue in most of these films) is to take something that seems most outside war—in its lack of practical use, its associations with emotional excess and interiority—and bring it within war's totalizing grasp. In many ways, I suggest, the problems of mobilizing music and mobilizing women (and other subjects deemed less "useful" or productive) are overlapping ones in these films. Most of all, they show how music was used to test the limits of "total war," and to conceptualize its new reach into all corners of life.

Total War

In recent years, scholars of World War Two literature and film have looked increasingly to the concept of "total war," using it to unpack subtle shifts in form and aesthetics that might seem peripheral to conflict. Literary critic Patrick Deer suggests that not only was culture transformed "into an instrument of warfare" in World War One and Two Britain, but that writers also struggled "to capture their own sense of the totality of modern war."[2] In his study of

[2] Patrick Deer, *Culture in Camouflage: War, Empire, and Modern British Literature* (New York: Oxford University Press, 2016), 5.

wartime British cinema, Kent Puckett suggests that its foregrounding of cinematic style was a way of resisting "the concept of totality, calling attention to the particular and the uncounted as political, ethical, and aesthetic values."[3]

For these critics, the "totality" of total war and its reach into every area of cultural life are crucial features. As they observe, though, the term "total war" can carry a confusing variety of meanings. According to the literary critic Paul Saint-Amour, "total war" is often understood as the loss of limits on violence itself, culminating in the genocide and nuclear attacks of World War Two.[4] Relatedly, the term can refer to the erosion of distinctions between combatants and civilians as legitimate objects of attack, particularly under the conditions of aerial bombardment, a defining new feature of early twentieth-century warfare and a major trope in discussions of total war. Sometimes, as Saint-Amour suggests, it refers to the "industrial and ideological mobilization of entire populations."[5] However, he also points out that the term "total war" refers not to a reality—in ways that would allow us to identify this or that conflict as an example—but to a concept, a doctrine, or an ideology. Ironically, it is one with many limitations, most notably its elision of colonial wars. As a *doctrine*, its genesis is fairly clear: it was spawned in the middle of World War One, developed throughout the interwar period (partly by way of imperial struggles for dominance), and reached its height in World War Two.[6]

The military historian Richard Overy makes a similar set of observations in *Blood and Ruins: The Great Imperial War 1931–1945*, but he also has a more ready definition of what total war means. Tracing the concept from the Great War through the late 1930s and early 1940s, he explains its powerful ideological force.

> The concept of "total war" became a self-fulfilling prophecy, an infectious cliché, like the war on terror or cyberwar in the twenty-first century. As a result, no state or armed force thought they could risk avoiding the

[3] Kent Puckett, *War Pictures: Cinema, Violence, and Style in Britain*, 1939–1945 (New York: Fordham University Press, 2017), 11.

[4] Paul K. Saint-Amour, *Tense Future: Modernism, Total War, Encyclopedic Form* (New York: Oxford University Press, 2015), 57. Also see Puckett, *War Pictures*, 8–9.

[5] Saint-Amour, *Tense Future*, 55–56.

[6] Ibid., 58–60. Saint-Amour traces the concept to French World War One writing, especially Léon Daudet's *La guerre totale* (1918). For other writers, the key text is *Der totale Krieg* (1935) by Erich Ludendorff, a central German architect of World War One. See Richard Overy, *Blood and Ruins: The Great Imperial War 1931–1945* (London: Allen Lane, 2021), 379.

> mobilization of all the social, material and psychological energies of the nation in the pursuit of victory in a modern war.[7]

For Overy, the defining tenet of total war was that victory depended on the mobilization of every resource of the nation. Such resources included materials, transport, food, labor, culture, even feelings or affects—anything that could be used. And it involved expanding the definition of what *could* be used, just as it meant searching "for ways to mobilize new sources of labour at the margins of the employable population."[8] For Overy, World War Two saw "the near universal belief that national survival in total war depended on utilizing the human and material resources of the nation to the fullest possible extent. Failure to do so meant probable defeat."[9] This idea of *using everything* thus took on the force of a moral imperative, in some ways displacing the more abstract idea of victory itself.

In my own story, it is this definition of total war as the totalizing demand for usefulness—the mobilization of all resources—that is most relevant. The British experience of such mobilization in World War Two was extreme and prolonged, compared to the other unoccupied Allied democracies. Not only did the British "home front" (civilian participation in the war effort) take on huge importance, but civilians also experienced air raids and the threat of direct attack, especially during the 1940–1941 Blitz, when German bombers targeted British cities and towns. British women were conscripted for both labor and the auxiliary services in World War Two, introducing a significant reconfiguration of women's relationships to citizenship and public utility. Women also saw combat at anti-aircraft sites, as well as volunteering as air raid wardens and ambulance drivers.[10] The war involved massive movements of people within Britain, displaced by both bombing and war work. Rationing and other restrictions touched all corners of private life as industrial production was pressed toward military ends.[11] Britain also mobilized its empire, as Overy points out, calling on Dominion and colonial forces and labor, often "for what were essentially imperial campaigns."[12] The

[7] Overy, *Blood and Ruins*, 380.
[8] Ibid., 416.
[9] Ibid., 376
[10] Ibid., 392.
[11] For a comparative discussion of wartime rationing and consumption, see Overy, *Blood and Ruins*, 407.
[12] Ibid., 389.

British experience thus brings into peculiar focus the pressing dilemma of total war for a democratic nation, as incisively identified by Puckett: commitment to total war was both required for the preservation of the nation and in conflict with its basic values.[13]

In his account of the concept of total war, Overy draws in part on a 1941 text by Cyril Falls, a British military historian and the military correspondent for *The Times* throughout World War Two. It seems worth pausing over this text here, to help flesh out a public discourse about this dilemma of total war in Britain. In *The Nature of Modern Warfare*, based on a series of public lectures, Falls begins by expounding the new "doctrine of total war," touching on the familiar themes of aerial bombardment, attacks on civilians, and the forsaking of the "laws of war" in a kind of return to barbarism.[14] "But of course," he continues, "total war implies something more than mere lack of restraint or scruple. It also implies the devotion of every section of the nation, every phase of its activity, to the purpose of war" (7). What it adds up to is a "a new philosophical conception of warfare, as a state of hostility independent of acts of violence" (9).

For Falls, modern warfare was less about fighting and more about relentless, everyday calibrations of use value. It required not only using everything, but thinking about how everything one produced, however useful, prevented the production of something potentially more useful. Even in Britain, he suggested, which might be accused of being "backward and half-hearted in organizing itself for the struggle" compared to Germany, total war involved the reorganization of all aspects of society (10). "Finance, industry, commerce, agriculture, art and literature in some degree, science, architecture, on the productive side, and at the other end consumption in a thousand forms are regulated by the requirements of warfare" (11). Falls tried to preserve some private space of thought from the reach of total war, but even this appears a little precarious: "Liberty of thought remains, in my view, untouched, but liberty of expression is restricted—very much less in our country than in the totalitarian States, which naturally provide the extreme examples of the conduct of total war—yet still forcibly restricted" (11). Total war extended not only to material resources, but also to emotional and intellectual ones, hence the importance of propaganda: "We have to appeal to

[13] Puckett, *War Pictures*, 2, 19, 34–35.
[14] Cyril Falls, *The Nature of Modern Warfare* (London: Methuen, 1941), 1, 5–7.

mass-minds as well as to fight and to forge weapons. For that reason we have to make them admit the merit of our ideals, and that seems to require a fuller definition of war aims than has yet been given" (14). Most striking is Falls's observation of the damaging nature of the very concept of total war, even as he explained the necessity of embracing it.

> The very fact that this total war exists in itself threatens the destruction and implies the doom of civilization. It is not merely that civilization is hurt and bruised by contact with warfare, as in the past; it is that civilization and total war cannot long exist together. In total war civilization can hope at best to live on its fat; it seems to possess a good store, but there is no telling how long it will last.[15]

He concluded, in words that will resonate across the films discussed in the following pages, that "war has become not merely a danger, a check to progress, a destroyer—whatever you have called war in the past—but also a veritable negation of organized life, that is, death" (19). For Falls, total war conceptually belonged to the totalitarianism democracies were fighting against, leaving those democracies in an impossible bind.[16]

In the following chapters, I trace how music became an important site for thinking through this dilemma, posing central questions about what, if anything, was left untouched by the demands of total war, or even alive at all. At the same time, I suggest how total war's unbounded demands for usefulness and productivity saturated thinking about music itself.

Music in World War Two

Despite the fact that it deals with popular discourses and the medium of film, this book mainly addresses the place of art music in World War Two.[17] As Annegret Fauser points out in her panoramic study of music in the wartime United States, "for all the scholarly emphasis on popular culture in the

[15] Ibid., 18–19.

[16] This formulation is indebted to Puckett's central argument about wartime British film (*War Pictures*, 2), which resonates with Falls's concerns.

[17] For an overview of scholarship on music in World War Two, see Pamela M. Potter, "Introduction: Music and Global War in the Short Twentieth Century," in *Music in World War II: Coping with Wartime in Europe and the United States*, ed. Pamela M. Potter, Christina L. Baade, and Roberta Montemorra Marvin (Bloomington: Indiana University Press, 2020), 4–16; Also see Kate Guthrie, "Soundtracks to the 'People's War,'" *Music & Letters* 94 (2013): 326–327.

wartime period, what in fact distinguished musical life in the United States during World War II from other times of war was the significant role assigned to classical music: in 1940s America it had a cultural relevance and ubiquity that is hard to imagine today."[18]

If that was the case in the United States, it was even more so in Britain. Popular music was a powerful tool for morale, as Christina Baade has shown in her study of the BBC's turn to popular music in wartime.[19] But studies by John Morris and Jörn Weingärtner have also examined how musical high culture (or "good music," as administrators often referred to it) was cast as propaganda, morale booster, spiritual sustenance, and necessary escape by a whole range of state-supported institutions, many of them newly founded in World War Two.[20] Scholars have also long noted a wartime expansion of audiences for art music (especially orchestral music) as part of a broader democratization of the arts.[21] Myra Hess's daily lunchtime concerts at the National Gallery are an especially persistent icon of this new "hunger for music" (to use a phrase common at the time).[22] Some revisionist accounts have questioned to what extent this widespread public appetite for art music was real or a projection of elites eager to make a case for their preferred cultural forms.[23] This theme of cultural democratization, after all, is closely allied with the dominant myth of "The People's War," in which World War Two was cast as a unifying force bringing together British people across social and economic divides—a myth that has been similarly called into question,

[18] Annegret Fauser, *Sounds of War: Music in the United States During World War II* (New York: Oxford University Press, 2013), 4.

[19] Christina L. Baade, *Victory Through Harmony: The BBC and Popular Music in World War II* (New York: Oxford University Press, 2011).

[20] Jörn Weingärtner, *The Arts as a Weapon of War: Britain and the Shaping of National Morale in World War II* (London: Tauris Academic Studies, 2006); John Morris, *Culture and Propaganda in World War II: Music, Film and the Battle for National Identity* (London: I. B. Tauris, 2014).

[21] Guthrie, "Soundtracks to the "People's War," 327. Also see Heather Wiebe, *Britten's Unquiet Pasts: Sound and Memory in Postwar Reconstruction* (Cambridge: Cambridge University Press, 2012), 24–33; F. M. Leventhal, "CEMA and the Arts in Wartime: 'The Best for the Most,'" *20th-Century British History 1* (1990): 289–317.

[22] In 1939, for instance, *The Times* noted "the present hunger for music, unsatisfied by the iron ration issued by the B.B.C." ("'In Tempore Belli': Occasional Music," *Times*, October 7, 1939, 4), while an article across the page announcing the new National Gallery concerts mentioned the "starvation of the spirit of the people" and the need for "spiritual refreshment" through music ("National Gallery in War-Time," *Times*, October 7, 1939, 4).

[23] Nick Hayes, "More than 'Music-While-You-Eat'? Factory and Hostel Concerts, 'Good Culture' and the Workers," in *"Millions Like Us"? British Culture in the Second World War*, ed. Nick Hayes and Jeff Hill (Liverpool: Liverpool University Press, 1999), 211. Also see Guthrie, "Soundtracks to the "People's War," 327.

especially as scholars become more attentive to who was included in this projected "People" and who was not.[24] Some skepticism along these lines is certainly well-grounded. Nonetheless, the persistent concern with art music across a variety of official and less official discourses is a striking phenomenon of wartime Britain.

World War Two was a major turning point for state support of the arts in Britain, a nation historically hostile to any state intervention in culture, as Weingärtner has argued.[25] Such initiatives (including the National Gallery concerts) were aimed in part at solving the problem of unemployed musicians and artists, especially in the wake of the "cultural blackout" in the war's first unsettled weeks.[26] But their goals quickly became more ambitious. The Council for the Encouragement of Music and the Arts (CEMA), which would become the Arts Council of Great Britain in 1946, was founded in early 1940.[27] Then operating under the auspices of the Board of Education, CEMA's aims were broadly educational, and the original emphasis was on promoting amateur activity in the arts. The decision to provide concerts—as well as theater, ballet, and art exhibitions—was based directly on the success of the National Gallery concerts and responded to the "almost pathetic hunger for such provision" they showed, in the words of Lord De La Warr, the President of the Board of Education.[28] Classical concerts were also provided by the Entertainments National Service Association (ENSA), created to provide entertainment for the armed forces.[29] These wartime initiatives, of course, built on a longer history of constructing art music as socially

[24] See especially Sonya O. Rose, *Which People's War? National Identity and Citizenship in Wartime Britain 1939–1945* (Oxford: Oxford University Press, 2003); Stephen Bourne, *Under Fire: Black Britain in Wartime 1939–45* (Cheltenham: The History Press, 2020).

[25] Weingärtner, *Arts as a Weapon of War*, 3. Also see Simon McVeigh, "A Free Trade in Music: London During the Long 19th Century in a European Perspective," *Journal of Modern European History* 5, no. 1 (2007): 67–94.

[26] Weingärtner, *Arts as a Weapon of War*, 50–51.

[27] CEMA was initiated by a private foundation, the Pilgrim Trust (funded by the American Edward Harkness), which approached the Board of Education with an offer of £25,000 if they would agree to administer the funds. In general, CEMA embraced a model of public–private cooperation, working closely with local arts, educational, and social services organizations, many of which were privately run. See Weingärtner, *Arts as a Weapon of War*, 55–56.

[28] De La Warr to Thomas Jones, December 13, 1939, quoted in Weingärtner, *Arts as a Weapon of War*, 56.

[29] The most comprehensive account of ENSA, by its founder, is Basil Dean, *The Theatre at War* (London: George G. Harrap and Co. 1956). On its first classical concerts, see p. 214.

useful and as a powerful tool for citizenship, both within Britain and beyond.[30] Private initiatives to enrich and improve people's lives through music and the other arts abounded in late nineteenth- and early twentieth-century Britain, including institutions like Lilian Baylis's Sadler's Wells and the Old Vic (which developed into major national institutions of the postwar period under the new regime of arts funding). But the condition of total war brought these initiatives under the purview of the state, at the same time rendering commercial and public interests newly imbricated.

Nonetheless, musical high culture in World War Two Britain mainly had an oblique relationship with war rather than functioning as overt propaganda. This is a phenomenon that Deer's notion of "war culture" helps to elucidate. He uses this term to suggest the lack of boundaries between official propaganda and the wider culture in times of war, especially in 1930s–1940s Britain, with its "unprecedented, and often uneasy, attempts to colonize and monopolize the cultural field" for the purposes of war.[31] As Deer points out, official attempts to reach into every corner of culture were closely linked with an enormous "culture boom" in World War Two Britain; even when not explicitly concerned with war, arts and literature were shaped by new habits of thought and feeling. Within musical culture, emphasis on the performance and circulation of standard repertory (including Austro-German music, unlike in World War One), rather than the composition of new music, might be seen as one aspect of this diffuseness.[32] Composers themselves, moreover, often insisted on art music as fundamentally apart from war. Ralph Vaughan Williams, for instance, saw a wartime role for composers in writing music for amateurs, but he also drew a line when it came to music as "art" rather than craft. He wrote in his 1940 article "The Composer in War Time,"

[30] The classic source on related interwar movements is D. L. LeMahieu, *A Culture for Democracy: Mass Communication and the Cultivated Mind in Britain Between the Wars* (Oxford: Clarendon Press, 1988). Also see Kate Guthrie, "Awakening 'Sleeping Beauty': The Creation of National Ballet in Britain," *Music & Letters* 96 (2015): 432–436; and *The Art of Appreciation: Music and Middlebrow Culture in Modern Britain* (Berkeley: University of California Press, 2021). On French precedents, see Jann Pasler, *Composing the Citizen: Music as Public Utility in Third Republic France* (Berkeley: University of California Press, 2009), 83–86.

[31] Deer, *Culture in Camouflage*, 5.

[32] On the wartime acceptance of Austro-German music and musicians, see especially Laura Tunbridge, *Singing in the Age of Anxiety: Lieder Performances in New York and London Between the World Wars* (Chicago: University of Chicago Press, 2018), 34–37, 130–155; Morris, *Culture and Propaganda*, 34–37, 130–155.

> It is certainly, to my mind, one of the glories of the art of music that it can be put to no practical use. Poets can be used for propaganda, painters for camouflage, architects for machine-gun posts, but music is purely of the spirit and seems to have no place in the world of alarms and excursions. Would it not indeed be better for music to keep out of the struggle and reserve for us a place where sanity can again find a home when she returns to her own?[33]

Nonetheless, even as something remote from war, art music *could* be put to use. Performing Beethoven and Bach—and performing it well—was a way of demonstrating an internationalism antithetical to Nazism, for example.[34] It also demonstrated fortitude and a commitment to maintaining the standards of civility even in a time of war. As Kenneth Clark put it when describing the National Gallery concerts: "To maintain this sense of quality, this feeling that there are standards which must survive all disasters, is the supreme function of the arts in wartime."[35] Both Clark's and Vaughan Williams's comments (as well as the persistent metaphor of hunger) also take on a different sense of urgency when read alongside Cyril Falls's statements on the costs and dangers of total war. Music, seen in this light, sustained those diminishing stores of "fat" on which "civilization" was forced to live in total war, counteracting its necessary "negation of organized life."[36]

Music and Propaganda in Wartime British Film

If composers tended to resist a propagandistic role, British filmmakers more openly embraced it. In doing so, they also developed a distinct style, leading scholars to see World War Two as a high point for British cinema. As an English-language tradition, overwhelmed from the start by competition from Hollywood even for its own domestic audience, British cinema faced the constant challenge of distinguishing itself. Antonia Lant writes,

[33] Ralph Vaughan Williams, "The Composer in War Time," *The Listener 23* (May 16, 1940): 989. On the conflicted relationship between composers and propaganda in World War Two Britain, see Kate Guthrie, "Propaganda Music in Second World War Britain: John Ireland's Epic March," *Journal of the Royal Musical Association* 139, no. 1 (2014): 137–175, especially 138–139.

[34] On this phenomenon in the context of Lieder performance, see Tunbridge, *Singing in the Age of Anxiety*, 134.

[35] Kenneth Clark, "From the National Gallery," in *National Gallery Concerts in Aid of the Musicians Benevolent Fund, 10th October 1939–10th October 1944* (London, 1944), 6.

[36] Falls, *Nature of Modern Warfare*, 19.

"The desire for a distinct national style has always been part of the British cinema endeavor, but at no time was this project more urgent, nor the existence of British cinema more imperiled, than during" World War Two.[37] In responding to demands to reflect wartime realities and to represent the nation to itself, it forged a distinct cinematic language and identity.[38] Puckett goes a step further, calling attention to the deeply "eccentric" style with which British film-makers responded to and registered the surrealness and ideological demands of war.[39]

Film carried such weight in propaganda efforts in part because it was uniquely situated to reach a broad British public. The cinema audience was huge. As James Chapman has noted, the 1943 Wartime Social Survey found that 32% of the British population went to the cinema at least once a week.[40] When they did, they were shown Ministry of Information (MoI) documentary and propaganda films (which cinemas had agreed to include in every program) alongside the features they came for.[41] Moreover, the lines between entertainment and propaganda, or indeed between features and documentaries, were very fuzzy in wartime. Films were enmeshed in the propaganda goals of the state, even when made by private studios for entertainment purposes. All films needed to be approved by the MoI's new Films Division, but studios were also at the mercy of the MoI for resources including film stock, transport, studio space, and actors.[42] Major studios such as Gainsborough, known mainly for escapist fare such as woman's pictures and costume dramas, introduced propaganda elements into their films. The MoI also directly commissioned films, both from private studios and from the Crown Film Unit, as John Grierson's GPO Film Unit was named after it came under the auspices of the MoI Films Division in early 1940. That same year, the MoI issued a set of directives for the British film industry that shaped it for much of the war, written by Kenneth Clark, head of the National Gallery but also briefly head of the MoI Films Division. As Chapman

[37] Antonia Lant, *Blackout: Reinventing Women for Wartime British Cinema* (Princeton: Princeton University Press, 1991), 4. Also see Andrew Higson, *Waving the Flag: Constructing a National Cinema in Britain* (Oxford: Clarendon Press, 1995).

[38] Lant, *Blackout*, 6.

[39] Puckett, *War Pictures*, 2.

[40] James Chapman, "British Cinema and the People's War," in *"Millions Like Us"? British Culture in the Second World War*, ed. Nick Hayes and Jeff Hill (Liverpool: Liverpool University Press, 1999), 41.

[41] James Chapman, *The British at War: Cinema, State and Propaganda, 1939–1945* (London: I. B. Tauris, 1998), 93–94.

[42] Higson, *Waving the Flag*, 217–218. On the complex relationship between the MoI and commercial studios, see Chapman, *British at War*, 58–85.

describes, Clark's Programme for Film Propaganda drew on the three propaganda themes outlined by the MoI—"What Britain is fighting for," "How Britain fights," and "The need for sacrifices if the fight is to be won."[43] Clark suggested that documentaries were suited to the latter two while feature films were best suited to the first theme, presenting a compelling portrait of British life, history, and value.

This first theme—"What Britain is fighting for"—was the propaganda goal to which music was also most obviously suited, helping to illustrate traditions and cultural values at stake in the war effort in both documentary and feature films. But music and sound played a prominent role across all three types of propaganda films. Many wartime British films foregrounded music and sonic experiment, from the popular songs of *We'll Meet Again* (1943) to film scores by Vaughan Williams and William Walton in *49th Parallel* (1941) and *Henry V* (1944). Propaganda and documentary films by Michael Powell and Emeric Pressburger (including *49th Parallel*) and Humphrey Jennings, among others, are characterized by innovative treatments of sound and elaborate soundscapes, and include complex meditations on cultural tradition by way of music and sound.[44] Meanwhile, an emerging genre of films deployed piano concertos (preexisting or newly composed) and musician characters; they relied heavily on their music for both plot and public appeal, often featuring the music in advertising and tie-in recordings.[45] These concerto films suddenly became hugely popular in World War Two Britain, establishing their own set of conventions and compelling film-makers to add concertos to the most unlikely narratives. Moreover, this tradition began to wane soon after the war (as discussed in Chapter 5), even as the concertos it helped popularize continued to feed a heavily commercialized postwar concert culture that played on their cinematic associations.[46]

[43] Chapman, "British Cinema and the People's War," 44.

[44] Anita Jorge, "Liminal Soundscapes in Powell & Pressburger's Wartime Films," *Studies in European Cinema* 14, no. 1 (2017): 22–32; Anita Jorge, "A 'Symphony of Britain at War' or the 'Rhythm of Workaday Britain'? Len Lye's *When the Pie Was Opened* (1941) and the Musicalisation of Warfare," in *Soundings: Documentary Film and the Listening Experience*, ed. Geoffrey Cox et al. (Huddersfield: University of Huddersfield Press, 2018), 220–239. On Powell and Pressburger's sonic experiments in their wartime films, also see Chapter 5.

[45] See K. J. Donnelly, *British Film Music and Film Musicals* (Basingstoke: Palgrave Macmillan, 2007), 19, 24, 50; Kenneth Shenton, "From A to B," *British Music* 17 (1995): 56; Jan Swynnoe, *The Best Years of British Film Music, 1936–1958* (Woodbridge: Boydell, 2002), 66.

[46] For some later examples, see Donnelly, *British Film Music and Film Musicals*, 24. On this postwar concert trend, see Heather Wiebe, "Music and the Good Life in Postwar Britain: The Phenomenon of Eileen Joyce," in *The Oxford Handbook to Music and the Middlebrow*, ed. Kate Guthrie and Christopher Chowrimootoo (online edn, Oxford Academic, December 19, 2022), https://doi.org/10.1093/oxfordhb/9780197523933.013.6, accessed June 30, 2023.

The phenomenon of the concerto film is not restricted to British film. Indeed, its roots arguably lie in Hollywood films such as *Intermezzo* (1939) and *The Great Lie* (1941). The Hollywood tradition continued in postwar films such as *Hangover Square* (1945) and *Deception* (1946), both concerned (explicitly or implicitly) with wartime trauma.[47] It also intersected with other music-themed films such as *Humoresque* (1946) or the hugely successful Chopin biopic *A Song to Remember* (1945). Together, these 1940s films raise a shared set of concerns around gender, cultural value, middlebrow culture, and the deployment of Late Romanticism and Romantic tropes. Both Peter Franklin and Ivan Raykoff have fruitfully explored these concerns in a wider historical and Hollywood-centric context, while Heather Laing has done so with more attention to 1940s British film, including two of the films on which I focus.[48] In *Mobilizing Music*, I address some of these same issues, but am more centrally concerned with how British films respond to and elaborate the all-consuming demands of total war.

Why would wartime British films turn so often to the piano concerto in particular? In addition to its popular appeal and public address, the genre's focus on the relationship between individual (soloist) and collective (orchestra)—and its endless variations on how that relationship could be navigated—allowed it to speak to central concerns around the mobilization of civilians in World War Two. Moreover, it thematizes this relationship visually as well as sonically, in ways film could exploit. As Joseph Kerman has noted, "Concertos not only bring dissimilar musical forces into play, they also enact scenes of human activity. Men and women and groups are brought into conjunction, cooperation, confrontation."[49] Such scenes could speak richly to wartime mobilization, which created urgent demands for cooperation but also raised questions about the space for private lives, feelings, and aspirations within these larger demands.

[47] Lloyd Whitesell, "Concerto Macabre," *The Musical Quarterly* 88 (2005): 167–203. Also see Ivan Raykoff, "Hollywood's Embattled Icon," in *Piano Roles: A New History of the Piano*, ed. James Parakilas (New Haven, CT: Yale University Press), 270–282.

[48] Franklin, *Seeing Through Music*; Peter Franklin, "Modernism, Deception, and Musical Others," in *Western Music and Its Others: Difference, Representation, and Appropriation in Music*, ed. Georgina Born and David Hesmondhalgh (Berkeley: University of California Press, 2000); Raykoff, "Hollywood's Embattled Icon," 270–282; Ivan Raykoff, *Dreams of Love: Playing the Romantic Pianist* (New York: Oxford University Press, 2014); Ivan Raykoff, "Concerto con Amore," *Echo* 2, no. 1 (2000), https://echo.humspace.ucla.edu/issues/concerto-con-amore/, accessed May 1, 2022; Heather Laing, *The Gendered Score: Music in 1940s Melodrama and the Woman's Film* (London: Routledge, 2007). Laing discusses *Dangerous Moonlight* (pp. 147–170) and *Love Story* (pp. 11–138).

[49] Joseph Kerman, *Concerto Conversations* (Cambridge: Harvard University Press, 1999).

The figure of the pianist—and the piano itself—are also important elements in the concerto's wartime appeal. In Raykoff's panoramic essay on the piano in film, war is a constant theme, with the instrument functioning as a figure of nostalgia and vulnerability: "the piano becomes an embattled Romantic icon, threatened just as love (humanity), freedom (desire), tradition (history), and democracy (or whatever applicable political ideal) come under attack."[50] The pianist, meanwhile, is heroic (in the mold of Chopin's Polish revolutionary persona) but is also often broken or defunct, as Raykoff observes.[51] In wartime film and reality, this pianist was often female, further complicating this dynamic. The female concerto soloist was hardly a new phenomenon in the 1940s. As Tia DeNora and Katherine Ellis have pointed out, female pianists have historically had a significant presence on the concert stage, even in the public genre of the concerto.[52] But, as DeNora notes, there has always been a tension between female performance and the heroic, spectacular, and virtuosic role of the soloist in nineteenth-century concertos in particular.[53]

Both this tension and the brokenness Raykoff observes were key to wartime British films, and both took on additional weight in the context of mobilization, where everything and everyone needed to be restored to productivity. In the films I discuss—including documentaries—the pianist is insistently marked as broken or liminal in various ways. The male pianist-composers include a Polish refugee and Black colonial subject, but most of the musicians are women—Jewish women, working-class Australian women, sick and dying women, and, in one case, a ghost. Their music both gives voice to their liminality and enables their recuperation and reincorporation.

Many of the films I explore here function within a version of what Lauren Berlant, in the context of 1940s US films, calls "women's culture," the first major example of a "mass-marketed intimate public." In Berlant's account, women were identified as a "bloc of consumers" to be sold a set of texts and products that claimed to "express those people's particular core interests and desires"; as participants in "women's culture," they were thus made to "*feel*

[50] Raykoff, "Hollywood's Embattled Icon," 268.

[51] Ibid., 279–282.

[52] Tia DeNora, "The Concerto and Society," in *The Cambridge Companion to the Concerto*, ed. Simon Keefe (Cambridge: Cambridge University Press, 2005), 27–30; Katherine Ellis, "Female Pianists and Their Male Critics in Nineteenth-Century Paris," *Journal of the American Musicological Society* 50 (1997): 353–385.

[53] DeNora, "Concerto and Society," 28–30; Ellis, "Female Pianists," 361–362.

as though it expresses what is common among them."[54] The ways in which propaganda films managed and accessed feeling were inseparable from the broader commercial cultures in which they operated. Indeed, they help show the entanglement of mobilization—with its reach into every corner of social, domestic, and emotional life—and an expanding capitalist culture with a similarly totalizing reach. Despite (or perhaps because of) their "juxtapolitical" status, the strategies Berlant describes could be inflected toward propaganda goals—one reason, perhaps, that the MoI was so eager to co-opt the film industry. The shared feelings projected in British woman's pictures had much to do with the experience of war, but also with the fantasies of attachment and the management of disappointment that Berlant describes.[55] One thing I excavate in this book, then, is a kind of wartime "women's culture," where total war intersects with an "intimate public" whose role in this new kind of warfare was under constant negotiation.

The Feeling of Wartime

Bringing together a range of approaches from sound studies and affect theory as well as histories of emotion and psychiatry, *Mobilizing Music* traces the important role music played in articulating the pressures on feeling, intimacy, and interiority in total war. It also suggests how music and sound were used to explore the shifting nature of feeling itself in wartime.

The feeling of wartime is famously difficult to capture, partly because of its diffuseness, but also due to its ephemerality and postwar mythologization. In his 1989 book *Wartime*, Paul Fussell attempted an analysis of the "psychological and emotional culture" of World War Two, creating a panoramic portrait of transatlantic wartime culture to show how war pervaded emotional experience.[56] Taking a cue from Fussell, Mary Favret writes of the ways war saturated culture in earlier periods as well. "However fragile or compromised," she writes, "the psychological and emotional culture called

[54] Lauren Berlant, *The Female Complaint: The Unfinished Business of Sentimentality in American Culture* (Durham, NC: Duke University Press, 2005), 5.
[55] Ibid., 10, 15.
[56] Paul Fussell, *Wartime: Understanding and Behavior in the Second World War* (New York: Oxford University Press, 1989), ix.

wartime provides its own responses and sometimes its own resistance to the destructiveness of war."[57]

These accounts and approaches are useful both in understanding aspects of the wartime culture I discuss—especially women's experience of war away from the battlefront—and in delineating what seems more specific to 1940s Britain. Favret mainly deals with an early nineteenth-century experience of "war at a distance," where war was ignorable but nonetheless invaded thought and feeling far away from battlefronts. That experience is certainly relevant to World War Two Britain, as radio in particular brought news of distant battles to the private spaces of the home—a persistent trope in 1940s film. For many people, though—perhaps even *most* people—war was *not* ignorable. Even for those who never directly experienced attack or threat on the home front, it invaded and reorganized every aspect of private and domestic life.

Perhaps more suggestive for my account is Favret's discussion of war's formational role in the development of Romanticism, a movement that haunts the films I discuss here; they are persistently concerned with the musical language of Late Romanticism and Romantic tropes of the heroic pianist, both of which read as residual remnants of a culture under threat. For Favret, Romantic interiority itself is enmeshed in wartime. Even in the early nineteenth century, she writes,

> recognition of the global sweep of the war lent only new urgency to the cultivation of an interiority which comprehended the interior spaces of England itself, its cottages and hearths, its "domestic quiet," but also, and increasingly, its inner psyche.... If, as George Lukács argued, the "inner life of a nation is linked with the modern mass army in a way it could not have been" prior to the French Revolution, the inner life of individuals cannot escape this militarized context. Indeed, ... wartime makes it hard to determine whether or not those psychic spaces had been conjured precisely to register war's intrusion.[58]

[57] Mary A. Favret, *War at a Distance: Romanticism and the Making of Modern Wartime* (Princeton: Princeton University Press, 2009), 18.

[58] Favret, *War at a Distance*, 25, quoting Georg Lukács, *The Historical Novel* (Lincoln: University of Nebraska Press, 1983), 24.

The films of the 1940s raise similar questions about the relationship between war and interiority, particularly in their prominent scenes of listening to music. In these films, such scenes of listening—alone and in groups, to Mozart, Beethoven, or Rachmaninoff—become a way to stage psychic, domestic, and national interiority.

In addition to the approaches modeled by Favret and Fussell, the history of psychiatry offers another productive way of approaching the feeling of wartime. Recent studies of World War Two psychiatry have done much to show how the emotions of wartime became objects of management, both on the battlefront and on the home front. The war years saw a huge growth of psychiatry, closely allied with military discipline. As Joanna Bourke has observed, World War Two psychiatry "conformed effortlessly to the military demands of rationalization, standardization, and hierarchical discipline."[59] Film was a major vehicle for the dissemination of psychiatric expertise, for both military personnel and civilians.[60] Even on the home front, experts deployed psychiatry to discipline emotions, especially anxiety and fear—"the most dreaded natural wartime emotions," as observed by Michal Shapira.[61] I address these psychiatric discourses most directly in Chapter 4, where I aim to excavate some of the feelings they tend to elide and to suggest the problematic place of women's wartime experience within them. But they also emerge more peripherally elsewhere, especially in relationship to sound studies and the debilitating effects of the sound of air raids on civilian populations—a central concern within wartime psychiatric discourse, as both Shapira and James Mansell have discussed.[62]

In *Mobilizing Music*, I also explore how concerns with music and sound intersected with a wartime understanding of feeling and morale as forces beyond the personal. While morale—and music's role in sustaining it—has long been a major theme in studies of World War Two, scholars have recently approached morale as a more diffuse and unmanageable force, informed

[59] Joanna Bourke, "Disciplining the Emotions: Fear, Psychiatry and the Second World War," in *War, Medicine and Modernity*, ed. Roger Cooter, Mark Harrison, and Steve Sturdy (London: Sutton, 1998), 225–238, here 232.

[60] See Noah Tsika, *Traumatic Imprints: Cinema, Military Psychiatry, and the Aftermath of War* (Berkeley: University of California Press, 2018). Tsika mainly focuses on American psychiatry in World War Two, but, as he points out, this drew heavily on British models developed earlier in the war.

[61] Michal Shapira, *The War Inside: Psychoanalysis, Total War, and the Making of the Democratic Self in Postwar Britain* (Cambridge: Cambridge University Press, 2013), 40.

[62] James G. Mansell, *The Age of Noise in Britain: Hearing Modernity* (Urbana: University of Illinois Press, 2017), 145–181.

in part by theories of affect. In his book *Cultural Feelings*, Ben Highmore returns frequently to World War Two Britain and its memory, tracking "a set of cultural feelings that were tied very specifically to . . . that vast military-industrial assemblage called World War II."[63] Highmore (following the lead of critics such as Sianne Ngai) uses the term "feeling" to connote something impersonal and material while also more socially constructed and historically rooted than is often suggested by the term "affect."[64] Ben Anderson has similarly turned to World War Two as a way of thinking through the relationship between politics and affect. Morale, he suggests, exemplifies the peculiar relationship between affect and power: affect is closely associated with an idea of excess—as a force that cannot be contained in individuals or objects, but rather one that exists in movement, and as something that cannot be assimilated to "systems of signification or narrativization."[65] On the one hand, affect offers a promise of liberation through this quality of excess, this unlocatability. On the other hand, Anderson argues, affect is harnessed by forms of power that exploit precisely this quality of excess in their own aspiration to boundlessness and complete saturation of life (169). The quality of excess shared by affect and power can be especially clearly seen, he argues, in attempts to foster morale in World War Two, where "an excessive state apparatus . . . functioned by tracking and synchronizing the excesses of affect" (163). Such approaches inform how I see music and sound working in relation to feeling and morale in wartime films, as a force that often goes beyond signification or individual emotion even while working on those planes as well.

As both Jim Sykes and Gavin Williams have recently pointed out, some of the major scholarship on sound and war has tended to focus on pain and trauma and on listening as an "act of survival," often privileging the battlefield over everyday wartime life and the experience of men over those of women and children.[66] In this regard, it might be said to follow a larger tendency to

[63] Ben Highmore, *Cultural Feelings: Mood, Mediation and Cultural Politics* (London: Routledge, 2017), 17.

[64] Ibid., 1–2; Sianne Ngai, *Ugly Feelings* (Cambridge: Harvard University Press, 2005), 25–27.

[65] Ben Anderson, "Modulating the Excess of Affect: Morale in a State of 'Total War,'" in *The Affect Theory Reader*, ed. Melissa Gregg and Gregory J. Seigworth (Durham, NC: Duke University Press, 2010), 161–186, here 162. Also see the more recent version of this chapter in Ben Anderson, *Encountering Affect: Capacities, Apparatuses, Conditions* (Farnham: Ashgate, 2014).

[66] Jim Sykes, "Ontologies of Acoustic Endurance: Rethinking Wartime Sound and Listening," *Sound Studies* 4 (2018): 37; Gavin Williams, Introduction to *Hearing the Crimean War: Wartime Sound and the Unmaking of Sense*, ed. Gavin Williams (Oxford: Oxford University Press, 2019), xxxi.

elide other wartime realities in favor of narratives of trauma and the image of the traumatized soldier. Roy Scranton has written about this tendency within American literature on World War Two in particular, suggesting how the "myth of the trauma hero" ensconced in the literary canon has come to obscure a broader experience of "totalized industrial war," emerging precisely in order to set aside the contradictions that experience raised.[67] *Mobilizing Music* unfolds a discourse that turns steadfastly away from such myths. This discourse locates the sounds and feelings of war in music and everyday life, using them to test and explore the reach of total war.

Music and Utility

In addition to asking what films might tell us about the feeling of war, I want to trace an argument over music's value and efficacy that developed in British films made during and immediately after World War Two. This cinematic discourse was in dialogue with a broader set of arguments about music's value in wartime, but it was also distinct, its groundedness in popular culture and media informing a different way of thinking about music and sound. In some ways, there is nothing very new about the models of musical utility at work in 1940s Britain. Music has long been seen to promote citizenship through a variety of means, both direct and indirect—by building a sense of social belonging and solidarity and by teaching individuals to discipline and refine judgments and emotions.[68] These are the kinds of benefits identified by Jann Pasler in a nineteenth-century French model of musical utility (which drew in turn on Enlightenment ideals), but they can also be seen to emerge in some of the discourses I examine, particularly in Chapters 1 and 2.[69] In Britain, music—especially amateur musical activity—had been promoted as a healthy and beneficial pastime throughout the nineteenth and early twentieth centuries, as social reformers sought to manage the relatively new problem of leisure for the urban working classes. This tradition, too, was

[67] Roy Scranton, *Total Mobilization: World War II and American Literature* (Chicago: University of Chicago Press, 2019), 7, 14.

[68] On this history, its problems, and new approaches to musical citizenship, see Martin Stokes, "The Musical Citizen," *Etnomüzikoloji Dergisi/Ethnomusicology Journal* 1 (2018): 15–30, and *Music and Citizenship* (Oxford: Oxford University Press, 2023).

[69] Jann Pasler, *Composing the Citizen: Music As Public Utility in Third Republic France* (Berkeley: University of California Press, 2009).

at work in the ways music was cast in wartime, when it addressed much the same problem of managing leisure and when boredom—due to blackouts, displacement, disruption of normal activities, and the perennial need to wait for alarms and signals—was seen as a particular problem.[70]

Music has also been cast as a "weapon" of war, offering another way of figuring its utility and efficacy. Scholarly discussions of morale and propaganda in World War Two often draw on this language of instrumentalizing and "weaponizing" music and the other arts.[71] The implication is that music was used (by institutions like the BBC, for instance) to directly shape thought and feeling in ways that supported the war effort. The instrumentalization of music as therapy also seems related to this idea, especially when it is caught up in the discourses of military psychiatry (as discussed in Chapter 4). Another, more material kind of weaponization is at work in some of the wartime films I discuss, recalling the models set out in Suzanne Cusick's work on music and torture, Martin Daughtry's on sound in the Iraq War, or Steve Goodman's on the broader weaponization of sound and vibration in contemporary culture.[72]

Arguably, though, the concept of total war also introduced new approaches to cultural utility that helped shape our own ways of thinking. George Yudice, for instance, has outlined a prevailing contemporary understanding of culture as a "resource for both sociopolitical and economic amelioration" to be "mobilized" and managed.[73] This understanding, he suggests, is subtly different from earlier notions of cultural utility, where culture was seen as providing "ideological uplift," transforming behavior, or producing "proper citizens" (much as Pasler describes music's utility in nineteenth-century France).[74] Yudice associates this idea with the recent past and with the globalized, post-Cold War environment that has emerged since the 1990s. "Without cold war legitimation," he suggests, which at least ensconced a certain ideal of artistic freedom, "there is no holding back utilitarian arguments

[70] Weingärtner, *Arts as a Weapon of War*, 54.

[71] See, for instance, Weingärtner, *Arts as a Weapon of War*.

[72] Suzanne G. Cusick, "Music as Torture/Music as Weapon," in *The Auditory Culture Reader*, ed. Michael Bull and Les Back (London: Routledge, 2015), 379–392; Martin Daughtry, *Listening to War: Sound, Music, Trauma, and Survival in Wartime Iraq* (New York: Oxford University Press, 2015); Steve Goodman, *Sonic Warfare: Sound, Affect, and the Ecology of Fear* (Cambridge, MA: MIT Press, 2012).

[73] George Yudice, *The Expediency of Culture: Uses of Culture in the Global Era* (Durham, NC: Duke University Press, 2003), 7, 4.

[74] Ibid., 10–11.

in the United States. Art has completely folded into an expanded conception of culture that can solve problems, including job creation" (12). Now usefulness—the ability to create change or improve lives—is a primary way of understanding culture's value and a condition of its support. One of the most distinctive aspects of this way of imagining culture, for him, is its totality, its insistence that everything is available for use. It involves "the penetration of capital logic into the as-yet-uncolonized recesses of life" (24). This obsession with totality, though, can be traced directly to the idea of total war. Indeed, while careful to state that his notion of culture is "not Heideggerian," Yudice draws explicitly on Heidegger's notion of "standing reserve," introduced in his 1954 essay "The Question Concerning Technology."[75] Here, according to Yudice, "nature becomes a resource, a means to an end. . . . Everything, including human beings, comes to be regarded as standing reserve ready to be used as resources."[76] As William Lovitt has suggested, Heidegger was drawing in turn from Ernst Jünger's 1931 article "The Total Mobilization," which grew out of his experience of World War One.[77] In many ways, I would suggest, the wartime discourses I examine were struggling to conceptualize this idea of music as resource and to work out its implications. They did so, moreover, in an environment that seems an early example of the one Yudice describes, where culture was supported and managed through complex webs of state, commercial, and private charitable interests, often for very direct purposes of "amelioration." In this sense, these wartime British films introduce problems of musical efficacy and the limits of usefulness that are still very much relevant, not least in the neoliberal British context in which this book was written, with its increasingly strident demands for use value by the public bodies founded in the 1940s.[78] More broadly, wartime attempts to use music to think through and about total mobilization, at a moment when it posed a new and urgent problem, still speak to how we conceptualize music's place in the context of an all-pervasive capitalism and the all-consuming social, political, and ecological demands of our own time.

[75] Ibid., 26. Yudice calls on Martin Heidegger, "The Question Concerning Technology," in *The Question Concerning Technology and Other Essays*, trans. William Lovitt (New York: Garland, 1977), originally published in 1954 and based on a series of lectures given in 1949 (William Lovitt, Introduction to *Question Concerning Technology*, ix).

[76] Yudice, *Expediency of Culture*, 26.

[77] Heidegger, *Question Concerning Technology*, 137, n. 21.

[78] For further thoughts on this, see Heather Wiebe, "Opera and Relational Aesthetics," *The Opera Quarterly* 35 (2019): 139–142.

Mobilizing Music

My narrative begins with *Listen to Britain* (1941–1942), a documentary made for the Crown Film Unit by Humphrey Jennings that presents a soundscape of everyday life in wartime, mixing art music, popular music, and industrial sounds. Looking particularly at its representation of Myra Hess's wartime National Gallery concerts—here, a performance of a Mozart piano concerto by Hess herself—I show how the film attempts to make space for introspection and melancholy, linking them to the work of war. *Listen to Britain* and the National Gallery concerts became touchstones for later wartime films, including *Millions Like Us*, a 1943 Gainsborough melodrama about women's mobilization. A comparison with this film, though, reveals a very different treatment of music in relation to wartime feeling, highlighting the challenges of incorporating art music into total war and the distinctiveness of the sonic logic that allows *Listen to Britain* to do so.

While Chapter 1 looks at the idealized forms of musical populism epitomized by the National Gallery concerts, the next chapter turns to their underside by way of the *Warsaw Concerto* (1941), a miniature concerto composed for the film *Dangerous Moonlight*. Richard Addinsell's *Warsaw Concerto* was one of the first pieces of film music to gain popularity on the concert stage, and created widespread controversy about the degeneration of orchestral culture in wartime. I both trace critical anxieties about the *Warsaw Concerto* and present an alternative perspective by way of one musician who regularly performed it in wartime tours, Eileen Joyce, a celebrated Australian pianist who can be heard in many film soundtracks of the 1940s and 1950s. Joyce embodied a type of populism widely held in suspicion, but she was also a model of aspiration and mobility, moving from poverty to wealth and from the imperial margins (she was born in Tasmania) to the metropolitan center. Turning to the audiences who embraced Joyce and the concerto and to *Dangerous Moonlight* itself, I trace a certain reflexivity about the issues of commodifying and mechanizing emotion that so worried its critics, suggesting how the *Warsaw Concerto* might cast light on the compressed space of feeling in wartime.

The damaged wartime pianist-composer, as well as the miniature concerto, are again at issue in two later films discussed in Chapter 3: the

Gainsborough melodrama *Love Story* (1944), with its terminally ill female pianist and her *Cornish Rhapsody*, and *Men of Two Worlds* (commissioned in 1942 and released in 1946), a feature film about an African pianist from Tanzania (then Tanganyika), commissioned as propaganda for British colonial policy. Both films begin with depictions of the same National Gallery concerts seen in *Listen to Britain* and draw on the earlier film's techniques. They go on, moreover, to grapple with a notion of musical efficacy that developed in documentary film, struggling to integrate it with more typically melodramatic modes of associating music with desire and escape while also addressing questions of how to mobilize subjects marked in various ways as liminal. Such questions extend to the making of *Men of Two Worlds*, which drew extensively on artists from London's diverse Caribbean and African communities. *Men of Two Worlds* brings into view complex issues of race and empire as they relate to the ideals of inclusiveness with which music was strongly associated in wartime, while *Love Story* suggests a certain resistance to mobilization, finding a positive role for music as escape even as it ultimately affirms music's role in total war.

Chapter 4 turns to the end of the war and two films from 1945, David Lean's iconic *Brief Encounter* and *The Seventh Veil*, the latter now more forgotten but then a huge box office success, internationally as well as domestically. Both feature canonical Late Romantic concertos (by Rachmaninoff, Grieg, and Tchaikovsky), performed on the soundtrack by Eileen Joyce. In both films, I argue, these are used to address issues around trauma and demobilization, particularly for women. I trace how they situate music as a tool in psychological treatment, in ways that engaged with discourses of military psychiatry (including military training films). Both films, I argue, deal with the emotional legacy of war, registering a gap in established discourses for representing women's experience in the new environment of total war.

In Chapter 5, I trace a postwar demobilization of music, turning away from the concerto film to two music-centered films from the later 1940s: *The Glass Mountain* (1949), with its Alps-inspired opera (composed in a lush Late Romantic style by Nino Rota), and Powell and Pressburger's ballet fantasy *The Red Shoes* (1948). Both films feature troubled male composers writing an opera in the context of a postwar return to normalcy, *The Red Shoes* dwelling on a process of demobilizing the arts in London, and *The Glass Mountain* on the more literal demobilization of its airman-composer hero. Both embrace music's role as a vehicle of fantasy in a way that rejects wartime strictures. Paradoxically perhaps, they also both use their composer characters to reassign music to English men, turning to opera to articulate a relationship between masculinity, excessive feeling, and authorial control while dwelling on the sacrifice of women to their demands. These films, I argue, reveal a preoccupation with the power assigned to music in World War Two, rendering music as a dangerous and deathly force—and in many ways inimical to a return to ordinary Englishness. In these films, we see the wartime mobilization of music coming to an uneasy end.

1

Music, Feeling, and Total War

Listen to Britain and *Millions Like Us*

> But of course total war implies something more than mere lack of restraint or scruple. It also implies the devotion of every section of the nation, every phase of its activity, to the purpose of war. It stands for something more still: a state of affairs in which conflicts of interest or will amounts to undeclared war. War thus has no definite beginning and perhaps no definite ending, though the start and finish of overtly violent acts can be exactly recorded.
>
> —Captain Cyril Falls, *The Nature of Modern Warfare* (1941), 7

In the mythology around World War Two Britain, Myra Hess's National Gallery concerts hold a prominent place. The series was founded in October 1939, immediately after the outbreak of war, when the Gallery was emptied of its collection and London's cultural life brought to a halt. In September, theaters and concert halls had been hastily closed, extreme blackout conditions imposed, and public gatherings prohibited. The National Gallery concerts constituted some of the first glimmers of normal cultural life in wartime.[1] They would continue to be held every weekday at lunchtime throughout the war, persisting even through the Blitz of 1940–1941, when London was regularly bombed. Hess's series was soon joined by similar ones instituted around London by other pianists, including Hilda Bor's at the Royal Exchange and Harriet Cohen's at the Dorchester Hotel (which she organized in exchange

[1] On the founding of the National Gallery Concerts, also see Laura Tunbridge, *Singing in the Age of Anxiety: Lieder Performances in New York and London Between the World Wars* (Chicago: University of Chicago Press, 2018), 148–152.

Mobilizing Music in Wartime British Film. Heather Wiebe, Oxford University Press.
DOI: 10.1093/oso/9780197631713.003.0002

for accommodation after her home was bombed, the Dorchester being well known as one of the safest buildings in London).[2] Unlike these, however, Hess's concerts quickly became established as an icon of national fortitude and of a new hunger for art music that transcended social divides. Much of that music, moreover, was Austro-German, situating the Gallery as a last refuge for a European culture under attack, while Hess (who was Jewish) was ensconced as a heroic national figure, putting British inclusivity pointedly on display.[3]

The concerts' image began to solidify already in 1939, when *Picture Post* described the queue outside the Gallery: "There are men and women, young and old, rich and poor waiting patiently in the cold up the steps of the Gallery and along the pavements . . . to hear Bach, Beethoven, Brahms, Chopin and Schumann. . . . Strange things happen in wartime."[4] A similar account was offered slightly earlier by Kenneth Clark, the director of the National Gallery. He described the audience for Hess's first concert, "sitting on the floor and standing all around the walls" after its 700 seats unexpectedly filled up:

> Young and old, smart and shabby, Tommies in uniform with their tin hats strapped on, old ladies with ear trumpets, musical students, civil servants, office boys, busy public men, all sorts had come, because they were longing for something to take them out of the muddle and uncertainty of the present into a world where even the most tragic emotions have dignity and order.[5]

Clark's account, set out in *The Listener* less than a month after the concerts began, would long define the terms in which they were understood and valorized. However, the concerts' reputation rests even more heavily, if less explicitly, on the wartime documentary films of Humphrey Jennings—films that, as Angus Calder has argued, have had an outsize role in the postwar "myth of the blitz" more broadly, their images circulating widely

[2] Harriet Cohen, *A Bundle of Time: The Memoirs of Harriet Cohen* (London: Faber and Faber, 1969), 299. On the Dorchester, see Matthew Sweet, *The West End Front: The Wartime Secrets of London's Grand Hotels* (London: Faber & Faber, 2011), 89–91.

[3] Tunbridge, *Singing in the Age of Anxiety*, 153–154. Austro-German music remained a cornerstone of the repertoire in World War Two Britain, in contrast to World War One, as has been widely discussed. See especially Tunbridge, *Singing in the Age of Anxiety*, 132–133, 153–157; John Morris, *Culture and Propaganda in World War II: Music, Film and the Battle for National Identity* (London: I. B. Tauris, 2014), 34–37, 130–155.

[4] "Music Among the Masters," *Picture Post*, November 11, 1939, quoted in Nick Hayes, "More Than 'Music-While-You-Eat'? Factory and Hostel Concerts, 'Good Culture' and the Workers," in *"Millions Like Us"? British Culture in the Second World War*, ed. Nick Hayes and Jeff Hill (Liverpool: Liverpool University Press, 1999), 211. See Hayes (p. 211) for other examples.

[5] Kenneth Clark, "Concerts in the National Gallery," *The Listener* 22 (November 2, 1939): 884.

as transparent documents of historical reality despite their status as highly constructed state-sponsored propaganda.[6]

Jennings—a poet, sociologist, surrealist painter, theater designer, and filmmaker—was one of the most important directors working for the Crown Film Unit (CFU), the wartime incarnation of John Grierson's GPO and the more experimental wing of the Ministry of Information's (MoI) Films Division. Jennings featured Hess and the National Gallery concerts in multiple projects, starting at the height of the Blitz. The first was an uncompleted documentary short, "National Gallery 1941." This grew into *Listen to Britain* (1942), which features Hess's performance of a Mozart concerto with the Royal Air Force (RAF) orchestra in a long segment at its climax.[7] Jennings also returned to the National Gallery concerts in two projects near the end of the war: a short film, *Myra Hess* (1945), in which she performs the first movement of Beethoven's "Appassionata" Sonata, as well as *A Diary for Timothy* (1946), featuring the same performance. This preoccupation with the National Gallery concerts might be seen simply as recognition of their value as propaganda and morale booster. I would suggest instead, though, that these films keep returning to the National Gallery concerts as a problem to be solved, an itch to be scratched.

This is especially the case in *Listen to Britain*, an 18-minute film that absorbed the National Gallery performance into a panoramic portrait of the sounds of everyday life in wartime.[8] In the words of one early blurb, "It is a Sound Report of a people at war."[9] Made with the editor Stewart McAllister, *Listen to Britain* is a montage of the sounds and images of wartime, tracing the life of the nation from one afternoon to the next, without narrative or voice-over. (In this sense, it is a more sound-centered variation on the 1920s "city symphony" film.[10]) In a dense series of shots (more than two hundred,

[6] Angus Calder, *The Myth of the Blitz* (London: John Cape, 1991), 229–231. Calder provides a succinct account of Jennings, *Listen to Britain*, and their important role in wartime propaganda (pp. 229–244).

[7] "National Gallery 1941" (April 28, 1941), Box 1, Item 7, Humphrey Jennings Collection, British Film Institute Special Collections (hereafter BFI Special Collections).

[8] *Listen to Britain*, dir. Humphrey Jennings, Crown Film Unit, 1942, in *Listen to Britain and Other Films by Humphrey Jennings* (Chatsworth, CA: Image Entertainment, 2002, DVD); also available on BFI Player. The essential account of *Listen to Britain* from a musicological perspective is David Rosen, "The Sounds of Music and War: Humphrey Jennings's and Stewart McAllister's *Listen to Britain* (1942)," in Cliff Eisen, ed. *"Coll'astuzia, col giudizio": Essays in Honor of Neal Zaslaw* (Ann Arbor: Steglein, 2009), 390–428.

[9] Box 1, Item 7, Humphrey Jennings Collection, BFI Special Collections. This document appears to be a draft of the core information for the film's publicity. The published advertising uses the blurb "The music of a people at war" instead.

[10] There is a direct connection to this tradition by way of Jennings's mentor, the Brazilian director Alberto Cavalcanti. Keith Beattie, *Humphrey Jennings*, British Film Makers (Manchester: Manchester

organized into seventeen sequences),[11] natural sounds mix with urban and industrial noise, planes, trains, radio, overheard speech, and all kinds of music. At its climax are two concert scenes: a lunchtime performance at an armaments factory by the entertainers Flanagan and Allan, followed by the concert at the National Gallery, by far the longest sequence in the film as well as its conceptual kernel. If (as discussed in the Introduction) the ideology of total war had at its core the "mobilization of all the social, material and psychological energies of the nation in the pursuit of victory," this film might be seen as a sonic portrait of these mobilized energies.[12] Strangely, it places a Mozart performance at their heart.

Why does the film work so hard to embed the National Gallery concerts in the noise and everyday music of wartime? In some ways, *Listen to Britain* echoes Clark's account of the concerts, using the Mozart performance to endow wartime emotions with "dignity and order," to recall his words. In other ways, though, it departs from that more conventional account significantly. The film both places music "out of the muddle and uncertainty of the present" and somehow, sonically, right in the middle of it.[13] In doing so, it extends the dignifying powers of music to *all* the sounds of war, even the noise of the factory or a mine; conversely, the sonic materiality of wartime noise—the idea that this noise is *doing* something—is also extended to music. If, as a number of scholars have explored, writers and artists turned to panoramic vision and encyclopedic form as a way of grappling with the totality of total war, *Listen to Britain* reveals a different approach to this problem, using sound and hearing to conceptualize war's all-pervasive force.[14] At the same time, the film's struggle to place art music within the sonic space of war suggests how music might act as a test of war's boundlessness.

University Press, 2010), 61, 69. See also Erik Barnouw, *Documentary: A History of the Non-Fiction Film*, 2nd rev ed. (Oxford: Oxford University Press, 1993), 73–74.

[11] Jim Leach, "The Poetics of Propaganda: Humphrey Jennings and *Listen to Britain*," in *Documenting the Documentary: Close Readings of Documentary Film and Video*, ed. Barry Keith Grant and Jeannette Sloniowski (Detroit: Wayne State University Press), 146.

[12] Richard Overy, *Blood and Ruins: The Great Imperial War 1931–1945* (London: Allen Lane, 2021), 380.

[13] Clark, "Concerts in the National Gallery," 884.

[14] On panoramic and aerial vision in World Wars One and Two, see especially Patrick Deer, *Culture in Camouflage: War, Empire, and Modern British Literature* (Oxford: Oxford University Press, 2009), 15–105. Deer highlights the new importance of listening in the *Second World War*, by contrast, on page 25. On narrative form, see Paul K. Saint-Amour, *Tense Future: Modernism, Total War, Encyclopedic Form* (New York: Oxford University Press, 2015).

From the National Gallery to "A Sound Report of a People at War"

According to Crown's final report on *Listen to Britain*, its origins lay in a 5-minute film script commissioned "on the theme 'R.A.F. Fighters and R.A.F. Music.'"[15] The report also notes the working titles "National Gallery" and "Tin Hat Concerto" (recalling Clark's 1939 description of the concerts), all of which suggests an original focus on the RAF orchestra playing in the National Gallery sequence. When Jennings expanded this original concept into a longer film, though, he did not enlarge on the original theme of music and the forces. Instead, he developed it into a portrait of music in everyday wartime life. A May 1941 treatment for the film, then entitled *The Music of War*, sums up its themes.

> More than ever when men are flying through the night and women are away from their homes and their children, their hearts have need of music. All kinds of music—classical music, popular music, home-made music, the nostalgic music of a particular region and just plain martial music to march and work to. For music in Britain to-day is far from being just another escape: it probes into the emotions of the war itself—love of country, love of liberty, love of living, and the exhilaration of fighting for them.[16]

The film had thus morphed into a statement on the essential nature of music in wartime, exploring the relationship between music and the "emotions of the war"—emotions that it did not just express, but "probed," as if music were a kind of analytical tool. This approach resonates with Jennings's work as a founding member of Mass Observation, an organization that attempted to track public feeling through surveys, reports, and diaries. The film is another kind of report, a "sound report," on the *feeling* of war. Moreover, the "emotions of the war itself" turn out to be much harder to pin down in *Listen to Britain* than is suggested by this rather pat list—love of country, love of liberty, love of living, and the exhilaration of fighting for them. In their kinetic quality and their unrootedness in individual subjects, they are

[15] INF6/339, The National Archives of the UK (hereafter National Archives). To my knowledge, none of the existing literature on *Listen to Britain* draws on this substantial Ministry of Information file. The treatment for "National Gallery 1941" (April 28, 1941) is also held in Box 1, Item 7, Humphrey Jennings Collection, BFI Special Collections.

[16] "The Music of War: Treatment" (May 23, 1941), Box 1, Item 7, Humphrey Jennings Collection, BFI Special Collections.

not even properly emotions at all, but rather moods, feelings, or affects.[17] Importantly, this May 1941 document also turns to the idea of women, "away from their homes and their children." Written just as British women were being required to register for war service after April 1941—culminating in their limited conscription in December 1941—this treatment works actively to include women in its account of Britain at war, perhaps informing its shift to a focus on music and feeling in everyday wartime life.[18]

In the final version of the film, it includes not just all kinds of music, but also the noise of industry, transport, and fighter planes, as well as the gentler sounds of nature and radio broadcasts, to produce a dense montage of the sounds of the home front. Jennings's experimental treatment of sound in *Listen to Britain* has been seen in part as simply augmenting his customary use of visual montage.[19] Many of his wartime films use montage to suggest an ideal of unity in diversity, often with a little more emphasis on the latter. Kent Puckett suggests that Jennings's films are an example of "official eccentricity," using montage to "imagine Britain . . . as a collection of distinct and idiosyncratic fragments, images, and perspectives."[20] His use of montage has also been seen as an attempt to produce a democratic form of propaganda, polysemic and open to interpretation.[21]

While the film was not alone in its experimentalism, it did fall somewhat outside the norm, both for the MoI and for the Crown Film Unit, which was responsible for its more ambitious documentaries. In general, the MoI favored a straightforward and informational approach in its documentary films.[22] Jennings was a bit of an outlier: "the unrepentant impressionist of the

[17] This observation relies on an established but also somewhat problematic understanding of emotion versus affect, seen, for instance, in Steve Goodman, *Sonic Warfare: Sound, Affect, and the Ecology of Fear* (Cambridge, MA: MIT Press, 2012), xiv. Rei Terada describes how "emotion appears inseparable from expression and subjectivity," while seeking ultimately to debunk that link (*Feeling in Theory: Emotion After the 'Death of the Subject'* [Cambridge, MA: Harvard University Press, 2001], 6). See also Sianne Ngai, *Ugly Feelings* (Cambridge, MA: Harvard University Press, 2005), 25–27.

[18] Sonya O. Rose, *Which People's War: National Identity and Citizenship in Wartime Britain, 1939–1945* (New York: Oxford University Press, 2003), 109. Starting in April 1941, women had to be registered for employment, although employment was still voluntary. In December 1941, conscription took effect for single women aged 20–30.

[19] Andrew Higson, *Waving the Flag: Constructing a National Cinema in Britain* (Oxford: Clarendon Press, 1995), 202.

[20] Kent Puckett, *War Pictures: Cinema, Violence, and Style in Britain, 1939–1945* (New York: Fordham University Press, 2017), 15, 14.

[21] Beattie, *Humphrey Jennings*, 71, 75.

[22] On the MoI's preference for either straightforward exhortation or, increasingly after 1942, factual information, see James Chapman, *The British at War: Cinema, State and Propaganda, 1939–1945* (London: I. B. Tauris, 1998), 107–108.

Crown Film Unit" as one contemporary put it.[23] *Listen to Britain* was typical of his films in its focus on civilians and the home front and its attention to culture as an object of defense, but its complete avoidance of voice-over and narrative rendered it especially ambiguous. Indeed, a spoken introduction clarifying the film's message was added before its release, at the insistence of commercial distributors, according to Crown's records.[24] A number of critics at the time—especially those most closely engaged with documentary—saw *Listen to Britain* as self-indulgent in its experimentalism and ineffective as propaganda. The documentary film-maker Edgar Anstey described it as "the rarest piece of fiddling since the days of Nero," complaining, "it will not encourage anyone to do anything at all."[25] An American trade journal had a similar verdict: "As an essay in modern documentary screencraft it will please the 1942 equivalent of the avant garde. It is clear that the CFU boys thoroughly enjoyed making it; the experimental manipulation of sound-track and picture, the cutting, and the atmosphere of nostalgia are characteristic." But "as propaganda," it concluded, it was "obscure and scanty."[26]

By many accounts, however, audiences were more receptive. Like other MoI shorts, *Listen to Britain* was widely distributed in British cinemas, all of which had agreed to play MoI films in each program.[27] There are listings from around the country of *Listen to Britain* being shown before films such as Marlene Dietrich's *Manpower* or the cowboy musical *Down Mexico Way*; in such listings, it was often assigned its own time and given a descriptive tag like "the spirit of wartime Britain."[28] The MoI also had a system of

[23] Forsyth Hardy, "The British Documentary Film," in *Twenty Years of British Film 1925–1945*, ed. Michael Balcon (London: Falcon Press, 1947), 59.

[24] "Listen to Britain (National Gallery) (Tin Hat Concerto)," INF 6/339, National Archives. This document, Crown's final report on the project, states "Upon completion, Crown had overspent and the distributors asked for an introductory commentary," noting that this led to further expenditure being approved in order to make the introduction.

[25] Edgar Anstey, *The Spectator*, March 13, 1942 (*Listen to Britain*, press cuttings, British Film Institute Reubens Library [hereafter BFI]).

[26] A. F., *Motion Picture Herald*, March 14, 1942, 554 (Box 2, Item 20, Humphrey Jennings Collection, BFI Special Collections).

[27] Chapman, *British at War*, 93–94. Chapman notes that the MoI started off producing 5-minute shorts, with cinemas agreeing to set aside 5-minute slots before features, later moving to 15-minute films that would change monthly (pp. 93–108). The shift to 15-minute films might help explain *Listen to Britain*'s expansion from a 5-minute film, although the new policy did not technically take effect until after it was made.

[28] Examples include "Tatler," *Manchester Evening News*, July 7, 1942, 2; *Sevenoaks Chronicle and Kentish Advertiser*, July 17, 1942, 2; *Stirling Observer*, August 25, 1942, 6. *Listen to Britain* was distributed commercially by British Lion, which created its own set of publicity materials for the film, featuring the tag "The music of a people at war . . . the sound of life in Britain, by night and by day" and casting it as "a worthy box-office successor to 'Target for To-night' and 'Ferry Pilot,'" both more informational documentaries about military efforts (*Listen to Britain*, press cuttings, BFI).

"non-theatrical distribution," presenting programs of shorts in villages and factories (using its own mobile film units) and in cinemas outside of normal showtimes;[29] loaning films to schools, women's organizations, youth clubs, and military units (both at home and overseas); and sending them for distribution in neutral and allied countries.[30] (Although not primarily aimed at overseas distribution, *Listen to Britain* was sent overseas, including to the United States, where it was distributed by the American Office of War Information, having been refused by all American theatrical distributors.[31]) Across these different venues, *Listen to Britain* seemed to resonate with audiences, especially British ones, as indeed did most of Jennings's films. In surveys, Tom Harrisson recalled, Jennings "was one of those whose films were most effective public wise,"[32] while the head of Crown, Ian Dalrymple, recalled that "the films with most impact" consistently came from Jennings.[33] Roger Manvell, who traveled with the MoI's mobile film unit, reports of Jennings's films: "I can testify personally that they were the ones of all we constantly showed that most immediately stirred emotions not only in the West Country but in the far tougher Northeast of Britain."[34] *Listen to Britain* was particularly effective in provoking such an emotional response. Helen Forman, who also worked with the MoI, recalled,

> All sorts of audiences felt it to be a distillation and also a magnification of their own experience of the home front. This was especially true of factory audiences. I remember one show in a factory in the Midlands where about

[29] For instance, *Listen to Britain* was shown within a free weekly series of films presented by the MoI in Bristol in summer 1942, in connection with an effort to encourage people to stay home for their holidays ("'Stay-at-Home' Film Shows," *Western Daily Press*, July 25, 1942, 4).

[30] Helen Forman, "The Non-Theatrical Distribution of Films by the Ministry of Information," in *Propaganda, Politics and Film, 1918–45*, ed. Nicholas Pronay and D. W. Spring (London: The Macmillan Press, 1982), 223–230; Everett Lawson, "'Half-Crown' Film Unit," *Edinburgh Evening News*, March 19, 1942, 2.

[31] "Britain's Film Role in America," *Documentary Newsletter* 4 (February 1943): 173. The MoI categorized films as "O" ("sent overseas"), "O.O." ("primarily for overseas use"), or "O.O.O." ("exclusively for overseas use"); *Listen to Britain* was categorized as "O" (*Documentary Newsletter* 3 [May 1942]: 74). Crown's report on the film lists additional versions made for countries across liberated Europe in 1944, as well as versions for Spain, Portugal, Turkey, Argentina, and Brazil in 1942, and China in 1946: INF 6/339, National Archives.

[32] Tom Harrisson, "Films and the Home Front: The Evaluation of Their Effectiveness by Mass-Observation," in *Propaganda, Politics and Film, 1918–45*, ed. Nicholas Pronay and D. W. Spring (London: Macmillan Press, 1982), 235. Harrisson is referring to surveys by Mass Observation, an organization he co-founded with Jennings.

[33] Ian Dalrymple, "The Crown Film Unit, 1940–43," in *Propaganda, Politics and Film, 1918–45*, ed. Nicholas Pronay and D. W. Spring (London: Macmillan Press, 1982), 217.

[34] Roger Manvell, *Films and the Second World War* (London: Dent, 1974), 159.

> 800 workers clapped and stamped approval. Films got very short shrift if they touched any area of people's experience and did not ring true.[35]

Dalrymple suggested that it was also very successful with military units based overseas, for whom it had a different kind of emotional appeal: "*Listen to Britain* was particularly popular with those serving in Egypt and North Africa, with its nostalgic scenes . . . , and the visual proof that the spirit at home remained high and resolute."[36] Such impressions are confirmed by at least one letter to Crown, from a Leading Aircraftman stationed in Southern Rhodesia. He wrote,

> Last night at the local cinema I saw a British Unit film 'Listen to Britain.' I can safely say this is the best ever yet put on—and it was a great source of joy to me, and I can also speak the same for Rhodesian friends who were with me. Particularly did I enjoy Myra Hess and the R.A.F. orchestra playing (in part) a Mozart Piano Concerto. It was really a first class effort. I am sure such a film is a source of joy to we fellows who have been away for 2 years.[37]

It is this strong emotional connection that distinguishes *Listen to Britain* from other documentary propaganda. Its focus on music seems central to this effect. But so do the particular ways—largely unarticulated in these accounts—in which it embeds music in the sounds of a nation mobilized for war.

Feeling Connected: Music and the Sounds of War

In *Listen to Britain*, the sounds of war are not the sounds of violence or the battlefield, but those of everyday life for the whole population, including women and children, civilians and non-combatant war workers. In this sense, it anticipates recent calls within sound studies for a more expansive approach to the sound of war.[38] To some extent, the film's focus on the

[35] Forman, "Non-Theatrical Distribution of Films," 230.

[36] Dalrymple, "Crown Film Unit, 1940–43," 218.

[37] LAC G. Maurice Turner (RAF Station Kinnalo) to Griggs (CFU), August 4, 1942, INF 6/339, National Archives.

[38] See Jim Sykes, "Ontologies of Acoustic Endurance: Rethinking Wartime Sound and Listening," *Sound Studies* 4 (2018): 37; Gavin Williams, Introduction to *Hearing the Crimean War: Wartime Sound and the Unmaking of Sense*, ed. Gavin Williams (Oxford: Oxford University Press, 2019), xxxi.

home front might be seen to demand such an approach. The limits of wartime sound are challenged in multiple ways by World War Two and by the particular circumstances of the Blitz, in which the lines between battlefield and home, soldier and civilian were largely effaced. Even in this context, though, *Listen to Britain* is unusual. Contemporary representations of the sounds of war tended to focus on violence. For an example, one need only look to Jennings's earlier film *London Can Take It!* (1940, co-directed with Harry Watts), which also shared *Listen to Britain*'s sound editor, Stewart McAllister. One of the most important propaganda films about the home front, *London Can Take It!* represented Londoners' experience of the Blitz through images of their daily life, but the only *sounds* included (other than the prominent voice-over and, once, the chimes of Big Ben) were those of air raids themselves—sirens, explosions, the hiss of falling bombs, anti-aircraft gunners. This, the narrator observed, was the "symphony of war."[39]

Jennings himself seemed to be fascinated both with the new sounds of air raids and with their surreal juxtapositions with music.[40] He wrote in one 1941 letter,

> Queer life. We were recording Handel's Water-music (of all things) the other night at the Queen's Hall with the LPO—and the sound comes out from the loudspeaker in the sound-truck in the street. Near the end of the session there were "chandelier" flares overhead—lighting up the sky—the music echoing down the street: the planes booming and the particular air-raid sound: people kicking broken glass on the pavement.[41]

Despite this fascination, Jennings turns away from the sounds of air raids in *Listen to Britain*, presenting a strikingly different notion of the "symphony of war." Instead, the film focuses strictly on the sounds of the British war effort at home: munitions factories, trains, mining, farming, even aircraft, as long

[39] *London Can Take It!* dir. Harry Watt and Humphrey Jennings, Crown Film Unit, 1940, in *Listen to Britain and Other Films by Humphrey Jennings* (Chatsworth, CA: Image Entertainment, 2002, DVD). Also see James G. Mansell, *The Age of Noise in Britain: Hearing Modernity* (Urbana: University of Illinois Press, 2017), 145-146.

[40] On this point, also see Jefferson Hunter, *English Filming, English Writing* (Bloomington: Indiana University Press, 2010), 74, 77–78.

[41] Humphrey Jennings to Cicely Jennings, Easter Monday 1941, in Kevin Jackson, ed., *Humphrey Jennings Film Reader* (Manchester: Carcanet, 1993), 15. Jennings was recording the music for his film *Words for Battle*. The Queen's Hall itself was destroyed in an air raid shortly afterward, in May 1941. See Peter Stansky and William Abrahams, *London's Burning: Life, Death and Art in the Second World War* (London: Constable, 1994), 96–97.

as they are friendly. The sounds of air raids or other violent attack are systematically excluded.

The revised scope of wartime sound in *Listen to Britain* might be understood as part of a turn to women's role in total war. A closely related example is Len Lye's *When the Pie Was Opened* (1941), a MoI propaganda film that also explores the sounds and images of daily wartime life, in this case in the service of instructions for how to make a pie with limited rations.[42] This film similarly represents women as part of the war effort, showing how that effort extended to all areas of life even in the ostensible privacy of home. But even Lye's film includes the sounds of aerial bombardment, creating sonic connections between violent attack and women's everyday management of food resources. *Listen to Britain* is all the more telling in its avoidance of these sounds.

The noise of air raids and the feelings it prompted became the object of some official concern in wartime. As Michal Shapira has shown, such noise was felt to contribute to fear and anxiety; psychoanalysts and other experts even suggested tactics such as "blitz concerts"—using recordings of blitz sounds—in an effort to acclimate the listener to the sounds of air raids.[43] More broadly, as James Mansell argues in a discussion of *Listen to Britain*, the threat of air raids gave new importance to noise and listening, which became objects of management in new ways. He observes,

> The auditory culture of total war bound the hearer to the nation in ways that would have been inconceivable outside the conditions of aerial bombardment and fear of invasion.... Listening—to radio broadcasts, warning sirens, and other wartime sound signals—became a fundamental requirement of the wartime citizen, as did knowing when not to listen.[44]

For Mansell, *Listen to Britain* ultimately uses music as a reprieve from noise and encourages listening to the right things—not to the noise of war, but to the sounds of the community pulling together. For Ben Highmore, similarly,

[42] Anita Jorge, "A 'Symphony of Britain at War' or the 'Rhythm of Workaday Britain'? Len Lye's *When the Pie Was Opened* (1941) and the Musicalisation of Warfare," in *Soundings: Documentary Film and the Listening Experience*, ed. Geoffrey Cox et al. (Huddersfield: University of Huddersfield Press, 2018), 220–239. *When the Pie Was Opened*, dir. Len Lye, Ministry of Information, 1941 (BFI Player).

[43] Michal Shapira, *The War Inside: Psychoanalysis, Total War, and the Making of the Democratic Self in Postwar Britain* (Cambridge: Cambridge University Press, 2013), 40, n. 76.

[44] Mansell, *The Age of Noise in Britain*, 150.

Listen to Britain is about "the sensorial recalibration of the environment during wartime" at a moment when populations had to learn "feelings and responses that would somehow be adequate to the new circumstances" of aerial bombardment.[45] Specifically, he suggests, it is not so much about sounds as about listening and about learning new forms of attention while avoiding or managing introspection.[46] In this sense, it does a particular kind of "morale work."

But something about the sound of war in *Listen to Britain* is not fully accounted for by these readings, both of which take the film primarily as a lesson in wartime listening. Indeed, their attempts to fit the film into more conventional understandings of morale and wartime sound help reveal some of its idiosyncrasy. Far from avoiding introspection, as one might expect, *Listen to Britain* dwells extensively on introspection, melancholy, and nostalgia in its "report" on wartime feeling. And while Mansell's reading rests on the claim that "Jennings carefully separated noise and music on the sound track," as he did in earlier films, *Listen to Britain* is more interesting for the way it departs from this earlier approach.[47] It does exclude violent types of wartime noise, as discussed above. Once that exclusion is in place, though, it uses all the editorial powers at its disposal to render the noise of war as continuous with music.

The opposition between noise and music is the object of play throughout *Listen to Britain*. This is signaled from the start by the opening title's image of an intersecting anti-aircraft gun and violin (Figure 1.1), juxtaposed with an incipit from "Rule Britannia"; in a 1990 study that still stands as one of the most observant readings of the film, William Guynn went so far as to suggest that the breakdown of such oppositions constitutes "the film's symbolic project."[48] Indeed, if contemporary sound studies often suggests a dichotomy between sound as text or representation and as a sonic force,[49] *Listen to Britain* is suggestive in the ways it breaks down that dichotomy, grounding

[45] Ben Highmore, *Cultural Feelings: Mood, Mediation and Cultural Politics* (London: Routledge, 2017), 71, 63.

[46] Ibid., 67.

[47] Mansell, *Age of Noise in Britain*, 179. Jennings's *Spare Time* (1939) does separate noise and music in this way, as Mansell correctly observes, and in fact includes very little industrial noise, reserving it for a disruptive moment at the very end of the film when the noise of a coal mine marks the end of the leisure time that is the film's main subject. A telling comparison is *Listen to Britain*'s reuse of this same stock footage of the sounds of a mining shift's start, which are here more integrated with other sounds and simply mark a shift into night-time activities.

[48] William Guynn, *A Cinema of Nonfiction* (Rutherford, NJ: Fairleigh Dickinson University Press, 1990), 87. Also see his discussion of the opening title on page 78.

[49] See especially Goodman, *Sonic Warfare*, 10.

Figure 1.1 *Listen to Britain*, opening titles.

the experience of music in a transformed sense of the power of sound itself, in what might be called (borrowing Steve Goodman's term) an act of "affective mobilization."[50]

Listen to Britain labors to create a seamless web out of the sounds of music, nature, and machine. This is illustrated by the film's very opening segment. It begins with the sounds of trees and birds intermingling with the roar of Spitfires overhead before giving way to the noise of farm machinery. The hum of the Spitfires continues through the following shots, underlaying the sounds of the BBC news and images of a woman at home closing her blackout curtains, and then mingling with the music of a swing band—a sound advance overlaying outdoor shots of forces at leisure or preparing for night-time work—before that music finds its home in a longer sequence in a dance hall. The tune to which the dancers sing and whistle along is the "Beer

[50] Ibid., 3 (and elsewhere). The film might be seen to draw on what Goodman calls the "attractive" (versus. the "repulsive") "power of sonic force." He writes, "On the other side, we have a tactical deployment whose objective is that of intensification, the heightening of collective sensation, an attractive, almost magnetic, or vertical force, a force that sucks bodies in toward its source. . . . In this instance, the aim of mobilizing bodies extensively is accompanied and perhaps overridden by the primary objective of the intensive mobilization of affect" (p. 11).

Barrel Polka," described by Paul Fussell as "the Allied song of the war" and a staple of cinematic sing-alongs, its blatant escapism replacing the patriotic sentiments of earlier wars.[51] The music then fades and gives way to the industrial noise of mining and the sound of a transport train. The latter is overlaid with another musical sound advance, of a group of soldiers singing inside the train; their music fades and is overlaid with the noise of the signal and train once again, which then matches with the sounds of a factory in the following shot.

Throughout the film, sound is a force of connection. Even within scenes, sounds work to link bodies, spaces, and times, rendering immaterial the boundaries between them. Consistently, sounds also overflow scenes, arriving before or lingering after the shots to which they belong. The film abounds in acoustic mixes and dissolves, matching (where juxtaposed sounds rhyme or echo each other), asynchronous sound, confusions of sound sources, and effects of disacousmatization.[52] Such techniques are not unusual, of course, but they are used with a density and conspicuousness that is extreme.

One of the effects of these techniques is that sound is both grounded in particular places, bodies, and things, and also rendered somehow all-pervasive. In his study of McAllister, the film's editor, Dai Vaughan writes, "There is a constant sense that music and even synch sound-effects are lifted slightly away from the picture; and this is abetted in numerous details by the editing."[53] In other words, while the film almost always reveals a source for a sound (with the exception of radio sound, whose source is implied without necessarily being seen), this revelation tends not to fully resolve the mystery of its acousmatic status, suggesting an ultimately invisible force animating all sounds.[54] This idea is confirmed at the end of the film, the only moment when a source is never suggested, as an unseen choir

[51] Paul Fussell, *Wartime: Understanding and Behavior in the Second World War* (New York: Oxford University Press, 1989), 187.

[52] On some of these acoustic effects, see Guynn's extensive analysis in *Cinema of Nonfiction*, 69–148, especially his discussion of "acoustic matches," which includes both the type of reflection effects mentioned here and two other effects: misapprehension-correction and acoustic dissolves (pp. 120, 147).

[53] Dai Vaughan, *Portrait of an Invisible Man: The Working Life of Stewart McAllister, Film Editor* (London: BFI, 1983), 91.

[54] In this sense, the film reflects Mladen Dolar's proposition that "there is no such thing as disacousmatization," not only in the case of the voice; it suggests an ultimate animating source of all sound that cannot be seen. See Mladen Dolar, *A Voice and Nothing More* (Cambridge, MA: MIT Press, 2006), 70.

sings "Rule Britannia," as if emerging spontaneously from the landscape itself.[55]

The film's representation of the diffuse and connecting force of sound seems strongly shaped by radio's new pervasiveness in wartime. As Patrick Deer has observed of 1940s Britain, radio "shaped the sensory landscape of wartime like no other medium," providing a crucial sense of aural continuity amid disruption."[56] Radio's centrality to national life is more obviously thematized in Jennings's later film, *A Diary for Timothy* (1946), which includes scenes of disparate households listening to the same broadcast, the radio transforming isolated individuals and families into a community. No such conventional scenes of radio listening occur in *Listen to Britain*, but radio ends up pervading the film: in the sounds of the Greenwich time signal, sober news-reading, the nightly activity of the BBC Overseas service, or even specific programs.[57] One slightly baffled critic went so far as to propose that radio was the primary focus of the film: "What the picture presumably seeks to depict is the work of the BBC in disseminating news at home and propaganda abroad, in entertaining the men in uniform and the women at the machine bench."[58] And it certainly does use radio to represent an intimate connection between Britain and its far-flung empire, which provided so much of the human and material resources for its war.[59]

The film, then, helps to suggest the distinct importance of radio as a sonic tool for the management of morale in World War Two. As Ben Anderson observes, drawing on a 1941 issue of the *American Journal of Sociology* devoted to the concept of morale, radio promised "to synchronize a heterogeneous population through the attunement of bodies at a distance" and through its enabling of "certain collective affects."[60] Furthermore, in evoking these capabilities of radio sound, *Listen to Britain* also explores a related,

[55] On the "liberating" of sound in this scene, see Vaughan, *Invisible Man*, 92. On sonic plenitude and disjunction in the film, also see Beattie, *Humphrey Jennings*, 74, and Guynn, *Cinema of Nonfiction*, 93, 103.

[56] Deer, *Culture in Camouflage*, 132, 134. In this last observation, Deer is drawing on Paddy Scannell, *Radio, Television and Modern Life: A Phenomenological Approach* (Oxford: Blackwell, 1996), 37–48.

[57] Vaughan, *Portrait of an Invisible Man*, 92.

[58] A. F., *Motion Picture Herald*, March 14, 1942, 554 (Box 2, item 20, Humphrey Jennings Collection, BFI Special Collections).

[59] See Overy, *Blood and Ruins*, 388–390.

[60] Ben Anderson, "Modulating the Excess of Affect: Morale in a State of 'Total War,'" in *The Affect Theory Reader*, ed. Melissa Gregg and Gregory J. Seigworth (Durham, NC/London: Duke University Press, 2010), 179–180. Also see the more recent version of this chapter in Ben Anderson, *Encountering Affect: Capacities, Apparatuses, Conditions* (Farnham, Surrey/Burlington, VT: Ashgate; 2014).

more abstract idea about how morale works in total war—as an affective force that moves between individuals in a way that is fundamentally mysterious and diffuse.[61] In *Listen to Britain*, the boundlessness of sound becomes a way of conceptualizing this quality of morale itself. In its expansive approach to both the sound and the feelings of war, the film explores the expanded field of morale in total war.

The Music of War

Listen to Britain's representation of music is grounded in its broader rethinking of the nature of sound as a connecting force in national life, and as a figure of war's totality. Nonetheless, the film is deeply invested in *music* as a manifestation of sound with special properties and powers. Indeed, even the specific music heard in the film often has significance, and is the product of directorial decisions rather than happenstance. Jennings had a long-standing interest in music, not least from his early experience as a designer for productions of theater works by Purcell, Stravinsky, and Honegger.[62] Many of his documentaries focus especially closely on music, depending on it to provide unique insight into daily life. His developing concern with music in British life can be seen in the 1939 documentary *Spare Time*, which focused on the leisure activities of industrial workers across Britain. Its most infamous scene presented a rehearsal of "Rule Britannia" by a cotton workers' kazoo band, in ways that prompted criticism of Jennings as a patronizing observer of working-class culture but could also be seen to epitomize his surrealist sensibilities and a deflating approach to any grand patriotic sentiment.[63] Elsewhere in *Spare Time*, a miners' chorus rehearses Handel, with the pianist, arriving late, casually beginning to play while still standing and removing outer layers of clothing. Jennings's favored images of musical solidarity were transient and haphazard moments of sounding and listening. His films, including *Listen to Britain*, were filled with such moments. But if *Spare Time* featured music as leisure, he also cast music as a form of work. He did so most directly in an unfinished film project on the

[61] See Anderson, "Modulating the Excess of Affect," 170–171.

[62] Kevin Jackson, *Humphrey Jennings* (London: Picador, 2004), 5, 68, 72. As a student at Cambridge, Jennings was involved in the first British production of *The Soldier's Tale*, with Michael Redgrave and Lydia Lopokova, and a production of Purcell's *King Arthur*, both in 1928.

[63] Ibid., 215.

London Symphony Orchestra that documented the everyday activities of the group, constructing music as labor of an often grueling, mundane kind.[64] Elsewhere he showcased music as part of other kinds of work and the workplace. In *Fires Were Started* (1943), for instance, firemen fill long intervals of waiting for action with music-making.

All of these visions of music—as labor, as leisure, as art—are on display in *Listen to Britain.* The film explores the diverse functions of listening and music-making and the various ways in which they can be mobilized: increasing productivity, filling empty time, providing comfort or a restorative reprieve. Underlying all of these functions, though, is one central role: music has a special power to connect individuals to places and to larger groups. It acts as a kinetic force, coordinating bodies both in work and in play; while rarely expressive in any conventional sense, it creates affective alliances; it conjures distant people, places, and memories; through radio, it connects people around the nation and the empire.

Much of *Listen to Britain* features scenes of informal music-making and distracted listening. However, the film culminates in two artfully opposed concert scenes. One is a lunchtime concert at a factory canteen by the music hall entertainers Flanagan and Allen. The location is not disclosed in the film, but Crown's records reveal it as the Royal Ordnance Factory (ROF) at Hayes—a munitions factory with a large female workforce, in London's western suburbs.[65] The other is the performance of a Mozart concerto by Myra Hess at the National Gallery, less than twenty miles away. These scenes continue to foreground the idea of sound as a connecting force, but they also explore some more specific concerns with how people listen and what they listen to. They are highly constructed representations of music and listening, suggesting some of the constraints of—and the dangers that threaten—the particular image of collectivity and morale the film works to build. Indeed, with these scenes, the film seems to court the dangers of atomization, interiority, and melancholy—as well as the dangers of social and cultural hierarchies—only to absorb them into its sonic portrait of wartime life.

[64] Jennings's notes for this project are published in Jackson, *Humphrey Jennings Film Reader*, 118–156; Also see Jackson, *Humphrey Jennings*, 339.

[65] "Listen to Britain (National Gallery) (Tin Hat Concerto)" [final report], INF 6/339, National Archives. This report notes that the BBC was also recording this performance. Nick Holder notes that Flanagan and Allen performed at ROF Hayes for the BBC radio show Workers' Playtime (*The Royal Ordnance Factory at Hayes* [London: Museum of London, 2011], 27). On women at Hayes, see pp. 21–23.

The performance at the factory canteen puts music's power to build solidarity on display, but that power seems to depend here on a nostalgic and highly idealized vision of working-class popular culture. Flanagan and Allen were a throwback to the prewar past, and were a little old-fashioned even at their prime in the 1930s. Jennings chose them precisely for this reason, calling for "the nostalgic entertainment of the working-class Flanagan and Allen."[66] (Jennings called for other relics of Victorian popular culture elsewhere in the film, only to be stymied in his plans by the tastes and knowledge of his subjects.) The song they sing here, "Round the Back of the Arches," is a rewriting of their signature song "Underneath the Arches," from 1932. Whereas the Depression-era song dwelled on the image of homeless men sleeping under railway arches ("underneath the arches, we dream our dreams away"), the wartime song is nostalgic for home and old friends, looking forward to a time of being settled and surrounded by those friends once again, "when the storm clouds all roll over."

In this scene, the workers—male and female—are at first largely oblivious to the music and absorbed in their own tasks; only slowly do they begin to engage with the entertainers on stage. Indeed, the whole scene is structured to create a sense of cohesion emerging out of apparent atomization, through the force of music. After a set of unrelated exterior shots overlaid by the sound of the performance, we first see scattered individuals and small groups, occupied with the business of lunch, before the camera focuses its attention on the performers. Soon, there are close-up shots of one or two people listening, but still in a slightly distracted way as they smoke or chat, before we finally see a shot of the whole group, now all facing forward, moving and whistling together (Figure 1.2). It is an image of a dynamic collective, bound together in an affective alliance characterized by a kind of melancholy optimism.

The film then shifts seamlessly to a different lunch-time audience, now at the National Gallery, listening to Hess perform the first movement of Mozart's Piano Concerto in G major, K.453 with the RAF orchestra, the Queen conspicuously in attendance.[67] On one hand, there is a clear attempt to create continuity between the two concerts, and between this music and the industrial noise into which it eventually fades. This is evidenced in the

[66] "The Music of War: Treatment" (May 23, 1941), Box 1, Item 7, Humphrey Jennings Collection, BFI Special Collections.

[67] Queen Elizabeth (the Queen Mother) attended to mark Hess's recent award of a MBE, and Hess invited Jennings to film on that day, offering to play the Mozart concerto he had requested (Rosen, "Sounds of Music and War," 396).

Figure 1.2 *Listen to Britain*, canteen shot.

striking sound edit that connects the two scenes, in which "Underneath the Arches" seems to join the concerto already in progress, its final chord melding with the first chord of the Mozart excerpt. Like the ROF Hayes scene, the National Gallery scene, with its many people in uniform, casts the concert as a short, sustaining break from war work. It also highlights the integration of listening and daily activities, returning frequently to shots of people having tea and sandwiches (the Gallery ran a canteen for this purpose) on the vestibule stairs, where the music could be clearly heard. The scenes thus present different places and different workers, but essentially the same situation. However, the very carefulness with which the Mozart is sonically bound to the popular song that precedes it and the industrial noise that follows suggests some of the precariousness of this concert scene—the only one in the film featuring art music, the one that most conspicuously raises issues of class difference, and also the only one prominently featuring traces of damage and signs of immediate danger.

The Mozart concerto, performed at the film-makers' request, seems carefully chosen to manage some of this precariousness.[68] Orchestral music was unusual at the National Gallery concerts, which normally featured chamber music. But performing a concerto allowed the film to highlight both the RAF orchestra and the ideas of cooperation and coordination associated with the genre. As David Rosen recounts, Jennings had first considered including Bach's Fifth Brandenburg Concerto before settling on Mozart.[69] (Both, significantly, would avoid the emotional excesses of later concertos while also being suited to a smaller orchestra.) Jennings's collaborator, Joe Mendoza, recalls telling him, "You've got to have *human* music if you want to make a film about the meaning of music to ordinary people in the National Gallery.... Why don't you have a Mozart piano concerto? It's always a warm, friendly sound in the orchestra."[70] The first movement of the bright G major Concerto seems especially appropriate, its main theme presenting a refined, playful version of a military march.[71] "The music is in uniform too," as a draft script noted, referring perhaps to this military topic as well as to the uniformed RAF orchestra.[72] But the concerto could also be seen to offer some more significant contributions to the film's construction of wartime citizenship. Simon Keefe has gone so far as to suggest that Mozart's concertos offered their original audience "an excellent vehicle for learning about cooperation (or, more precisely, the quest for cooperation)"—a lesson as important for wartime civilians as for Mozart's Enlightenment listeners.[73] And the concerto offers another lesson especially suited to Jennings's approach, which (as Puckett notes) favors individual particularity and eccentricity over a totalizing homogeneity.[74] As James Hepokoski observes, the form Mozart adopts for his concerto first movements—including this one—is especially rigid and unwieldy, giving "the impression of passing through a preformatted check-list of concerto-specific tasks that must be accomplished in a certain sequence."[75] These constraints, though, prompt in Mozart ever

[68] See Rosen, "Sounds of Music and War," 396, 404–405.

[69] Ibid., 396.

[70] Ibid., 404–405, quoting Vaughan, *Invisible Man*, 85.

[71] See Charles Rosen, *The Classical Style: Haydn, Mozart, Beethoven*, expanded ed. (New York: W. W. Norton. 1997), 221.

[72] "National Gallery, 3rd Treatment, The Tin Hat Concerto," August 21, 1941, p. 3, INF6/339, National Archives.

[73] Simon P. Keefe, "Dramatic Dialogue in Mozart's Viennese Piano Concertos: A Study of Competition and Cooperation in Three First Movements," *Musical Quarterly* 83 (1999): 197.

[74] Puckett, *War Pictures*, 13–15.

[75] James Hepokoski, *Elements of Sonata Theory: Norms, Types, and Deformations in the Late-Eighteenth-Century Sonata* (New York: Oxford University Press, 2006), 470.

more ingenious individualized responses, in ways that suggest Jennings's ideal British response to wartime demands and constraints themselves. "One gets the impression," Hepokoski observes, that Mozart "has individualized as much as can be individualized, that taken together these works provide a treatise on how to refresh even the most rigid of schemes." It is another important lesson for the wartime citizen, and one very much at the heart of *Listen to Britain*'s vision of a nation of individuals mobilized for total war.

More than the film's other segments, the National Gallery sequence is closely governed by its music, which provides order and cohesion to a visually fragmented series of shots.[76] If the factory scene showed a clear process of integration through listening, the Gallery scene has a greater tendency toward diffuseness and atomization. Throughout the concerto's opening orchestral ritornello, the camera's eye seems oddly distracted, first alighting on the orchestra but then shifting quickly between shots of people eating and chatting, buying postcards, or looking at paintings. As the piano exposition begins, it focuses more closely on Hess and the seated audience in the central concert space, but then its focus moves a little anxiously between that audience and signs of threat—empty or sandbagged frames of paintings, water buckets in case of fire, and the damaged windows and dome of the Gallery itself. This anxiety appears prompted—or at least allowed—by the music, as the camera strays to these images in a transitional piano-orchestral passage that feels tonally and thematically unrooted. As Hess settles into a new theme securely anchored in the dominant, however, the camera returns to the performance space, fixing on different faces in the audience, as well as Hess's, in a steady rhythm of shots that matches that of the music.

These faces are noticeably more differentiated than the factory listeners in the previous scene: "Here," Jennings wrote of this scene, "for the purest of all music, the most mixed of all groups."[77] The film highlights this diversity by focusing on individuals and small groups of listeners, while the seated audience is rarely seen as a collective whole (there are just two short shots of the group, and those are from behind, possibly for practical reasons). If the audience is mixed, so are the modes of listening on display, in ways Jennings carefully dictated in the shooting script.[78] Some listeners look

[76] For an analysis of how shots are coordinated with the score in the entire scene, see Rosen, "Sounds of Music and War," 415–425.

[77] "The Music of War: Treatment" (May 23, 1941), Box 1, Item 7, Humphrey Jennings Collection, BFI Special Collections.

[78] The scene follows many of the details in the "National Gallery 1941" rough shooting script, which calls for shots of a "pair of ambulance drivers in uniform (girls from Station 76)" in the

Figure 1.3 *Listen to Britain*, listeners in the National Gallery sequence.

attentively at a score or a program, others look around or listen with faces covered, while a number of audience members appear to have their minds elsewhere (Figure 1.3). In a set of clearly staged shots, for instance, a well-dressed young woman in black stands alone, while the painting behind her suggests her thoughts turning to a soldier in battle; similarly, a member of the RAF's Polish squadrons stands near a painting of two little girls (Figure 1.4).[79] What is perhaps most striking about this scene, then, is that it allows an extraordinary amount of space for introspection as people listen quietly, some clearly lost in their own thoughts, some standing alone with images suggesting those absent or gone. Nonetheless, despite their diversity and

audience, as well as "a young girl music student, who is following with a score, a woman air-raid warden and an old man listening by himself with his hand over his eyes" (Jackson, *Humphrey Jennings Film Reader*, 24–25). Jennings shot some of the footage for this scene (including shots of the Queen) immediately after the concert rather than during it, allowing him to stage some of it.

[79] The "National Gallery 1941" rough shooting script calls for a shot of a "Polish Flyer standing against reproduction of Gainsborough's Artist's Daughters" and for a sailor (rather than a woman) next to an Uccello painting, both of which are the paintings seen here (Jackson, *Humphrey Jennings Film Reader*, 24–25).

Figure 1.4 *Listen to Britain*, introspective listening in the National Gallery sequence.

this element of introspection—typically seen as a threat to collectivity and morale—the audience is bound together in the act of listening and enveloped in that "warm, friendly sound" of the orchestra.

Jennings's representation of the National Gallery concerts is highly constructed, participating in a larger discourse that ensconced them as a display of social cohesion in diversity (within limits, as will be seen in Chapter 3), heroic endurance, and communal participation in a transcendent cultural idealism. But it also departs from this discourse in some subtle and important ways. Kenneth Clark claimed a higher, almost spiritual purpose for the concerts—"that of maintaining through beauty our faith in the greatness of the human spirit."[80] Writing much later, he recalled Hess as a heroic figure, a "conquering, radiant presence" in an "atmosphere of defeat and gloom." He described the first National Gallery concert as transformational, especially when Hess performed her arrangement of Bach's "Jesu, Joy of Man's Desiring."

> I stood behind one of the curtains, and looked at the packed audience. They had come with anxious, hungry faces, but as they listened to the music and looked at Myra's rapt expression, they lost the thought of their private worries. I had never seen faces so transformed, and said to myself "This is how men and women must have looked at the great preachers who gave them back their courage and faith."[81]

[80] Kenneth Clark, "From the National Gallery," in *National Gallery Concerts in Aid of the Musicians Benevolent Fund, 10th October 1939–10th October 1944* (London, 1944), 6.
[81] Kenneth Clark, "Music in Place of Pictures," in *Myra Hess by Her Friends*, ed. Denise Lassimonne and Howard Ferguson (London: Hamish Hamilton, 1966), 57.

Figure 1.5 *A Diary for Timothy*, listeners at the National Gallery.

For Clark, then, drawing on some traditional notions of cultural uplift, Hess's concerts allowed audiences to transcend both the circumstances of war and their own anxious condition. Clark's description of the concerts resonates closely with how Elaine Scarry describes the workings of morale. She suggests, "the notion of 'morale' still tends to have an aura of the spiritual, to signal some capacity for self-transcendence or form of consciousness different from the physical events."[82] She adds that this aspect of morale allows it to be associated with "benign activities" such as music. By this definition, though, morale—and music—are quite distant from the material realities of war.

Jennings's later film, *Diary for Timothy*, adheres more closely to Clark's description in its rendering of a Hess performance of Beethoven's "Appassionata."[83] One critic described it in terms much like Clark's, as displaying "the heroic face of Dame Myra Hess playing Beethoven to an ennobled audience steady while the bombs fall."[84] Focusing on a single row of listeners rather than the scattered audience of *Listen to Britain*, the camera slowly scans their rapt faces, casting the concert as an exercise in communal transcendence (Figure 1.5). *Listen to Britain*, though, is strikingly different, focusing instead on the everydayness of the occasion, the "human" sound of Mozart, and the diversity of the audience and the types of listening it displays.

[82] Elaine Scarry, *The Body in Pain: The Making and Unmaking of the World* (Oxford: Oxford University Press, 1985), 105–106. On this passage, also see Anderson, "Modulating the Excess of Affect," 174.

[83] *A Diary for Timothy*, dir. Humphrey Jennings, Crown Film Unit, 1946, in *Listen to Britain and Other Films by Humphrey Jennings* (Chatsworth, CA: Image Entertainment, 2002, DVD); also available on BFI Player.

[84] C. A., *New York Post*, December 28, 1946 (Box 1, Item 3, Humphrey Jennings Collection, BFI Special Collections). The sequence was filmed in late 1944, so the observation about bombs is slightly anachronistic and more applicable to *Listen to Britain*.

While it similarly casts Hess as heroic and her audience as ennobled, it does not quite content itself with a notion of music or morale as transcendence, in the sense of being *beyond* the reality of war. For no such thing is possible in the concept of total war—no beyond, no excess, no "outside to war," in Anderson's words.[85] Indeed, as the National Gallery scene ends, it goes out of its way to connect this "purest of all music" (to recall Jennings' description) with the noisy business of war.

Here, as the exposition of the concerto's first movement draws to a close, the camera moves out of the Gallery in a quickly changing series of shots that draw the eye upward before establishing a high perspective, floating above the city. (As Rosen notes, this shift from the interior to the exterior of the gallery occurs at a splice in the music, as it cuts from m.125 to m.153.[86]) The camera then focuses on the surrounding heights, bringing into view some potent signs and symbols of war—a barrage balloon, meant to defend from enemy aircraft, and the statue atop Nelson's Column, commemorating his unlikely victory in the Battle of Trafalgar—before looking down on the busy city. The scene ends with another shot of a barrage balloon and then shifts to a tank factory, as the concerto's orchestral ritornello fades away into the sounds of the factory. In planning stages, Jennings described an earlier version of this moment in especially evocative terms.

> The Spitfires and Hurricanes in the sun above the clouds and the smoke, are beautiful shining things, flying in a world very like the lyrical world of Mozart. And below them we can now see London, big as it is, as a grey smudge. And yet it is this grey smudge which is the main objective of the Luftwaffe in the Battle of Britain and which the RAF Patrols are protecting. And right down inside it, invisible from this height, is the National Gallery where hundreds of men and women still find time in their lunch-hour to listen to Mozart and to invigorate themselves for the final battle.[87]

The fighter aircrafts have been replaced with the barrage balloon—a less aggressive image—but the idea is the same: there are points of contact between the world of Mozart and the tools of war. And music is both "above the clouds and the smoke" and at the heart of the "grey smudge" of reality; moreover, it is

[85] Anderson, "Modulating the Excess of Affect," 171; also see Puckett, *War Pictures*, 10.
[86] Rosen, "Sounds of Music and War," 421.
[87] "National Gallery 1941" (April 28, 1941), Box 1, Item 7, Humphrey Jennings Collection, BFI Special Collections.

useful, uplifting, and invigorating, preparing citizens for battle—indeed, for the "final battle," with all the spiritual, apocalyptic overtones of that phrase.

The Mozart concerto is rendered as a particularly powerful sound in this sequence, able to transcend immediate realities and "invigorate" its listeners. Part of its power is that it is especially loosened from its visible source, tending instead to overflow the space of the concert itself. It is heard before the inside of the Gallery is seen and long before the performance itself is shown. And, as the camera leaves the Gallery, the music is still there, heard just as closely as it was before, as if omnipresent, even as the viewpoint ascends high above the city. One could hear it as emanating from the Gallery to pervade reality. But it could also be heard as music of the ether, to which the Gallery concert merely provides a kind of access point. The listeners and musicians are in this sense merely tuning in to a sound that is always there, as part of a sonic flux used to imagine the affects and energies of total war.

The National Gallery scene, then, introduces a potential gap between the art of music and the work of war only to cross it, creating sonic connections between them. But the scene is also the locus for music's peculiar power in the film. Its use of the Mozart concerto allows it to draw on notions of transcendence and ineffability to present music as all-pervasive and mysteriously omnipresent. And it creates a certain space for interiority and melancholy (if not for "private worries"), showing how they, too, can be brought inside the expanded space of total war without disrupting its totality.

The Feeling of Being "Where You Don't Want to Be"

Jacques Rancière has described *Listen to Britain* as a series of "peaceful moments" making for a paradoxical film about war; for him, it is made up of those "moments of suspension" that normally punctuate action.[88] It is partly this that allows melancholy to creep in, perhaps. To suggest so is to depart slightly from Ben Highmore, who observes that if Blitz-time morale work "included self-reflection, it wasn't the sort of self-reflection that could encourage introspection (melancholic or otherwise)."[89] Even in *Listen to Britain*, he adds, "reminiscences are fine but they must be managed," and they tend to be quickly displaced by "the business of moving forward."[90] The

[88] Jacques Rancière, *Film Fables*, trans. Emiliano Battista (Oxford: Berg, 2006), 17.
[89] Highmore, *Cultural Feelings*, 66.
[90] Ibid., 68.

film does perhaps treat reminiscence as something to be managed, but it is nonetheless pervaded by images of introspection, melancholy, and nostalgia, even amid sonic connection. To some extent the film might be seen to reserve such moments of introspection for members of the middle class—for the National Gallery scene, and specifically the airman and well-dressed young woman mentioned above—but it allows introspective listening and music-making for others as well. And if music's power to connect interiorities is at its most concentrated in the Mozart concerto, this power is also extended to other types of music.

In addition to these solitary standing figures in the National Gallery scene, a striking earlier scene shows a woman at home alone, first watching a group of children playing outside as the music of their game reaches her and then turning to a photo of a man in uniform, presumably absent. A synopsis from an earlier version of the film reads: "She stops for a moment—looks across to the mantelpiece, to a photo of a boy in a Glengarrie: a great wave of emotion sweeps over her—the sound of the Pipes played not in the hills of Scotland, but in the sand dunes of Syria, where her lad is away at the war."[91] Another scene features a group of female ambulance workers waiting at a station, dwarfed and out of place among monumental statues in the cavernous space of the Old Bailey, each involved in her own silent thoughts and activities while one woman sings slowly and uncertainly, accompanying herself on an out-of-tune piano (Figure 1.6). She is singing a melancholy Welsh folksong, "The Ash Grove." For Jennings's collaborator Mendoza, this song was about the feeling that "you are where you don't want to be."[92] Like Flanagan and Allen's song, it both remembers lost friends and imagines a reunion. Here, however, that reunion only seems possible in death or the imagination. In the film, the woman sings only the first verse, muddling the words, many of which she cannot quite remember. It ends:

> A host of kind faces is gazing on me.
> The friends of my childhood again are before me
> Each step wakes a memory as freely I roam.
> With soft whispers laden its leaves rustle o'er me

[91] "National Gallery, 3rd Treatment, The Tin Hat Concerto, 21/8/1941," INF6/339, National Archives. This episode was meant to be underlaid by bagpipes, but the production team was apparently unable to find any "Scottish pipers" available (INF5/82, National Archives).

[92] Joe Mendoza, communication with the author, in Vaughan, *Portrait of an Invisible Man*, 83 (also quoted in Rosen, "The Sounds of Music and War," 402).

Figure 1.6 *Listen to Britain*, singing "The Ash Grove" at an ambulance station.

The ash grove, the ash grove alone is my home.[93]

Feelings of melancholy, loss, and displacement are all given space here. (The final verse, which is not included in the film, is even more blatantly concerned with death and absence.) Such feelings emerge again when Canadian soldiers sing "Home on the Range" in another night-time scene of filling empty time, of being "where you don't want to be." In these scenes—all of which thematize displacement in various ways—music works to bind people together even in their isolation and to connect them to people and places from which war separates them. And while this "Ash Grove" episode is not linked in the same way as other potentially troublesome scenes of inwardness to the business of war—it is followed instead by a descent into night and the sound of radio voices reaching out in greeting, not unlike the sounds and faces in the song—there is a clear sense that melancholy is a legitimate

[93] "The Ash Grove," English words by John Oxenford, in *The Songs of Wales*, ed. Brinley Richards (London: Boosey & Co., 1873), 42–43.

wartime feeling, one that can be absorbed and can itself form a bond of connection.

Listen to Britain, then, is a morale-building film that finds space for sadness, inwardness, and melancholy, enfolding them in the sonic and affective flux of total war. To be sure, sadness is not the most disruptive feeling. Panic or fear, or indeed the more "minor" feelings (to cite Sianne Ngai) of anxiety or irritation—these would all be more difficult to assimilate. Melancholy, as Ngai points out, is still one of the "potentially ennobling or morally beatific states."[94] This is very much how it appears in *Listen to Britain*, and, with some careful navigation, even melancholy can be mobilized.

Millions Like Us (1943)

It is perhaps no surprise that a high-cultural figure like Jennings found space for art music in his version of propaganda. For films of a more popular orientation, art music was harder to associate with morale, as seen for instance in Vera Lynn's *We'll Meet Again* (1943), which explicitly posed popular music against an ineffective art music, making a case for the value of entertainment in wartime.[95] *Millions Like Us* (1943), a Gainsborough melodrama, did something similar but drew conspicuously on some of the techniques of documentary, especially *Listen to Britain*, even mimicking particular scenes and shots, as a number of scholars have pointed out.[96] A more straightforwardly successful propaganda film, it makes for a telling comparison with Jennings's documentary, revealing a clear rejection of its vision of art music and further suggesting the precariousness of the National Gallery scene.

Millions Like Us was commissioned by the MoI partly to create a more positive image of women's conscription and of factory work in particular.[97]

[94] Sianne Ngai, *Ugly Feelings* (Cambridge: Harvard University Press, 2005), 6.

[95] See Kate Guthrie, "Vera Lynn on Screen: Popular Music and the 'People's War,'" *Twentieth-Century Music* 14, no. 2 (2017): 245–270.

[96] Higson, *Waving the Flag*, 202, 226, 240; Morris, *Culture and Propaganda*, 151–152; Anthony Aldgate and Jeffrey Richards, *Britain Can Take It: British Cinema in the Second World War* (London: I. B. Tauris, 2007), 309. None of these accounts, though, points to the significant *differences* in how these films treat music. On the merging of documentary and melodrama in *Millions Like Us*, see especially Higson, *Waving the Flag*, 214–231. Also see Christine Gledhill, "'An Abundance of Understatement': Documentary, Melodrama and Romance," in *Nationalising Femininity: Culture, Sexuality and British Cinema in the Second World War*, ed. Christine Gledhill and Gillian Swanson (Manchester: Manchester University Press, 1996), 213–229.

[97] Sue Harper, "The Years of Total War: Propaganda and Entertainment," in *Nationalising Femininity*, 202–203. Also see Higson, *Waving the Flag*, 215; Antonia Lant, *Blackout: Reinventing Women for Wartime British Cinema* (Princeton: Princeton University Press, 1991), 63.

The story follows the young heroine, Celia, as she is conscripted to work in a Welsh munitions factory, moving away from home and living in a hostel with women representing a cross-section of British society, and eventually marrying a young Scottish pilot, Fred, only to lose him in battle. Andrew Higson argues that the film uses documentary's "modes of looking"—a particular kind of public, distanced gaze—to create a sense of the individual as part of the collective.[98] But what of documentary film's ways of hearing? In some ways, *Millions Like Us* draws on documentary in its treatment of sound, relying heavily on diegetic music.[99] It even recalls specific sonic effects and musical scenes in *Listen to Britain*: when music from a dance hall melds with industrial sounds as evening shifts into night, for instance, or women in a factory sing along to broadcast music. But *Millions Like Us* seems to draw the line at *Listen to Britain*'s representation of art music, presenting the inwardness or reflection that it might encourage as dangerous and self-indulgent. This is especially apparent in the two concert scenes prominently featured in the film. These clearly echo the factory canteen and National Gallery concerts in *Listen to Britain*, but, in *Millions Like Us*, the relationship between these two concerts is very different.[100]

The lunchtime canteen concert in *Millions Like Us* occurs at the very end of the film and acts as its emotional culmination soon after Celia hears that her new husband has died on a bombing mission.[101] As an entertainer sings a comic music hall song, Celia is at first an isolated figure in the midst of the large group; she pays little attention to the music and is instead absorbed in her own grief and fear and distracted by the sound of bombers flying overhead. But slowly, with the help of her friend, she begins to sing along, letting the music drown out the more frightening sounds above (Figure 1.7). The scene alternates between shots of her, increasingly absorbed in the group around here, and a shot of the mass, singing and whistling along, echoing precisely the collective shot of the canteen listeners in *Listen to Britain* (Figures 1.8, 1.2). A number of critics have remarked on this scene's subsuming of the individual into the collective as a marked departure from the conventions of

[98] Higson, *Waving the Flag*, 193, 194, 214.

[99] The soundtrack was largely the responsibility of Louis Levy, the music director for *Millions Like Us*, and at least some of the original music was by Hubert Bath (uncredited). See Jan G. Swynnoe, *The Best Years of British Film Music, 1936–1958* (Woodbridge: Boydell, 2002), 22, 233.

[100] Beattie notes the close relationship between the two canteen scenes in *Humphrey Jennings*, 80. On the canteen scenes in both films, also see Hunter, *English Filming, English Writing*, 222.

[101] *Millions Like Us*, dir. Sidney Gilliat and Frank Launder, Gainsborough Pictures, 1943 (BFI Player).

Figure 1.7 *Millions Like Us*, getting Celia to sing along.

Figure 1.8 *Millions Like Us*, canteen shot.

melodrama, highlighting how it draws on documentary modes to displace personal loss for what Christine Gledhill calls "a new form of desire—for the communal bond."[102] But what seems most striking about this scene, when compared to *Listen to Britain* as a whole, is both its stark denial of introspection and its representation of this denial as music's highest good.

The popular song used here, "Waiting at the Church" (1906), has a clear social function, promoting participation and group identity, much like in the parallel canteen scene in *Listen to Britain*. Other music used in the film is valued only to the extent that it has a clear instrumentality or legibility. In factory scenes, music is played to increase productivity and increase coordination. Other music is used as a simple signaling device: one brass-band piece (the "Post-Horn Galop," traditionally used to signal the end of dancing) tells the workers to evacuate when bombers are overhead, and a second (the "Colonel Bogey March") prompts them to return once it is safe. However, other types of music and listening are often more suspect, and aligned with "bad" or misdirected forms of desire. One scene mocks melodramatic musical conventions as the heroine fantasizes about a glamorous placement in the WAAF or the WRENS, imagining herself in flirtations and adventures and finally engaged to be married. These self-indulgent fantasies, which are brought short by the reality of her placement in a Welsh factory surrounded entirely by women, are accompanied by orchestral underscore (likely by the uncredited Hubert Bath, who worked in Gainsborough's music department) in a Late Romantic style, a type of music rarely heard elsewhere in the film.[103]

More surprisingly, canonical classical music also seems somewhat suspect in related ways. That is, the film finds itself unable to assimilate this music to a documentary mode, instead treating it within the musical logic of melodrama. This is clear in a scene earlier in the film in which Celia attends an orchestral performance. It parallels the National Gallery scene in *Listen to Britain* but almost systematically reverses its values.[104] While the National Gallery scene is rendered continuous with the canteen concert that precedes it in Jennings's film, heightening rather than contradicting its basic effect of solidarity, here art music seems starkly opposed to the group values of the canteen scene.

[102] Gledhill, "Abundance of Understatement," 221. Also see Higson, *Waving the Flag*, 243

[103] Higson, *Waving the Flag*, 230. On Bath's participation, see Swynnoe, *Best Years of British Film Music*, 22, 233.

[104] The parallel (but not the reversal) is also noted in Aldgate and Richards, *Britain Can Take It*, 309.

Planning to meet her new love interest Fred, Celia and a friend attend a concert at the local cinema. The billboard outside announces "The Metropolitan Symphony Orchestra conducted by Sir Herbert Tunbridge in a programme of popular classics," with guests the South Wales Workers Choir (followed the next week by the "All-Star Glittering Spectacle 'Thighs Right!'"). The concert, then, is not quite at the high-cultural level of the National Gallery performance. Indeed, the scene clearly references a different phenomenon of wartime musical democratization, the London Philharmonic Orchestra's tours of provincial music halls and cinemas (discussed in Chapter 2). Countering this slightly debased quality, though, the concert features perhaps the most elevated of the "popular classics," Beethoven's Fifth Symphony.[105]

As the performance of the Fifth begins, it prompts a shift into a self-consciously melodramatic mode. It seems to enable—and is certainly aligned with—Celia's utter distraction from the war effort and absorption in her personal desires and undisciplined feelings. When Fred fails to arrive, she leaves the concert at the very opening of the symphony (selfishly disrupting the other listeners) in order to call him. She becomes angry at his refusal to explain his absence, failing to consider the obvious—that he is being sent on a bombing mission, which he would be prohibited from telling her, especially over the phone. Hanging up on him, she returns for the lyrical second movement of the symphony, only to spend the entire movement indulging in self-pitying fantasies as the camera closes in on her tear-filled face: she imagines jumping to her death and a guilt-ridden Fred being rebuked by an inquest judge, in a parody of melodramatic excess. This is where listening to Beethoven leads in *Millions Like Us*.

One portion of the Fifth, though, is associated with the realities of war. Celia's fantasies and the second movement itself are abruptly cut off as the scene cuts to a shot of bombers flying overhead, which serves as the explanation for Fred's absence but also more broadly as a rejoinder to Celia's selfishness as she sits obliviously listening to the concert. This image of the bombers is accompanied by the rhythmic "fate" motif from the third movement, blared out on a single pitch in the horn—music that ends just as abruptly when the scene cuts back to the hall. Strangely, then, this music is not

[105] On the label "popular classics" in wartime (partly in relation to *Listen to Britain*), see Christina Baade, "Radio Symphonies: The BBC, Everyday Listening and the Popular Classics Debate During the People's War," in *Ubiquitous Musics: The Everyday Sounds That We Don't Always Notice*, ed. Marta García Quiñones, Anahid Kassabian, and Elena Boschi (London: Routledge, 2013), 59–71.

part of the performance. The jarring cut marks a shift in the music's mode of signification as well as its diegetic status as the film clearly draws on the wartime association of Beethoven's Fifth—and specifically the rhythmic motif heard here—with the Morse code for V (short-short-short-long), standing for Victory.[106] This association is confirmed when we hear this music again at the end of the film, very briefly: here, it emerges out of the collective singing of the canteen scene, now in the full orchestra and accompanying another scene of bombers overhead. In other words, this ending works sonically like the dissolve from Flanagan and Allen's song to the Mozart concerto in *Listen to Britain*, but instead of Mozart as an object of communal reflection, we have Beethoven instrumentalized as a legible signifier. The V motif is also heard during the opening credits, where it accompanies documentary footage of men and women leaving factories—the "millions like you" contributing to victory, as the onscreen text announces. In this more extended passage, the film score skips awkwardly between statements of the V motif, cutting the more uncertain passages that interrupt them in the opening of the third movement: it is clearly the motif itself that matters. Listening to the Fifth Symphony in general is associated with fantasy and indulgence. It is only this rhythmic pattern, with its legible message, that can be mobilized.

The film thus puts in stark relief the ways *Listen to Britain* works to make space for listening, for inwardness and reflection even under the conditions of mobilization and, indeed, in ways that support mobilization. This move depends on finding a new sonic logic, one that does not rely on the more straightforward logic seen in *Millions Like Us*. Binding introspection into its sonic web, *Listen to Britain* finds ways of binding the individual to the group without proscribing feeling as self-indulgence. Mobilizing music, feeling, and introspection all at once, it leaves little that cannot be absorbed or included in total war.

[106] See Matthew Guerreri, *The First Four Notes: Beethoven's Fifth and the Human Imagination* (New York: Knopf, 2012), 211–217.

2

"A Classic of the Masses"

The *Warsaw Concerto* and *Dangerous Moonlight*

One of the most polarizing musical developments in wartime Britain was the sudden popularity of the *Warsaw Concerto*, from the 1941 film *Dangerous Moonlight*.[1] In 1945, one critic recalled the "extraordinary phenomenon of the *Warsaw Concerto*, which brought The Piano Concerto to the notice of the man in the street."[2] Another spoke of it "sweeping the country from end to end as a musical craze rarely equalled."[3] But some also debated its benefits, asking if it helped introduce new audiences to "serious music" or simply fed them derivative dross. One simply declared, "the *Warsaw Concerto* in a concert programme is an atrocity."[4] Not just critics, but average listeners denounced it as dangerous: a letter to the *Birmingham Mail*, for instance, referred to it as "low-brow rubbish" and a "plague and menace in our social life," setting off a string of indignant responses in the following weeks.[5] Meanwhile, such hysteria overshadows the more modest claims of fans, such as one twenty-year-old cinema operator: "*Dangerous Moonlight* was the film which changed or should I say added something to the list of my hobbies. My first hearing of *Warsaw Concerto* caused my [*sic*] to take music more seriously. Since then I should say that music has played a very important part in my life."[6]

[1] *Dangerous Moonlight*, dir. Brian Desmond Hurst, RKO Radio Pictures, 1941 (Odeon Entertainment, 2010, DVD).

[2] Hubert Clifford, "Music from the Films," *Tempo* 11 (June 1945): 13.

[3] John Huntley, *British Film Music* (London: Skelton Robinson, 1947), 55.

[4] Ernest Irving, "Music and the Film Script," in *The British Film Yearbook 1947–48*, ed. Peter Noble (London: Skelton Robinson, 1948), 48.

[5] Readers' Letters: W. H. Bantock, "Light Music Wanted," *Birmingham Mail*, July 26, 1944, 3, and letters in July 29, 1944, and August 1 and 3, 1944, 3.

[6] J. P. Mayer, *British Cinemas and Their Audiences: Sociological Studies* (London: Dennis Dobson, 1948), 106.

Mobilizing Music in Wartime British Film. Heather Wiebe, Oxford University Press. © Oxford University Press 2024.
DOI: 10.1093/oso/9780197631713.003.0003

The *Warsaw Concerto* was a short one-movement work for piano and orchestra by Richard Addinsell. Duplicating in miniature the shape of a standard three-movement work, it was an early example of the "tabloid" or "capsule" concertos that soon became common in 1940s films.[7] In *Dangerous Moonlight*, it acted as a showpiece for the hero, a Polish pianist-composer exiled from Warsaw by the Nazi siege. Explicitly modeled on works by Rachmaninoff,[8] the *Warsaw Concerto* also takes a cue from the Grieg and Tchaikovsky concertos featured in some recent Hollywood films, including *Intermezzo* (1939) and especially *The Great Lie* (1941), which helped produce a string of popular adaptations of Tchaikovsky's First Piano Concerto and spurred new demand for the original.[9] Whatever its precedents, nobody seemed to have anticipated the *Warsaw Concerto*'s success. John Huntley suggested in 1947 that it was "the first piece of film background music to attract the attention of a very large and enthusiastic audience."[10] No recording of the music had been made for commercial release, and only after the fact did the studio issue both published arrangements and a recording taken directly from the soundtrack, performed by Louis Kentner—uncredited, apparently at his request—with the London Symphony Orchestra (LSO) conducted by Muir Mathieson.[11] Recordings quickly proliferated—many of them arranged for light music performers in cheaper 10-inch versions, with the short work fitting neatly onto two sides of a 78. By the end of 1942, there was one by Mantovani's Orchestra, Victor Young's Orchestra, and the piano duo Rawicz

[7] The only earlier one appears to be Jack Beaver's "The Portrait of Isla" in the British film *The Case of the Frightened Lady* (1940). See K. J. Donnelly, *British Film Music and Film Musicals* (Basingstoke: Palgrave Macmillan, 2007), 24.

[8] Christopher Robbins, *The Empress of Ireland: A Chronicle of an Unusual Friendship* (London: Scribner, 2004), 319. According to the director, Brian Desmond Hurst, Rachmaninoff had originally been asked to write the concerto, but the composer and the film director—who needed something in a mere six weeks—had rather different ideas about the time such a task would require. Hurst recalls approaching Addinsell with a score of Rachmaninoff's Second Piano Concerto and saying, "Don't exactly steal—add a little Tchaikovsky. That's the sort of thing I want." Also see the orchestrator's account: Roy Douglas, "The True Story of *The Warsaw Concerto*," in *The Best Years of British Film Music, 1936–1958*, ed. Jan G. Swynnoe (Woodbridge: Boydell, 2002), 215.

[9] See Ivan Raykoff, "Concerto con Amore," *Echo* 2, no. 1 (Spring 2000) [http://www.echo.ucla.edu/article-concerto-con-amore-by-ivan-raykoff/]. The *Daily Mirror* (London) reported in connection with *The Great Lie*, "So heavy was the demand for gramophone records of Tschaikowski's famous work that there was a famine in them," adding "Another record which caught the gramophone people on the hop was the popular 'Warsaw Concerto' featured in the Dangerous Moonlight' films. Sales have been phenomenal" ("'Good' Music Pushes out Swing," *Daily Mirror*, June 12, 1942, 7.)

[10] John Huntley, *British Film Music* (London: Skelton Robinson, 1947), 55.

[11] Ibid., 54. Huntley suggests that the recording was taken directly from recordings made during film production. Hurst's account concurs (Robbins, *Empress of Ireland*, 292). *Gramophone* reported that the recording (Columbia DX1062, 1941, 12-inch) was made "owing to public demand" (*Gramophone*, January 1942, 132).

and Landauer.[12] The work's popularity extended to the United States as well. By 1946, *Billboard*'s weekly charts of top classical records would more than once include the *Warsaw Concerto* in *two* of the top five spots.[13]

All of this success caused some consternation among critics. One, commenting on the lines of people waiting to buy the record, complained the piece was "no more than a pastiche of romantic concerto-writing; its melodies and main ideas are warmed-up clichés, it effects of brilliance are made from old recipes; in short it is all very second-hand."[14] Another wrote,

> Addinsell has recently made a bestseller of what his publishers call a "concerto" which he would be the first to admit shows resemblance to well-known tunes, one of which is by Rakhmaninov. The sub-Plimsollites stormed the music and gramophone shops for copies and records of the "concerto"; and the sales, I am told, far exceeded those of the model, while the success of the music reacted upon the film that contained it, probably doubling its box-office value.[15]

In other words, the *Warsaw Concerto* was widely seen as "kitsch," defined by Sam Binkley as "knock-off imitation luxury products, 'fine art' items crudely and glibly manufactured to resemble the posh, high art objects of the old aristocracy."[16] And it was critiqued along the standard lines Binkley describes, as derivative and inferior, indeed, "as a uniquely modern form of aesthetic corruption."[17] What made the *Warsaw Concerto*'s kitsch status even more

[12] Victor Young and His Concert Orchestra, Marlene Fingerle, Decca 18417 A, 1942; Mantovani and His Orchestra, Ivan Fosello, Decca F. 8021, 1941; Rawicz and Landauer, Columbia DB 2096, 1941. All three recordings can be found on www.archive.org. Also see "Light Music," *Gramophone*, March 1942, 168; "Light Music," *Gramophone*, November 1942, 78. I am grateful to Nick Morgan for helpful advice and information on some of these recordings.

[13] There is no equivalent source for British sales figures for 1940s recordings, and even *Billboard* classical charts only started in 1945. In September 1946, two of the top five "records by classical artists" were recordings of the *Warsaw Concerto*, by the Boston Pops and the Los Angeles Philharmonic (*The Billboard*, September 21, 1946, 24). The same two recordings were in the top five "albums by classical artists" in March (*The Billboard*, March 30, 1946, 30). Rachmaninoff's Second Piano Concerto is also a very dominant presence in *Billboard* charts of this period. On the massive popularity of the *Warsaw Concerto* in wartime on both sides of the Atlantic, also see Paul Fussell, *Wartime: Understanding and Behavior in the Second World War* (New York: Oxford University Press, 1989), 188.

[14] William McNaught, "Gramophone Notes," *Musical Times* 83 (March 1942): 83.

[15] Ernest Irving, "Music in Films," *Music and Letters* 24 (October 1943): 230.

[16] Sam Binkley, "Kitsch as a Repetitive System," *Journal of Material Culture* 5, no. 2 (2000): 132.

[17] Ibid., 133.

troubling, though, was that it was soon being heard in concert halls alongside the standard concertos it imitated.

On the one hand, the success of the *Warsaw Concerto* expanded commercial possibilities for film music, especially of a more serious variety. In press books prepared by studios' publicity departments, sections entitled "Exploitation" directed cinemas on how to promote products associated with the film. By the 1940s, Mary Ann Doane suggests, "the system of tie-ins and press books was fully in place, and the machinery of advertising had attained a fairly sophisticated form."[18] Music played a part in this system, but British films seemed to rely especially heavily on it in the wake of the *Warsaw Concerto*'s success. A string of piano concertos was written for British films—including *Cornish Rhapsody* for *Love Story*, *Baraza* for *Men of Two Worlds*, and *The Dream of Olwen* for *While I Live*—with a view to recording and publishing but also as a tool for advertising the film itself. On *Dangerous Moonlight*'s re-release in 1942, its press books began emphasizing the *Warsaw Concerto* as a major selling point of the film, giving it top billing (above the star, Anton Walbrook), and calling it "a firmly established classic—a classic of the masses."[19] Already in 1946, one critic used the term "exploitation" (in quotation marks, suggesting a specific reference to the language of the press books) to describe the larger relationship between film and concert music by way of publishing, identifying the *Warsaw Concerto* as a particularly insidious example.[20] Another, writing in 1947, suggested that the *Warsaw Concerto* helped establish this relationship.[21]

On the other hand, the *Warsaw Concerto*'s infiltration of the concert repertoire prompted a set of anxieties about the state of orchestral culture. It is not surprising, of course, that critics were suspicious of a work so obviously designed as a commodity and of the ways in which it blurred the boundaries between itself and the musical objects it imitated. But for many commentators, Addinsell's *Warsaw Concerto* was not categorically different from the rest of an increasingly standardized orchestral repertory of Beethoven symphonies and Late Romantic piano concertos. It was a symptom of a fundamental problem with contemporary orchestral culture.

[18] Mary Ann Doane, *The Desire to Desire: The Woman's Films of the 1940s* (Bloomington: Indiana University Press, 1987), 27.
[19] Exhibitor's Campaign Manual, *Dangerous Moonlight*, Pressbooks Collection (PBS-27260), British Film Institute Special Collections.
[20] Ernest Irving, "Music from the Films," *Tempo* 15 (June 1946): 12.
[21] Huntley, *British Film Music*, 54.

Thus William Glock could complain in 1942 about "the concert industry with its Tschaikowsky and Addinsell concertos, its denial of everything that could help English music in the future, its steady lowering of standards."[22] Glock's complaint is in a familiar vein of criticism. It is related to Adorno's critique (written not long after his move to Oxford) of much the same late-nineteenth-century repertory as satisfying "the demands of the cinema before the cinema was invented," and as being "part of the culture industry, even before the real consumers of the culture industry had come into existence."[23] But Glock's anxiety is also more specific to British music and its long history of a free-market approach to concert culture.[24] Some of the most prominent mid-century figures in the democratization of British musical high culture—Edward Dent, Wilfrid Mellers, even Benjamin Britten—were deeply suspicious of an orchestral culture they saw as commercialized and of its repertory of nineteenth-century classics; they advocated instead for forms of engagement less structured by commodification and for less familiar musical objects that might encourage these other forms of engagement.[25] Glock's complaint, moreover, highlights how some of these anxieties were exacerbated during World War Two, even as less commercial forms of cultural democratization seemed newly possible. Indeed, the *Warsaw Concerto* suggests the extent to which the "concert industry" Glock decries was shaped by the peculiar conditions of total war.

Looking at the *Warsaw Concerto* and how it circulated helps bring into focus the nebulous musical culture—so easily dismissed with a term like "the concert industry"—to which critics like Glock were responding. It also suggests some ways in which this culture was more complicated than its contemporary critics allowed. The first has to do with the particular place of indulgence—emotional or material—in wartime. This, after all, was a

[22] William Glock, *Observer*, June 12, 1942. Glock's preference for early and new music is well known, but his antipathy to nineteenth-century music seems largely due to these associations with a commodified concert culture.

[23] T. W. Adorno, "Commodity Music Analyzed" (1934–40), in *Quasi una Fantasia*, tr. Rodney Livingstone (New York: Verso, 1992), 42.

[24] Simon McVeigh, "A Free Trade in Music: London During the Long 19th Century in a European Perspective," *Journal of Modern European History* 5, no. 1 (2007): 67–94.

[25] On Dent's suspicion of "classics" as lending "themselves to commercialization," see Annegret Fauser, "The Scholar Behind the Medal: Edward J. Dent (1876–1957) and the Politics of Music History," *Journal of the Royal Musical Association* 139 (2014): 246–247. On Mellers, see Kate Guthrie, *The Art of Appreciation: Music and Middlebrow Culture in Modern Britain* (Berkeley: University of California Press, 2021), 136–171. On Mellers and Britten (further discussed below), also see Heather Wiebe, *Britten's Unquiet Pasts: Sound and Memory in Postwar Reconstruction* (Cambridge: Cambridge University Press, 2012), 16–20.

moment when luxury goods were not readily available, making music one of the few such luxuries on hand. It was also a time when individual freedoms were severely and explicitly curtailed, in ways that give the idea of emotional indulgence represented by music like the *Warsaw Concerto* a particular quality of contingency. Second, while critics rarely make this explicit, a closer look at how the *Warsaw Concerto* circulated suggests that it was especially associated with women, as both producers and listeners. Indeed, its very connection with film worked to signal a mainly female audience. Women were widely assumed to be the main consumers of film in wartime Britain (a 1943 Ministry of Information survey, for instance, showed film audiences to be disproportionately female).[26] In one major audience survey of 1948, it was female film-goers who most often pointed to their affection for the *Warsaw Concerto* and *Dangerous Moonlight*, and the voices that came to its defense—in letters to the editor, for instance—were also often those of women.[27] The new dominance of female pianists in wartime Britain also seems an issue, as we will see by looking at Eileen Joyce, one of the most popular and active pianists of the period, who regularly performed the *Warsaw Concerto* in concert from as early as 1942. In other words, if art music's commodification is often marked as feminine in mid-century critical commentary, looking closely at the *Warsaw Concerto* suggests that this is more than a metaphor or discursive strategy: actual women—and marketing strategies specifically directed at women—were at issue. Finally, the "concert industry" is marked by mobility: the physical mobility of touring musicians, improvised concert venues, and dislocated audiences of troops and mobilized civilians; the social mobility of aspirational listeners and performers (like Joyce); and the mobility of media involved in the *Warsaw Concerto*'s movement between film, recordings, radio, and concert halls. This idea of mobility was inscribed in *Dangerous Moonlight* itself, a film dizzily occupied with touring, travel, and displacement. All of these issues seem to lurk behind critics' anxious response to the *Warsaw Concerto*.

[26] Janet Thumim, "The Female Audience: Mobile Women and Married Ladies," in *Nationalising Femininity: Culture, Sexuality and the British Cinema in the Second World War*, ed. Christine Gledhill and Gillian Swanson (Manchester: Manchester University Press, 1996), 246. In 1949, the film critic Catherine de la Roche observed that 69% of British cinema audiences were women but that studios behaved as if the proportion were higher, and she complained about how this audience was addressed as a coherent and largely invented group: "That 'Feminine Angle,'" *Penguin Film Review* 8 (January 1949): 26–27.

[27] In the survey, three of the four respondents who mention the *Warsaw Concerto* are women (Mayer, *British Cinemas and Their Audiences*, 74, 169, 188, 106).

Most of all, I am interested in taking seriously wartime audiences' response and attachment to the *Warsaw Concerto*, partly by looking closely at its role and associations in *Dangerous Moonlight*, the plot of which was stubbornly ignored by music critics at the time. If critics worried about listeners being tricked and manipulated by this piece of compressed, synthetic Late Romanticism, perhaps the *Warsaw Concerto* also provides some insight into the feelings of wartime themselves as both grand and somehow reduced.

The Concert Industry

The popularity of the *Warsaw Concerto* was closely connected with an expansion of audiences for orchestral music in general during World War Two. This growth was accompanied by a perceived dependence on a small number of "popular classics," including the Tchaikovsky, Rachmaninoff, and Grieg concertos that Addinsell's work imitated and alongside which it was performed. Many critics and administrators enthusiastically welcomed this expansion as a sign of the democratization of high culture, but some also found cause for concern. Christina Baade sums up critics' and administrators' ambivalence about these developments, observing that "for many critics, the popular classics and their mass audience promised not a democratic utopia but an active threat to serious music."[28] Radio was one culprit, as Baade argues, but in many ways live performance was just as problematic in wartime, as orchestras attempted to meet new demand and toured widely—often presenting a limited repertory in less than ideal circumstances—in a struggle to survive. Critics regularly complained of a decline in performance standards and an overreliance on a small body of works, as well as the appearance of light works on otherwise "serious" programs. This is the musical culture Britten described in dismay when he returned to London in 1942.

> The first impression of the country is a sort of drab shabbiness. All the excitement of the "blitz" . . . has died down, & people seem very, very tired. Musical life doesn't really exist, except for this extraordinary demand for organised sound, which makes people crowd into the Albert Hall, to

[28] Christina Baade, "Radio Symphonies: The BBC, Everyday Listening and the Popular Classics Debate During the People's War," in *Ubiquitous Musics: The Everyday Sounds That We Don't Always Notice*, ed. Marta García Quiñones, Anahid Kassabian, and Elena Boschi (London: Routledge, 2013), 50–51.

> hear bad orchestras, conducted by mediocre conductors, under the worst acoustic conditions possible, play a few popular classics (mainly Beethoven, & then only 3, 5, or 7). Scarcely a musical life.[29]

In 1945, the American composer Hugo Weisgall complained further of a British orchestral culture blighted by the repetition of "old warhorses," especially piano concertos, concluding, "The 'Beethoven-Tchaikovsky-piano soloist disease' which has gripped the British . . . is directly attributable to the war."[30] A survey of British cultural and political events of 1943 reported the "boom in orchestral music" with some concern (and reported a similarly "confused" and "paradoxical" situation in earlier years of the war).[31] William McNaught writes,

> Full-sized professional orchestras were to be met with up and down the country competing for box-office favour, often clashing with each other's dates, imposing their own haphazard time-table on local musical life, and hurling symphonies and concertos at a vast new population that had had no previous experience of that order of music. This sudden propagation of the masterpieces was no bad thing in itself; nobody wished to complain that Beethoven was being listened to by more people than ever before. It was the misdirection of this new industry that aroused misgivings. The new audience was being taught to believe that the highest musical ideal lay in the colourful, emotional, and impressive effect produced only by a large and varied body of instruments. Moreover, this one-sided view was being further narrowed by a limited choice of music.[32]

These orchestras included not only established provincial and London groups, but even a new touring orchestra formed by a concert promoter to feed audience demand.[33] This is the wartime "concert industry" Glock was

[29] Benjamin Britten to Elizabeth Mayer, May 4, 1942, in *Letters from a Life, Vol. 2, 1949–1945*, ed. Donald Mitchell and Philip Reed (London: Faber, 2011), 1037.

[30] Hugo Weisgall, "English Musical Life: A Symposium, IV," *Tempo* 12 (September 1945): 9.

[31] W. McNaught, "Music," in *The Annual Register: A Review of Public Events at Home and Abroad for the Year 1943*, ed. M. Epstein (London: Longmans, Green & Co. 1944), 346; *The Annual Register: A Review of Public Events at Home and Abroad for the Year 1940*, ed. M. Epstein (London: Longmans, Green & Co. 1941), 337; *The Annual Register: A Review of Public Events at Home and Abroad for the Year 1941*, ed. M. Epstein (London: Longmans, Green & Co. 1942), 337.

[32] McNaught, "Music," *Annual Register 1943*, 346.

[33] Geoffrey Self, *Light Music in Britain Since 1870: A Survey* (Aldershot: Ashgate, 2001), 197–198. The concert promoter was Harold Fielding, who would later be Eileen Joyce's manager.

similarly decrying in 1942, and the *Warsaw Concerto* quickly came to stand for its most insidious developments.

Reflecting on this period in his *Social History of English Music* (1964), and quoting part of the passage above, Eric Mackerness observed a narrowing and commercialization of the repertory accompanying the expansion of audiences, whom he characterized as "a large and relatively unadventurous 'middlebrow' audience of catholic rather than discriminating taste."[34] (This audience was opposed in his account to idealized wartime visions of "ordinary people . . . anxious to educate themselves in the art of responding sensitively to the world's musical masterpieces.") For him, the success of the *Warsaw Concerto* perfectly demonstrated "the strength of 'middlebrow' taste in the 1940s," which he defined precisely as the inability to discriminate.

> Heavily romantic in style and technically brilliant, the "Warsaw Concerto" is comparable from a musical point of view with Gershwin's *Rhapsody in Blue*, but its significance—quite apart from its association with the cinema—lies in the fact that it was received with rapturous applause by audiences who were convinced that in responding to it they were enjoying authentic "classical" music. In the estimation of thousands the "Warsaw Concerto" was placed on the same level as the Grieg and Tschaikovski concertos, and was indeed frequently played along with them in the same programme. . . . Its triumphant success was due to the skill with which the composer managed to arouse the susceptibilities of the middlebrow audience—which is, in the last analysis, a product of the commercialism by which the present century of musical history is distinguished.[35]

What differentiated it from older and more harmless forms of light music, for Mackerness, was that it *tricked* "susceptible" audiences, pretending to be something it was not. As kitsch, it was manufactured to deceive.

In his 1946 book *Music and Society*, Wilfrid Mellers was even more pessimistic about the "great middlebrow public," which he, too, associated with music ranging from "middle period Beethoven, through the ubiquitous Tchaikovsky concerto and the Rachmaninov concertos, down to the Warsaw

[34] Eric David Mackerness, *A Social History of English Music* (London: Routledge & Kegan Paul: 1964), 270. Mackerness's account cites part of the *Annual Register* passage quoted above. For a related, more contemporary discussion, see Ross McKibbin, *Classes and Cultures: England 1918–1951* (Oxford: Oxford University Press, 1998), 386–390.

[35] Mackerness, *Social History of English Music*, 271–272.

one."[36] For Mellers, only the "lowest (Warsaw) level" was objectionable as music, but the new audience's experience of all of it was equally problematic. The central problem for Mellers, as for Mackerness, was this audience's perceived lack of discrimination: "the middlebrow 'orchestral' public is almost completely undiscriminating and will applaud everything within the accepted repertory more or less equally, whatever the merits or demerits of the performance."[37] But he was also concerned that these audiences were not experiencing "genuine musical culture" or indeed genuine feeling—that everything was somehow second-hand. Despite all efforts, they found "the struggle against cliché and stock-response, blared at them continuously through newspaper and loudspeaker, too much for their capacity to experience at first hand." They looked "to art as a means of escape," appreciating music mainly as an opportunity for "nostalgia or self-dramatization" and for "the day-dreams it gives rise to."[38] For Mellers, moreover, these problems associated with the repetition of familiar works were exacerbated by a fascination with star performers. In a 1944 article, he wrote of the virtuoso tradition as one that encouraged passivity—a great fault for Mellers, who emphasized education and participation in his commitment to providing access to the arts. For the "vast audiences" thronging "to hear a virtuoso play Chopin" or a " 'maestro' conductor performing Tchaikowsky, Wagner, and middle period Beethoven, not to mention Rachmaninov," Mellers wrote, music was "a means of sublimating the private failures, nostalgias and disappointments resulting from a lack of creativity, on however humble a scale, in his own life." This was musical culture as utterly passive, as a "supine relinquishment of the emotions along the channel of least resistance."[39]

Both Mellers and Mackerness, then, saw the *Warsaw Concerto* as part of a broader commodification of orchestral culture, feeding a passive and undiscriminating "middlebrow" audience looking for escape. Mackerness begins his account, though, with reference to the peculiarity of wartime orchestral activity—a context that has largely receded by the time he gets to the *Warsaw Concerto* and to which Mellers does not refer at all. Keeping this context in play suggests how the forces of total war intersected powerfully with those of

[36] Wilfrid Mellers, *Music and Society: England and the European Tradition* (London: Dennis Dobson, 1946), 13. For a related discussion of Mellers, also see Guthrie, *Art of Appreciation*, 136–137.
[37] Mellers, *Music and Society*, 15.
[38] Ibid., 13.
[39] Wilfrid Mellers, "Musical Culture Today: A Sociological Note," *Tempo* 7 (June 1944): 3–4.

commodification. It also might cast a different light on the "private failures, nostalgias and disappointments" Mellers attributed to a lack of creativity in 1944.

One performer at the center of the wartime orchestral culture that so concerned these critics was the Australian pianist Eileen Joyce. She played regularly with touring orchestras, often including the *Warsaw Concerto* in her programs alongside standard Late Romantic concertos. Joyce was precisely the type of star virtuoso Mellers worried about, and she epitomized the "Beethoven-Tchaikovsky-piano soloist disease" that Weisgall saw gripping the British. Looking more closely at Joyce's work can help provide a fuller picture of this area of activity, beyond critics' broad complaints about "middlebrow" audiences and limited repertory. It might also help recover some voices drowned out by this critical censure and a different perspective on the audiences and performers drawn to the *Warsaw Concerto*.

By the late 1940s, Joyce was one of the most famous pianists in Britain, with a distinctly popular appeal. Her fame was based largely on her work in film (especially *Brief Encounter* and *The Seventh Veil*, both from 1945), but also her repertory of Late Romantic concertos and her own rags-to-riches story. Born in poverty in rural Tasmania, she was a model of mobility and self-made success for an aspirational audience.[40] But, in the early 1940s, Joyce was just beginning to forge this role as a celebrity pianist. Trained at the Leipzig Conservatory (thanks to funds raised by Australian supporters) and given the imprimatur of London's premier teacher Tobias Matthay (with the help of Myra Hess), she started out in the early 1930s with a modern repertory, including Prokofiev's Third Piano Concerto (1921) and Shostakovich's First Piano Concerto (1933), the British premiere of which she gave in 1936. In many ways, the war reshaped Joyce's career, providing opportunities to make a living that she—a single mother after her estranged husband died in action in 1941—assiduously took advantage of, as one 1946 profile observed with surprising forthrightness.

> A singer or instrumentalist who can stand the strain has been able to make money steadily throughout the war. It is astonishing the number of avenues

[40] For more on this and on Joyce's postwar fame, see Heather Wiebe, "Music and the Good Life in Postwar Britain: The Phenomenon of Eileen Joyce," in *The Oxford Handbook to Music and the Middlebrow*, ed. Kate Guthrie and Christopher Chowrimootoo (online edn, Oxford Academic, December 19, 2022), https://doi.org/10.1093/oxfordhb/9780197523933.013.6, accessed June 30, 2023.

> available, over and above the concerts given in the big halls: local oratorios, special recitals, school visits. Into this world plunged Eileen Joyce, with terrific energy, and a wardrobe which caught the eye of women in the audience.[41]

At the same time, wartime conditions also worked to standardize her repertory, and she relied increasingly on a small group of Late Romantic concertos. Her wartime repertory was what Donald Brook referred to as "a fine selection of the more popular classics": from Grieg and Rachmaninoff to Gershwin's *Rhapsody in Blue* or the *Warsaw Concerto*.[42] The showiness of the repertory was matched by her appearance: despite austerity measures, she managed to procure elaborate gowns for her wartime tours, supplied by Norman Hartnell, then the Queen's dressmaker.[43] Both worked to relieve the prevailing "shabbiness" Britten noted in 1942. Like the *Warsaw Concerto* itself, she came to represent for some critics the underside of the democratization of high culture. As an ambitious and mobile woman, working-class and from the margins of empire, she embodied the very tension between incursion and aspiration that characterized new audiences' forays into art music.

Joyce was a featured performer with perhaps the most important touring orchestra in wartime, the London Philharmonic (LPO), which was displaced from its home at the bombed Queen's Hall. Its struggles are documented in the 1943 film *Battle for Music,* which reenacts its crisis in 1940 and its ensuing tour, using members of the orchestra and many of the figures involved, including Joyce.[44] As portrayed in the film, the LPO was in danger of disbanding when the war began and was saved partly through the efforts of J. B. Priestley and the bandleader and impresario Jack Hylton, who organized a tour around provincial music halls. The film and the tour it documented thus involved the leading British spokesman of the literary middlebrow and a working-class bandleader who had long attempted to bridge jazz and high culture, most famously with a big band performance of Stravinsky's *Mavra*

[41] Gordon Beckles, "Top of the Class no. 12: Eileen Joyce: 'The Girl at the Keyboard,'" *Leader*, January 5, 1946, 17, Eileen Joyce Collection, Callaway Centre Archive, University of Western Australia.

[42] Donald Brook, *Masters of the Keyboard* (London: Rockliff, 1946), 171.

[43] Richard Davis, *Eileen Joyce: A Portrait* (Fremantle, WA: Fremantle Arts Centre Press, 2001), 102.

[44] *Battle for Music: The London Philharmonic Orchestra at War*, dir. Donald Taylor, Strand Film Company, 1943 (Broxburn UK: Panamint Cinema, 2013, DVD). See John Morris, *Culture and Propaganda in World War II: Music, Film and the Battle for National Identity* (London: I. B. Tauris, 2014), 39–44.

at the Paris Opera House.[45] In *Battle for Music*, Joyce recreates an important 1940 fundraising concert hosted by Priestley, in which she performed the Grieg piano concerto. (Piano concertos in general feature prominently in the film, which also includes Benno Moiseiwitch performing Rachmaninoff's Second Piano Concerto.) Joyce also joined the orchestra on tour, playing up to three concerts a day in music halls and cinemas as well as concert halls. *Battle for Music* cast the LPO's tour in idealistic terms: as a testament to the survival of culture itself and as providing much-needed refreshment in wartime. At one point in the film, for instance, the conductor Malcolm Sargent pronounces from the stage: "Why, here are we, the London Philharmonic Orchestra and I, touring up and down the country from town to town giving concerts almost every night, and hundreds, thousands of war workers and members of the forces have found in music the best recreation for their tired minds and bodies."[46] As we have seen, though, many critics were more skeptical about the benefits of this frenetic activity and about the extent to which it was driven by financial pressures—pressures that were all too clear in the case of the LPO.

While the *Warsaw Concerto* represented Joyce's most conspicuous inclusion of "commercial" music in her concert repertory, she was often to be found in a cross-over area between art and popular music. Throughout the war, she regularly performed under the auspices of the Entertainments National Service Association (ENSA), even though this was mainly an organization for popular entertainers (a second organization, the Council for the Encouragement of Music and the Arts, was responsible for providing classical concerts). When ENSA decided it needed to provide more substantial musical offerings, particularly for its officers, Joyce performed in its very first concert of "serious music" for military personnel in October 1940.[47] She continued to perform in events that attempted to bridge popular and classical music, usually in the role of the "highbrow."[48] In 1941, for instance, the bandleader Geraldo (conservatory

[45] On Hylton's *Mavra*, see Andy Fry, *Paris Blues: African American Music and French Popular Culture, 1920–1960* (Chicago: Chicago University Press, 2014), 82–85. On Priestley, see John Baxendale, "Priestley and the Highbrows," in *Middlebrow Literary Cultures: The Battle of the Brows, 1920–1960*, ed. Erica Brown and Mary Grover (Basingstoke: Palgrave Macmillan, 2012), 69–81.

[46] *Battle for Music*, 01:00:18, also quoted in Morris, *Culture and Propaganda in World War II*, 48.

[47] Basil Dean, *The Theatre at War* (London: George G. Harrap and Co. 1956), 214. The concert took place at Aldershot Garrison. ENSA's Music division was run by the record producer Walter Legge and its Bands division by Jack Hylton (as Chairman, with Geraldo as supervisor), both prominent supporters of art music for broad audiences.

[48] Kate Guthrie and Christina Baade have discussed wartime efforts to both bring together and demarcate art music and popular music (or music and entertainment, as they were often called) by the BBC, ENSA, and CEMA. See Christina Baade, *Victory Through Harmony: The BBC and Popular*

trained himself) presented an orchestral concert at the Albert Hall called "Music in the Modern Form," in which Joyce performed the first movement of Grieg's Piano Concerto "cheek by jowl with a 'swing' version of 'Tea for Two.' "[49] This, according to the *Liverpool Post*, was "another of the current attempts to make the best of both worlds—of music and of popular entertainment."[50] Even Joyce's association with Shostakovich's First Piano Concerto (which she recorded in 1941) might be seen as consistent with her middlebrow status. As Pauline Fairclough has argued, Shostakovich was seen by interwar British critics as a composer of "deliberately vulgar, crass music."[51] He was another representative of the most pernicious forms of populism, of the state-subsidized rather than the commercial order. Critics derided his Fifth Symphony as being "like thin and sentimental Tchaikovsky in his worst moments" and as made up of "eclectic" and "rubbishy musical material."[52] The Concerto, with its mix of jazz and lush lyricism, might be seen to illustrate the worst of these tendencies. The *Times* certainly thought so, observing in the review of Joyce's British premiere that it "descends at times to something perilously like café-music," while the slow movement was "dull and vapid."[53] Even when performing the most challenging music, then, Joyce could be associated with an empty populism.

Indeed, her playing was often seen as emotionally vacant and lacking in interpretive nuance. One critic suggested in 1945 that her style was "notable for technical virtuosity rather than for an awareness of the emotional subtleties of the music."[54] A 1941 Mozart recording (later much admired by Glenn Gould) was described as "impeccable" and avoiding "romance," with the cumulative effect of being "correct but rather empty."[55] Her entry

Music in World War II (New York: Oxford University Press, 2011); Kate Guthrie, "Vera Lynn on Screen: Popular Music and the 'People's War,'" *Twentieth-Century Music* 14, no. 2 (2017): 245–270.

[49] "Music Grave & Gay," *Liverpool Daily Post*, December 8, 1941. On this concert, also see Baade, "Radio Symphonies," 66.

[50] She also appeared with Geraldo and his orchestra in a concert for the BBC Forces Programme (*Radio Times*, December 8, 1941). On Geraldo and ENSA's BBC broadcasts, see Dean, *Theatre at War*, 272–280, especially p. 279.

[51] Pauline Fairclough, "The 'Old Shostakovich': Reception in the British Press," *Music and Letters* 88 (2007): 268.

[52] Ibid., 270, quoting W. J. Turner, *New Statesman and Nation*, December 2, 1939, 787. Nicolas Nabokov also seemed to link Shostakovich with the middlebrow in an American postwar context: see Ian Wellens, *Music on the Frontline: Nicolas Nabokov's Struggle Against Communism and Middlebrow Culture* (London: Routledge, 2002), 103–113.

[53] 'Week-End Concerts," *Times*, January 6, 1936, 10.

[54] Clifford, "Music from the Films," 11–12.

[55] "The Gramophone: A Piano Recital," *Times*, August 6, 1941, 6. Glenn Gould, *The Glenn Gould Reader*, ed. Tim Page (Toronto: Lester & Orpen Dennys, 1984), 33. The recording is of Mozart's Sonata in D Major, K. 576.

in *Grove* (1954), written at the height of her fame, deplored her appeal to "the indiscriminate concert-going crowds" but remarked on the "extraordinary, almost mechanical accuracy" of her early performances, adding "If she did not give evidence of strong musical feeling, she showed a remarkable capacity for learning any work she was required to play, however difficult, and giving a polished performance of it."[56] While her tendency toward detachment might seem an odd match for her Late Romantic repertory, such comments worked to foreground the notions of commodification and "second-hand" feeling increasingly attached to this repertory, and inscribed the idea of mechanical reproduction into Joyce's playing itself.

With her spectacular dresses, her virtuoso repertory, her brilliant but inexpressive playing, and her touring performances in commercial venues, Joyce was in many ways the bad double of Myra Hess, whose National Gallery concerts represented the most idealized form of musical populism. The fact that Hess was an early supporter of Joyce and that Joyce regularly contributed to the National Gallery concerts complicates this opposition but does not fundamentally undo it. As David Savran suggests, "the cachet of highbrow culture was dependent on its purported refusal of commodity status and its ability to function as a signifier of cultural purity, consecration, and asceticism, during a period marked by the widespread and unprecedented availability of luxury goods."[57] These terms—purity, consecration, and asceticism—recall those used to describe Hess and the music she played. The National Gallery concerts' association with "quality" and "standards" (as discussed in Chapter 1) had much to do with Hess herself, her commitment to "the very best music,"[58] and her resistance to more spectacular models of the concert pianist. Hess was not known for virtuosity but rather for soberly expressive playing and an austerity matched by her modest appearance and tendency to wear all black.[59] In the war years, she was associated with the height of the Austro-German canon, particularly music by Bach, Beethoven, and Mozart. (Notably, the only concertos she ever performed at the National

[56] Eric Blom, "Eileen Joyce," in *Grove's Dictionary of Music and Musicians*, ed. Eric Blom (London: Macmillan, 1954), vol. 4, 672.

[57] David Savran, *A Queer Sort of Materialism: Recontextualizing American Theater* (Ann Arbor: University of Michigan Press, 2003), 5.

[58] Myra Hess, "A Great Adventure," in *National Gallery Concerts in aid of the Musicians Benevolent Fund, 10th October 1939–10th October 1944* (London: National Gallery, 1944), 3.

[59] See Bruce Simonds, "Myra in America," in *Myra Hess by Her Friends*, ed. Denise Lassimonne and Howard Ferguson (London: Hamish Hamilton, 1966), 44.

Gallery were by Mozart or Bach.[60]) She preferred music that "was not mere glitter" in the words of one writer, who observed that her technique "does not shine as such, because it is wholly devoted to the true uses of technique as a means of interpretation."[61] Ensconced at the National Gallery, Hess represented the very opposite, too, of Joyce's ceaseless mobility as she toured up and down the country.

Joyce's association with the *Warsaw Concerto* helps ground the phenomenon of its success in the activities of wartime touring orchestras and their efforts to expand their reach by performing in unorthodox venues, as well as attempts by Joyce and others (such as Hylton and ENSA) to cross high and popular culture. It also suggests how a figure like Joyce—a working-class woman trying to make a living as a professional musician—might be an object of some of the anxieties circulating around the *Warsaw Concerto* and "middlebrow" audiences.

A closer look at her concerts also reveals a self-consciousness about the *Warsaw Concerto*'s status that belies critics' anxieties. Addinsell's work was quite clearly marked as different from the standard repertory, its cinematic origins consistently highlighted in programs and local reviews. In Joyce's touring concerts with the LPO and the LSO, the *Warsaw* was generally set apart, presented as a short, entertaining part of a more serious program. One LPO concert program, for instance, includes careful analytical notes for most of the works performed, but not for the *Warsaw Concerto*. It merely provides some information about Addinsell, who is described as working for the Army Film Unit, and states, "He was one of the first to insist on a place for serious music in British films, and the 'Warsaw Concerto,' specially written for 'Dangerous Moonlight,' is perhaps the first piece of film music which has gained an existence apart from the medium for which it was written."[62]

Reviews of Joyce's touring performances made such distinctions even more clearly; they also show that debates about the *Warsaw Concerto* played out in local discourses, not just in the pronouncements of elite critics, and that audiences could be expected to be aware of them, often participating themselves. Some reviewers simply dismissed the work as film music, one commenting, "The programme maintained a discreet silence about this

[60] Denise Lassimonne and Howard Ferguson, eds. *Myra Hess by Her Friends* (London: Hamish Hamilton, 1966), 109–111.

[61] Simonds, "Myra in America," 45.

[62] Thomas Russell, notes for the London Philharmonic Orchestra, Blackpool Opera House, November 15, 1943, Eileen Joyce Collection, Callaway Centre Archive, University of Western Australia.

work and we will follow its good example. We are informed that it is film music. It sounds like that."[63] Another observed more generously, "Its connection with the cinema, and the criticism that it is 'so much after Tchaikovsky' do not hide the fact that it is a clever little composition of warm colour, and melody of broad and noble effect."[64] One more ambitious reviewer summed up the debates for the readership of the *Staffordshire Advertiser*:

> The inclusion of Richard Addinsell's 'Warsaw' Concerto in serious programmes has been the subject of much controversy. Of course it is not a concerto at all, and belonging, as it does, entirely to the cinema, it has little interest for such as me, particularly as I am not told what the story surrounding it is all about. But we have to remember that many of the people now flocking to orchestral concerts are not impelled by a deep love of great music, and I see no reason why they should not be given something occasionally which appeals because of its romantic cinema associations. "Live and let live" is still a good motto. The "Warsaw" music in any case is quite innocuous: it cannot possibly lower anyone's standard of taste, and there is always a chance that the other music may raise someone's.[65]

One thing even the lowliest of reviewers seemed to share is this assumption that the cinema had nothing to do with them and that they could not possibly be expected to know what *Dangerous Moonlight* was about. Such automatic dismissiveness of both film in general and the *Warsaw Concerto* in particular sometimes raised the ire of listeners, who seemed to have a clear-eyed sense of its status. One such listener, identified as Mrs. Irene Bracegirdle, wrote in response to the first reviewer quoted above:

> Sir,—Your reporter's supercilious attitude towards Richard Addinsell's "*Warsaw Concerto*" is very unfair. It is wrong to boycott a work because it is dubbed "film music". What of William Walton, who has composed for several films? Why trample down a piece of music which, though small and insignificant in comparison with the Rachmaninov Concerto, has given pleasure to millions of people, and to people who like the best in music? . . . Mr. Addinsell's music is unknown to me, but, though I may

[63] "Music in Rochdale: The Wessex Philharmonic Orchestra," *Rochdale Observer*, April 24, 1943.
[64] "Orchestral Festival's Fine Start," *Gloucestershire Echo*, September 29, 1942.
[65] "Bournemouth Philharmonic Orchestra," *Staffordshire Advertiser*, November 28, 1942.

> perhaps never like another of his pieces, his "*Warsaw Concerto*" will always give me pleasure, and I feel confident I express the feelings of many.[66]

Pleasure in something relatively small and insignificant—that is what the *Warsaw Concerto* provided, according to this listener, for both her and many others.

Indeed, contrary to critics' concerns about the popular masquerading itself as high art, the extent to which the *Warsaw Concerto* did *not* present itself as "great music" seems striking. It is blatantly Romanticism reduced, offering something imitative and second-hand. Looking closely at its use in *Dangerous Moonlight*—which surely shaped audience understanding even as it utterly bypassed critics—further suggests a certain reflexivity about its reduced status.

"Perhaps That Music Will Bring Back a Lot of Things"

If the *Warsaw Concerto* could serve as a shorthand for everything wrong with British musical culture, *Dangerous Moonlight* as a whole presents its own anxieties about the fate of Late Romanticism—and indeed, of musical greatness—in wartime. The derivative quality of the *Warsaw Concerto*, which struck so many critics as naively embraced, is in some ways thematized in the film, creating a persistent tension between feeling and mechanicity, repetition and authenticity. To the extent that the concerto does represent a set of ideals—of selfhood, beauty, romance, heroism, and even greatness—it is always contingent, out-of-place, and under threat.

The film itself has a barely suppressed camp aesthetic, in ways that perhaps speak to its queer-cultural origins. Its director, star, and composer were all gay men, and (except for Addinsell) they were to some extent cultural outsiders as well. As created by Anton Walbrook—an operetta star before fleeing Austria due to his Jewish ancestry—the film's heroic pianist comes across as feminized and theatrical, in ways the Northern Irish director Brian Desmond Hurst actively tried to keep in check. Reminiscing about filming with Walbrook, Hurst recalls,

[66] Letter to the editor, *Rochdale Observer*, May 8, 1943. This writer is quite critical of Joyce's performance of the *Warsaw Concerto*.

> In one scene he had to say, "I'm handsome, full of charm and a wonderful musician." I thought he was doing this in an extremely feminine way and tried every word I could think of to explain this to him diplomatically—the term "camp" had not yet been invented. . . . Finally, I lost patience: "Anton, it's just too damn sissy!"[67]

The *Warsaw Concerto*'s kitsch status contributes to the film's camp aesthetic. But as kitsch, it can be read in a more recuperative mode than its wartime critics would allow. Binkley has defended kitsch as a style that "celebrates repetition and conventionality as a value in itself," employing "the thematics of repetition over innovation, a preference for formulae and conventions over originality and experiment, an appeal to sentimental affirmation over existential probing." For Binkley, kitsch "works to re-embed its consumers, to replenish stocks of ontological security, and to shore up a sense of cosmic coherence in an unstable world."[68] Both calling on a heroic past and rendering it as miniaturized, accessible, and conventional, the tabloid concerto offered a kind of embeddedness that could counteract the radical change, uncertainty, and scarcity of wartime. At the same time, the *Warsaw Concerto* is not so straightforwardly celebratory as Binkley's model suggests, betraying a simultaneous sense of melancholy and loss.

Dangerous Moonlight is overtly occupied with the dangers of war and with a tension between the artist as something special to be protected and his duty to fight. This results in some generic instability, its prominent vein of melodrama mixed with more "masculine" scenes of military struggle and camaraderie. Indeed, as Heather Laing has pointed out, the film throws together such an array of wartime tropes and conventions that it ends up struggling to communicate anything coherent, not least about music.[69] Its generic and narrative confusion is intensified by a dizzying mobility; its characters are always on the move—Warsaw, Romania, New York, an American tour, a British airbase, and finally London—and often strikingly out of place. The hero is the Polish pianist Stefan Radetzky, a pilot in the Polish Air Force. After the Siege of Warsaw, he makes his way to the United States, marrying an intrepid

[67] Robbins, *Empress of Ireland*, 320. (This passage is cut in some American editions.) On Walbrook and operetta, see http://operetta-research-center.org/adonises-operetta-re-encounter-adolf-wohlbruck/ (accessed April 6, 2019).

[68] Binkley, "Kitsch as a Repetitive System," 135.

[69] Heather Laing, *The Gendered Score: Music in 1940s Melodrama and the Woman's Film* (London: Routledge, 2007), 148–149, 170. Laing provides a much fuller account of the film and its

American reporter, Carol Peters, whom he first encountered during the siege. In the still neutral United States, he tours incessantly, raising funds for Polish relief. For British audiences, Radetzky would have recalled the Polish virtuoso, composer, and statesman Ignacy Jan Paderewski (1860–1941), who had represented Poland abroad during both World Wars One and Two, visiting the United States in 1941 and serving as Chairman of the wartime Polish parliament in London.[70] (Paderewski had also appeared in the 1937 film *Moonlight Sonata*, playing himself.) But in the film, Radetzky is dissatisfied with merely performing and returns to battle as a pilot, only to be brought down almost instantly (in a long aerial sequence that is the film's main claim to longevity). Radetzky miraculously survives, but remembers nothing. Sent to a hospital in Blitz-besieged London, he pecks away at the piano, watched over by a despondent Carol; she sings him the melody of his own *Warsaw Concerto* until finally the music (and his memory) returns to him in a rush.

The film begins with the amnesiac Radetzky in London, casting the whole of its narrative as flashback. That flashback, in turn, is constituted by the *Warsaw Concerto* and marked by the unusual absence of voice-over.[71] The concerto becomes both a tool and an object of memory: the elusive thing that Radetzky has lost and the means by which he will remember everything else. The use of flashback is of course common in 1940s films, especially film noir and melodrama. In Maureen Turim's account, flashback is not merely a narrative gimmick: it has everything to do with constructions of memory, its repetitions elaborating both "a nostalgic desire" to revisit the biographical and historical past and a psychoanalytical understanding of trauma.[72] This therapeutic use of flashback is often applied to wartime trauma in 1940s films: Turim discusses the example of *So Proudly We Hail* (US, 1943), for instance, where flashback provides "a stage in a cure for battle shock."[73] *Dangerous Moonlight* also offers an example of flashback as

score, with particular attention to issues of masculinity and how music articulates the relationship between Radetzky and Carol (pp. 147–171).

[70] Ivan Raykoff explores Radetzky's connection to Paderewski, as well as Chopin and Liberace (also of Polish ancestry), who often performed the *Warsaw Concerto*: "Hollywood's Embattled Icon," in *Piano Roles: A New History of the Piano*, ed. James Parakilas (New Haven, CT: Yale University Press, 2002), 278.

[71] On this absence of voice-over, see Laing, *Gendered Score*, 149–150.

[72] Maureen Turim, *Flashbacks in Film: Memory and History* (New York: Routledge, 1989), 119.

[73] Ibid., 130–131. Also see Chapter 4 for further discussion of flashback's association with psychiatric treatment.

therapy, albeit in a less straightforward way. Its replay of the biographical past is simultaneously concerned with a larger social and cultural trauma, caught up as it is in the conflicts of World War Two and the sense of a civilization under threat.

That sense of threat is thematized from the very first moments of the film. In the hospital in which it opens (in November 1940, we're told, the tail-end of two months of intense bombing of London), Radetzky's amnesia offers a frightening figure of erasure. (*Dangerous Moonlight* itself was made during the Blitz, and, according to Hurst, filming was frequently interrupted by bombing, with the costumes and dressing rooms at one point completely destroyed.[74]) At the hospital, we first see Radetzky as an elegant automaton. His amnesiac playing—a telling parody of Second Viennese School atonality, here speaking to his loss of self—continues to sound in the background as two nurses discuss the crash that left him in this state. "What's the good of being alive if you don't know who you are," they ask, while hoping for a night of relief from the bombs. The importance of Radetzky's recovery is elaborated when his doctor and a visiting specialist arrive to consult about his treatment. As they listen to his incessant musical nonsense, filtering into the doctor's office from across a courtyard, the specialist comments ironically, "Stefan Radetzky the great Polish pianist in one of his own original compositions," adding more seriously,

SPECIALIST: "I've often heard him play."
DR. LONGMAN: If we could get him better, I should feel that we'd *done* something for the world, something for . . . well you know what I mean."
SPECIALIST: Ah, if you feel like that too, we'll get him better alright, even if it takes a miracle or an act of God. I just don't like the idea of another great artist finishing up in a home.

The reference to a "great artist" suggests a conventional nod to protecting art or humane culture writ large, but they are otherwise tellingly vague on what precisely the stakes are in Radetzky's recovery. Moreover, any claims to greatness for the concerto are somewhat undone by the Specialist's earlier reference to his idea for Radetzky's piano cure, inspired by a similar experiment in which children were given their old

[74] Robbins, *Empress of Ireland*, 319.

toys to play with—"I figure giving him this piano is pretty much the same thing," he observes.

As the doctors ruminate on Radetzky's recovery, they suddenly hear a familiar set of chords. At first, there is a slight confusion about the sound source as one of them is fiddling with the knobs of the radio. But a process of deacousmatization quickly follows. They turn off the radio and the lights, open the black-out curtains, and, after listening for a moment, identify the music as his *Warsaw Concerto*—"I've got the records!" exclaims the doctor. They move across the courtyard to peer in at Radetzky, remarking hopefully, "Perhaps that music will bring back a lot of things." What they see, however, is not precisely a redemptive return to consciousness. The pianist plays as if in a trance, motionless except for his arms, his face utterly blank; as he plays, the camera closes in on that expressionless face, and it is gradually obscured by a scene of destruction—the site of trauma—while the sound of bomb-blasts threatens to drown out the music. It is a curious scene. If the doctors' conversation mourned the loss of the concerto (even while it remained available in mechanically reproduced form), Radetzky's replay seems to represent something less than recovery, at least in these first moments. He merely repeats what was once meaningful, in a way that is now automatic, mechanical, abdicated: like repetition under hypnosis. Even once the entire flashback is over and we return to Radetzky in the hospital, he is still playing in this automatic way, until the music suddenly stops. Only then do we see a full recovery: a grand restoration of feeling, selfhood, and memory in the midst of war.

Even when Radetzky is not in this amnesiac state, he and his concerto seem set apart and out of place—things of the past. This is clear from the very beginning of the flashback, where we see Warsaw in ruins: buildings collapsing, fires erupting, the sound of bombs in the air. Across these ruins, Carol picks her way. Hearing someone playing the piano, she finds shelter in a partially bombed house and discovers an elegant young pilot at a grand piano, in a room that is the epitome of aristocratic sophistication except for the gaping holes and broken windows. In the ruined Warsaw, Radetzky appears on the scene like a remnant of another world, one in the midst of being destroyed. He and his concerto are ghostlike presences. Later appearances of Radetzky in the modern world of his American wife always seem a little off, Walbrook's refined, exoticized figure fitting oddly into a rustic cabin or an industrialist's library. As Rachmaninoff said of himself in 1939 Hollywood, he is "a ghost in a world grown alien."[75]

Perhaps more strangely, the concerto also seems detached from Radetzky himself, rather than being cast as the expressive voice of the Romantic artist.[76] When we first see him playing it in Warsaw, in his flashback, he seems utterly removed from both the surrounding scene of chaos and the concerto itself, chatting and smoking as he plays a work he has just begun composing. He then goes on to forget the concerto entirely, well before his traumatic plane crash (making that the second time it is forgotten). Even its "love theme"—inspired by Carol and associated with their romance throughout the film—seems less to express his feelings for her than the idea of "loveliness" she embodies, as Radetzky repeatedly makes explicit.[77] Their romance, moreover, is highly compressed, like the love theme and the concerto itself—after all, Radetzky says, "there's a war on"—contributing to a sense of the reduction of grand feeling as well as its detachment from an expressive subject.

In the film, then, the concerto is presented as slightly distanced from wartime reality, like a damaged remnant from a world that is largely lost. It represents less escape or emotional plenitude than a kind of stranded object in the midst of war. The film also thematizes the concerto's own status as an object of reproduction—when the doctors mention the records, or when there is confusion about where the sound of the concerto is coming from, or, most disconcertingly, when Radetzky himself plays it automatically without yet seeming to know who he is. The idea of mechanical repetition is further thematized in the scene immediately after the concerto's introduction, when the first few bars of Chopin's "Military" Polonaise are played as a chime-like loop on Polish radio to signal a resistance that was knowingly futile.[78] Even within the film, then, there is something about reduction, reproduction, and

[75] Rachmaninoff (1939), in Sergei Bertensson and Jay Leyda, *Serge Rachmaninoff: A Lifetime in Music* (New York: New York University Press, 1956), 351, quoted in Peter Franklin, "Modernism, Deception, and Musical Others," in *Western Music and Its Others: Difference, Representation, and Appropriation in Music*, ed. Georgina Born and David Hesmondhalgh (Berkeley: University of California Press, 2000), 145.

[76] In Laing's reading, Radetzky's music does act as a more straightforward means of expression, often replacing words in ways that illustrate his masculine restraint (*Gendered Score*, 152). However, she also highlights some complications to its expressiveness that might support my own reading of his music as more detached (pp. 156–159, 167), including the fact that when he most clearly plays as an expression of otherwise silent grief—at the death of his best friend Mike—it is a sentimental tune borrowed from Mike, not his own music.

[77] On the appearances of the "love theme" throughout the film, see Laing, *Gendered Score*, 157–167.

[78] Reports abound of this having happened during the Siege, from as early as 1939 ("Life on the Newsfronts of the World," *Life*, October 2, 1939, 14).

displacement at issue in the *Warsaw Concerto*. Indeed, perhaps that is why it relies on an obviously fake concerto in the first place.

It might be too much to suggest that with the *Warsaw Concerto*, *Dangerous Moonlight* offers a reflection on the debased state of Romanticism itself and the reduced space for fantasies of feeling or the self. It would thus demonstrate the kind of reflexivity about the experience of modernity (as opposed to the "formalist self-reflexivity" normally associated with modernism) that Miriam Hansen found in classical cinema and famously labeled "vernacular modernism."[79] But the film does seem to attach its concerto to notions of emptiness in some striking ways. It also anticipates and reinforces the way the concerto circulated in wartime reality, playing with the idea of its own reproduction and mechanicity. At a more basic level, *Dangerous Moonlight* suggests some of the meanings attached to the concerto for audiences—meanings ignored by critics who ostentatiously denied any knowledge of the film's content. Through the film, the concerto was associated with the experience of World War Two itself and with the survival of some remnant of selfhood—or at least of "loveliness"—in wartime. If critics dismissed audiences for being attracted to the *Warsaw Concerto*'s "romantic cinematic associations," its ability to induce escape or daydreams, or its (false) value as "serious" music, perhaps audiences were more interested in its status as a product of war (in reality as in fiction) and in the smallness of the pleasures it offered.

[79] Miriam Hansen, "The Mass Production of the Senses: Classical Cinema as Vernacular Modernism," *Modernism/Modernity* 6, no. 2 (1999): 69, 59–60.

3

Recuperating Selfhood

Love Story and *Men of Two Worlds*

Myra Hess's wartime concerts at the National Gallery served as a powerful image of solidarity and endurance—an image that spanned both popular culture and official discourse. In Humphrey Jennings's documentary *Listen to Britain* (1941), as seen in Chapter 1, these concerts were used to situate music as a special force of national belonging. But they also appear prominently in two more unlikely and very different films, the Gainsborough melodrama *Love Story* (1944) and the ambitious colonial propaganda feature *Men of Two Worlds* (1943–1946).[1] Both begin with the central character performing at a National Gallery concert, and both feature a tabloid concerto in the mold of the *Warsaw Concerto* (discussed in Chapter 2). These films attest to the cultural pervasiveness of Hess's wartime concerts, showing the extent to which they and the associated image of the heroic pianist had become conventions of wartime film. But if the National Gallery concert had become somewhat of a cliché by this point—a touchstone of wartime imagery—in these films it also signals an underlying concern with the question of music's efficacy.

Love Story begins with the heroine performing her final concert at the National Gallery. Thinking she needs to do more for the war effort, she has decided to join the Women's Auxiliary Air Force (WAAF), against the protests of her manager and the audience. Before she can enlist, though, she finds out she has a life-threatening heart condition and retreats to Cornwall, where she falls in love with an injured pilot and writes her *Cornish Rhapsody*—a tabloid concerto composed by Hubert Bath. This idyll is interrupted when, in a gesture of self-sacrifice, she recklessly decides to tour with

[1] *Love Story*, dir. Leslie Arliss, Gainsborough Pictures, 1944, in *The Margaret Lockwood Collection* (ITV Studios, 2008, DVD); *Men of Two Worlds*, dir. Thorold Dickinson, Two Cities, 1946 (BFI Player, https://player.bfi.org.uk/free/film/watch-men-of-two-worlds-1946-online).

Mobilizing Music in Wartime British Film. Heather Wiebe, Oxford University Press. © Oxford University Press 2024.
DOI: 10.1093/oso/9780197631713.003.0004

the Entertainments National Service Association (ENSA), playing popular songs for troops around North Africa. Finally, she returns to her own music, in a performance of the *Cornish Rhapsody* at the Albert Hall, and thereby to love and to Cornwall.

A National Gallery concert also opens *Men of Two Worlds* (1943–1946), commissioned by the Colonial Office and the Ministry of Information (MoI) and directed by Thorold Dickinson, with a score by Arthur Bliss. Again it is 1944. The pianist this time is Kisenga, a London-trained musician from Tanganyika (now Tanzania), playing his own concerto, *Baraza* (another tabloid concerto, by Bliss). After his concert, signing autographs for his English fans, Kisenga reveals that he, too, is leaving his musical career to do something more useful—to the dismay of his manager—and is returning to Africa to be a teacher. "You have a duty to music, Mr. Kisenga, to *English* music," one admirer protests. "I'm *needed* in Africa," he responds, "as an African, to teach." In the end, though, it is his music that has efficacy, in this case of an almost magical order. Despite his own illness and self-doubt, the choral symphony he writes in his home village works to bring his community together, dispelling the malevolent forces represented throughout the film by a competing music, preventing his own death, and enabling the colonial project of moving his village out of a disease-infested area to a new, "modern" community.

These are both confused films, in their different ways. This is partly because they are *about* confusions of identity—to do with gender, race, and colonial subjectivity—in the face of overwhelming and conflicting national demands. They also dwell on a tension between the demands for self-sacrifice and the importance of selfhood, associating music with the latter and suggesting that the recuperation of the self can be necessary for the larger social good. Most of all, though, they suggest how music might be used to test the limits of mobilization. Music poses the question of what can be made useful or productive and how, and what happens when usefulness is demanded of everything, particularly when usefulness is defined as helping to fulfill the purposes of the state. *Love Story* is explicitly concerned with wartime mobilization and with the demands of total war. But *Men of Two Worlds* is similarly concerned with how to mobilize populations in service of the state, in this case in projects of colonial development. In an extension of domestic wartime technocracy, the colonial state both represented and served by the film sought to reorganize East African communities, rendering them more easily managed for the purposes of delivering health and education services, and thereby more economically productive. Most of all it sought to mobilize Africans themselves in this project. Meanwhile, the mobilization of Black citizens and colonial subjects for the British war effort was managed with some ambivalence, with the British relying heavily on Africans for military labor in the colonies even while using informal color bars to limit the full participation of people of African and Caribbean descent in British units from the Royal Air Force (RAF) to the Women's Land Army.[2] In both of these films, music and the musician—in both cases insistently marked as weak or damaged—become figures for exploring the problem of how to mobilize what was imagined as liminal or unproductive, whether that was feeling itself or people marginalized on the basis of gender, race, or ability.

Love Story and Music as War Work

Love Story was both made and set in 1944, and it reflects on a kind of exhaustion that seems a feature of this moment. As Richard Overy notes, there were "signs of growing demoralization" in Britain and the United States in 1944, after years in which "total war became a way of life."[3] This exhaustion with the conditions of total war is sometimes obscured by the flurry of postwar planning in these years, but it is clearly apparent in women's fiction. A particularly rich example is Sylvia Townsend Warner's "Poor Mary" (1945), one of a series of stories she wrote for *The New Yorker* about the wartime lives of British women. Late in the war, an enlisted woman who has been working in a factory goes to visit her husband, a conscientious objector assigned to farm labor. Estranged by their differing views and concerned by the absurd appearance of a wife in uniform visiting her pacifist husband, they have never bothered to visit each other before. Now she shows up in some despair. "When I get out of the army," she declares, "I shall come out healthy, hideous, middle-aged, and without an interest in life. And there will be hordes and hordes of me, all in the same boat." "You'll take hold," he reassures her, "you'll

[2] On the difficulties encountered by Black Britons attempting to enlist or volunteer, see Stephen Bourne, *Under Fire: Black Britain in Wartime 1939–45* (Cheltenham: History Press, 2020), 47–55. Also see Richard Overy, *Blood and Ruins: The Great Imperial War 1931–1945* (London: Allen Lane, 2021), 390. On British recruitment in African colonies, especially for military labor, see Ibid., 389–390, and David Killingray, *Fighting for Britain: African Soldiers in the Second World War* (Woodbridge: Boydell & Brewer, 2010).

[3] Overy, *Blood and Ruins*, 431.

get interested in something or other. Probably you'll fall in love, and make a fresh start."[4] The story's concern is in part with demobilization, but also, I think, with a prevailing affect of the moment—a lack of attachment to life, born of the all-consuming demands of war work. It is this lack of attachment that music seems to address in *Love Story.*

Love Story is a Gainsborough "woman's picture"—featuring the studio's star Margaret Lockwood, doubled on the piano by Harriet Cohen—that combined melodrama with "home front" realism. However, compared with *Millions Like Us*, for instance—another Gainsborough "home front" film, discussed in Chapter 1, with the same musical team of Bath and music director Louis Levy[5]—it leaned much more toward melodrama, indulging in unlikely plot twists and emotional excess, in a hybrid that met with popular success and acute critical embarrassment. One reviewer commented, "I expect it's absurd, but I wake up in the night wishing that an English company hadn't made *Love Story*. . . . We hear a lot about the desirability of putting ordinary English life into films. Can this be the result?"[6] Indeed, part of the oddness of *Love Story* is that it engages with realism while asserting what we might call the values of melodrama, making it very different from related hybrids like *Millions Like Us.*

By the values of melodrama, I mean something like the utopianism of entertainment as described by Richard Dyer, or the sentimentality of "women's culture" as discussed by Lauren Berlant. For Dyer, entertainment presents "the image of something better to escape into, or something we want deeply that our day-to-day lives don't provide"; through non-narrative signifiers like music, it presents "what utopia would *feel* like rather than how it would be organized."[7] That involves both a transparency and an intensity of feeling—the "experiencing of emotion directly, fully, unambiguously, 'authentically,' without holding back."[8] For Berlant, mid-century "women's culture" similarly circulates around fantasies—of feeling, of emotional transparency and recognition, of the "good life"—that provide a relief from the disappointment of the present and from political realities that create barriers to women's

[4] Sylvia Townsend Warner, "Poor Mary," in *English Climate: Wartime Stories* (London: Persephone Books, 2020), 194.

[5] Jan G. Swynnoe, *The Best Years of British Film Music, 1936–1958* (Woodbridge: Boydell, 2002), 22, 233.

[6] *Time and Tide*, October 14, 1944 (*Love Story*, press cuttings, British Film Institute Reubens Library [hereafter BFI]).

[7] Richard Dyer, *Only Entertainment* (London: Routledge, 1992), 20 (emphasis added).

[8] Ibid., 23.

flourishing.[9] This is "fantasy as a mode of disappointment management or adaptation and of interruption of the realism of the present."[10] At the same time, for Berlant, such fantasies can themselves be constraining, tending to promote "normativity as the basis of feminine optimism."[11] In *Love Story*, music is central to these fantasies. It first resists the idea of music as "war work"—as useful or elevating rather than expressive—and instead affirms the importance of escape to an alternative world of emotional plenitude, attachment, and self-fulfillment based on individual desires; it then attempts, however awkwardly, to saddle this fantasy to the purposes of war, making it useful after all.

Normative femininity is very much at issue in *Love Story*, and very much a fantasy in the context of a more fundamental wartime confusion about feminine identity. As Pam Cook has noted, the period "gave rise to a number of different, often contradictory, representations of femininity," and Gainsborough woman's pictures, including *Love Story*, "work through these conflicts, bringing contradictions to the surface."[12] Indeed, *Love Story* takes to absurd extremes the figure of the "mobile woman," described by Antonia Lant as an expression of "femininity's unstable wartime nature."[13] Not only is the narrative concerned with the heroine's deployment; in more literal ways, too, she is on the move. She is shown in buses, trains, planes, military caravans, even a donkey cart, while almost never appearing in a private or domestic space; indeed, she seems to have no home at all, spending much of the film living in a hotel. Her physical transience is matched by a tendency to transform in appearance and to some extent character, shifting from sober, utilitarian clothing to glamorous evening gowns and girlish dresses, from hard-working heroine to seductress to self-sacrificing lover. Indeed, she even has two names—her stage name, Felicity Crichton, and the name she goes by for much of the film, Lissa. The heroine's odd shifts in persona suggest the film's confusion about the roles women should occupy. But they also suggest a loss of self—a loss of expression and attachment amid the pressures of war—that the film seeks to address.

[9] Lauren Berlant, *The Female Complaint: The Unfinished Business of Sentimentality in American Culture* (Durham, NC: Duke University Press, 2008), 2–5.

[10] Ibid., 24.

[11] Ibid., 22.

[12] Pam Cook, *Screening the Past: Memory and Nostalgia in Cinema* (London: Routledge, 2004), 83.

[13] Antonia Lant, *Blackout: Reinventing Women for Wartime British Cinema* (Princeton: Princeton University Press, 1991), 66.

That loss of self, feeling, and connection is first articulated, oddly, through the brief opening scene at the National Gallery concert, conventionally a potent site of national belonging. In Jennings's documentary *Listen to Britain*, as argued in Chapter 1, the National Gallery concerts provided a rich space of feeling and connection. In *Love Story*, however, they are treated as a site of emotionally impoverished realism, in what reads partly as an indictment of the concerts themselves and partly as an indictment of the values of collectivity ensconced in documentary film.

Indeed, *Love Story* might be seen to comment directly on *Listen to Britain*, knowingly contradicting its reading of the concerts. For a start, *Love Story*'s opening sequence uses some shots that are identical, clearly relying on the same stock footage of the National Gallery—the same bus rolls by, the same people are still sitting in the square outside. The organization of those shots also seems to call on Jennings's film, suggesting more than an accidental relationship. After the opening credits (accompanied by the lush *Cornish Rhapsody* and shots of Cornwall), *Love Story* begins outside the National Gallery before the concert, with a shot of a barrage balloon and then Nelson's Column—the same images with which the National Gallery scene *ends* in *Listen to Britain* (including the exact same shot of Nelson), in reverse order. A clock strikes one (as in all such scenes) and the requisite poster for the lunchtime concerts is shown outside the gallery, the heroine Felicity Crichton's name clumsily plastered in giant letters beneath Hess's. The commentary on *Listen to Britain* continues in the following scene, when the heroine attempts to join the WAAF. She is asked by an impressed secretary if she has ever performed with Flanagan and Allen, the music hall duo, in what can be read on one level as a comic confusion of high and low, but on another as a gesture to the Flanagan and Allen performance that precedes the National Gallery concert in *Listen to Britain*, and thus as a more pointed gesture to its exalted claims for art music and its vision of national community. It is all the more striking, then, that the opening scene of the film sets aside Jennings's central claim that music in wartime is "far from being just another escape," valorizing it precisely on the grounds that it *is* an escape while also rejecting it as inadequate.[14]

The National Gallery scene itself presents the wartime musician as a self-sacrificing figure, heroic in some ways but also diminished and to some

[14] "The Music of War: Treatment" (May 23, 1941), Box 1, Item 7, Humphrey Jennings Collection, British Film Institute Special Collections (hereafter BFI Special Collections).

extent ineffective. The heroine's sober black day dress might be seen as a reference to Hess herself, but more broadly, she is a portrait of self-erasure. As she delivers a rather anodyne performance of Chopin's "Revolutionary" Étude, the audience appears uninspired and uninspiring. It consists mostly of women in civilian clothing; some are doing needlework or knitting or discreetly nibbling at sandwiches. These are hardly the rapt listeners seen in Jennings's *Diary for Timothy* (1946), or even the delighted ones seen in *Listen to Britain* (see Chapter 1). The lack of uniformed personnel, meanwhile, also suggests a certain irrelevance to the war effort. When the heroine's manager comes on stage to make an announcement, he both defends music as "war work" and suggests some of its shortcomings:

> Miss Crichton does not agree with me that the happiness and relaxation her skill can bring to people, longing for a brief escape from the grimness of today, is the best sort of war work she can do [applause]. And so you have heard her play for the last time. She is giving up her music for the duration. She is determined to do something more directly connected with the war effort.[15]

These are fairly modest claims—music as an escape, bringing happiness and relaxation. One problem in the scene, though, is that music does not seem to be providing *much* of an escape. It is just more grimness—from the dutiful performance of Chopin to the distracted audience and their mundane activities—in ways that perhaps speak to a sense of tedium at this late stage of the war. From the heroine's point of view, moreover, the whole thrust of the scene is toward self-denial and sacrifice, from her stage name to her black dress and self-deprecating manner to the fact that she is playing Chopin rather than her own music, as she does elsewhere in the film. If music is to become war work—at least on these terms, the scene suggests—it might as well be given up altogether.

Love Story is hardly the first wartime film to voice doubts about the validity of art music as war work. Even *Battle for Music*, the 1943 documentary about the London Philharmonic Orchestra (LPO; discussed in Chapter 2), explores anxieties that music is not a worthwhile war activity, if only to allay them. At one point in the early days of a tour, one of the younger musicians

[15] *Love Story*, 0:02:30.

suggests it was all a mistake.[16] "[T]here are more important things to do at the present time than play music," he suggests. "Beat Jerry first and *then* listen to music." His despair is met with various arguments, most of them revealingly vague: you can't "lose faith" in what you are "living and fighting for," one musician says. Another musician suggests that the LPO is an institution that takes a long time to build and cannot be replaced—echoing the real-world rhetoric around the orchestra as a national treasure to be preserved—and another suggests that it is as essential as "books or schools." But what settles the argument is a bit of Nazi radio propaganda the musicians hear at this moment, taunting the British as culturally bankrupt and praising German support for the arts. All in all, it is not the most convincing set of arguments, and the idea of music's utility plays oddly little role (except, perhaps, in the vague comparison to books and schools). Ultimately, the verdict is clear: playing music is valid war work and constitutes a type of heroism. But that defense depends on the idea that music is not just a "brief escape," as it is described in the opening scene of *Love Story*. For J. B. Priestley in *Battle for Music*, music provided "courage and inspiration," and "noble refreshment of the spirit" in wartime.[17]

In *Love Story*, on the other hand, art music imagined as war work seems to provide little to others or to the musician. In place of the idea of music as war work and self-sacrifice, it goes on to launch a defense of music in a melodramatic mode—music as feeling and as unfettered expression, in an environment of restraint and self-erasure. While the film remains committed to duty and sacrifice, it also insists on survival—and a kind of selfishness and indulgence in pleasure—as compatible with duty, and even useful or necessary. Pam Cook writes that, in *Love Story*, "Female desire is first mobilized, then channeled by the presentation of two paths: sacrifice or self-interest"; for her, the film manages to keep these two paths in tension without resolving their conflicts.[18] I might put this a little differently. The film plays with a classic conflict between duty and desire, but with a few telling variations. First, what is opposed to duty is not so much desire as feeling more broadly, and the ability to express feeling. Indeed, the opposition might also be understood

[16] *Battle for Music: The London Philharmonic Orchestra at War*, dir. Donald Taylor, Strand Film Company, 1943 (Broxburn, UK: Panamint, 2013, DVD). This episode is also quoted and discussed in John Morris, *Culture and Propaganda in World War II: Music, Film and the Battle for National Identity* (London: I. B. Tauris, 2014), 43–44.

[17] *Battle for Music*, quoted in Morris, *Culture and Propaganda*, 44.

[18] Cook, *Screening the Past*, 87.

as one between the corporate values of documentary and the ideals of self-hood ensconced in melodrama. Second, music can be associated with either pole—duty or feeling—although it is distinctly unsatisfactory as a performance of duty. And third, the opposition finally collapses when feeling—and music as feeling—is revealed as compatible with duty and in fact necessary for its fulfillment.

The *Cornish Rhapsody*

It is only once the film leaves the world of war-besieged London and the National Gallery concerts—which is also the world of documentary realism here—that we are introduced to its musical centerpiece. The *Cornish Rhapsody* is another miniature piano concerto in a lushly expressive late-Romantic style—"drip and Tchaikovsky again" commented one film critic, asking "how many miles to Warsaw?"[19] But unlike the *Warsaw Concerto* in *Dangerous Moonlight*, it does not even have a minimal function as war work in the film, becoming associated mainly with idyllic escape and excessive feeling, as its title suggests. Having been rejected by the WAAF because of a newly discovered heart condition, the heroine, Lissa, removes to Cornwall with the goal of enjoying what little time she has left. The hotel where she stays is a world apart, and news of the war only occasionally intrudes.[20] In Cornwall, she falls in love with a mysteriously undeployed young man—Kit, who turns out to be an injured pilot, going blind as the result of a crash—and, inspired both by her new happiness and by her natural surroundings, she begins to compose her *Cornish Rhapsody*. The film makes its meanings absurdly explicit when Lissa gives Kit a demonstration of its musical themes, all based on their recent visit to the Cornish headlands: one is the seagulls, another the waves, "and this," she says, playing the main theme, "to express some of the emotions I felt at the time." She adds, "If I could express them in words, I wouldn't have to write music."[21] The music's association with nature and freedom is consolidated in a climactic scene at a primitive outdoor theatre (the Minack Theatre, built for outdoor Shakespeare performances), perched on a cliff with the sea in view.

[19] William Whitebait, *New Statesman*, October 21, 1944 (*Love Story*, press cuttings, BFI).
[20] See Lant, *Blackout*, 73.
[21] *Love Story*, 0:25:00.

But at this point near the end of the film, the *Cornish Rhapsody* is suddenly abandoned and the film pivots back to self-sacrifice, musically and dramatically. Leaving Cornwall, in a complicated secret bargain to allow Kit to have sight-saving surgery, Lissa returns to music as war work once again. She decides to go ahead with the ENSA tour that was planned before her terminal diagnosis. In a montage of her tour—briefly returning to the aesthetic world of documentary—we see her traveling around North Africa in airplanes and military caravans, exhausted and unhappy. And instead of performing her own music—or even Chopin—she finds herself pounding out the chords for a singalong version of "Dear Old Blighty," broadcast on the BBC. Even more clearly than in the National Gallery scene, music as war service is a joyless affair—the problem, in other words, was not with art music but with the very idea of music as work and as self-denial rather than self-expression or self-fulfillment. And this vision of music is rejected once again. At the end of this sequence, Lissa returns to England, performing her *Cornish Rhapsody* at the Albert Hall (where the scene was actually filmed).[22] Her own music becomes aligned not with war work but with a return to herself and the fulfillment of her own aspirations. These aspirations are professional ones in the first instance—performing at the Albert Hall has long been a career goal, she says—and in the process of pursuing them she fulfills her romantic desires as well. The performance serves as an occasion for a reunion with Kit, all misunderstandings suddenly dispelled. After his successful surgery, moreover, he is now returning to duty, and the last image in the film is of Lissa back in Cornwall, waving to fighter aircraft flying overhead. This turns out to be her true contribution to the war effort, in a subsidiary role. Kit's return to service is enabled by her sacrifice, but his rehabilitation more broadly seems to be enabled by her love and her music.

For some critics, the value of that music lies in its harnessing of nature. K. J. Donnelly observes, her music "appears to be an emanation of both nature and Lissa's desire" and "thus functions to associate and unite elemental natural forces and female desire."[23] Heather Laing suggests that through her music Lissa "becomes the voice of the land and sea" and transfers their strength to Kit, thus symbolizing "the recuperative powers of female love for

[22] "Albert Hall used for 'Love Story,'" in Eagle-Lion Distribution, *Love Story* [Pressbook], 8, Pressbooks Collection, BFI Special Collections.

[23] K. J. Donnelly, *British Film Music and Film Musicals* (Basingstoke: Palgrave Macmillan, 2007), 51.

war-damaged men"; the *Cornish Rhapsody* itself, in its joint association with both primitive nature and feminine desire, thus has a restorative force.[24]

But the importance of the *Cornish Rhapsody* also seems to lie in its status as an expression of the (female) self; as such, it is placed in tension with the idea of self-sacrifice throughout the film. In the publicity for *Love Story*, its distributor placed a heavy emphasis on the *Cornish Rhapsody* as a publicity tool. It attempted to relate the *Cornish Rhapsody* directly to women's wartime experience, in part by insisting on its source in Lissa herself (eliding its actual male authorship) and by associating it strongly with feeling. The "Exploitation" package for *Love Story* suggests in one passage that the music was "written by Lissa as an expression of her feelings" and, in another, that Lissa "pours out her feelings in life and love in the composing" of it.[25] This focus on the *Cornish Rhapsody* as an expression of feminine feeling extends throughout the publicity. A story for press distribution states, "she is inspired to write a piano concerto into which her love for Kit, her feeling of freedom underneath the Cornish skies, the emotion inspired in her by the grandeur of the rocky coast and the sea, the sadness that her life may be ended, just as she has found love, are all poured." The package also outlined how cinemas might present a live performance of the *Cornish Rhapsody* in advance of the film, accompanied by a slide show of "Cornish Scenery to 'dress' the music." The slide show included the following text:

> Into this music she [Lissa] has woven her dreams of "what might have been" intermingled with expressions of her love for the beautiful Cornish countryside midst which their mutual love blossomed and fought to find its logical conclusion.
>
> Yes! A woman's soul went into this rhapsody.... "The Cornish Rhapsody" she named it, thinking of the rugged moorland, rolling hills and sleepy hamlets of that part of England which gave it birth.
>
> So her Love Story is not tragic, for a woman's heart will always find consolation in beauty and draw forth courage and comfort in adversity (haven't we seen it so often in these days—do we not know someone who is doing so this very moment?).

[24] Heather Laing, *The Gendered Score: Music in 1940s Melodrama and the Woman's Film* (London: Routledge, 2007), 126. See also Rachel Moseley, "A Landscape of Desire: Cornwall as Romantic Setting in *Love Story* and *Ladies in Lavender*," in *British Women's Cinema*, ed. Melanie Bell and Melanie Williams (London: Routledge, 2009), 82.

[25] Eagle-Lion Distribution, *Love Story* [Pressbook], 13, 12, Pressbooks Collection, BFI Special Collections.

> Therefore let us listen to A "Cornish Rhapsody," written by Lissa: it is her Love Story set to music, and realise that music enables her to forget herself, whilst so many of us struggle to find means of expressing ourselves, even in words.[26]

These statements are not particularly coherent, but they do return again and again to the idea of music as an expression of a woman's heart, soul, and dreams. Their preoccupation is with the feelings of individual women (treated as a marketing group, in the manner of an "intimate public") in response to wartime circumstances.[27] In "enabling" Lissa to "forget herself"—that is, in the peculiarly paradoxical sense of the phrase, to forget duty and restraint and the wartime demands for self-sacrifice—it allows her precisely to remember the self she had forgot and to express it freely.

The slideshow's gesture to a shared wartime problem with expression seems more than empty publicity. The problem of blocked expression is in fact central to the film, as it has been to the melodramatic mode in general since its origins in the late eighteenth century, according to Peter Brooks's classic account.[28] The plot circulates around the characters' inexplicable refusal to tell each other central facts about themselves—that she is dying, that he is going blind. While both circumstances are treated as melodramatic absurdities, they obviously gesture to wartime realities of trauma and uncertainty. The couple's failure to address these realities leads to further confusion when they pretend to be noncommittal about their relationship because their own futures are so uncertain. Music is what finally allows transparency. And this is a benefit for Kit as well as Lissa. Indeed, this is how music ends up rehabilitating Kit, the slide show text seems to indicate: with "no means of expression, he is bewildered, heart-riven, lonely in the midst of his Love Story until he hears Cornish Rhapsody and at last learns and understands the depths of Lissa's heart."[29] Music is what enables emotional recognition, and this, in turn, is what seems to save Kit in this account.

In the end, the film reasserts the call of duty: between their reunion and the next scene, the couple is separated again, Kit returning to the air and Lissa to Cornwall. But for the first time, the film's pivot to duty and

[26] Eagle-Lion Distribution, *Love Story* [Pressbook], 14, Pressbooks Collection, BFI Special Collections. The idiosyncrasies of typography are in the original text.

[27] On "intimate publics" and women's culture, see Berlant, *Female Complaint*, viii, 2–3.

[28] Peter Brooks, *The Melodramatic Imagination: Balzac, Henry James, Melodrama, and the Mode of Excess* (New Haven, CT: Yale University Press, 1976), 4.

[29] Eagle-Lion Distribution, *Love Story* [Pressbook], Pressbooks Collection, BFI Special Collections.

self-sacrifice is accompanied by the *Cornish Rhapsody*. Rather than being grounded in self-erasure, a reinvigorated usefulness is grounded in a call to life and attachment. As Antonia Lant suggests, *Love Story* asks "its audience to accept emotional loss, separation, and uncertainty about the future while still demanding its commitment to 'living through.'"[30] This idea of "living through" is summed up by Kit when he and Lissa reunite at the Albert Hall, in a statement underlaid by an orchestral version of the *Cornish Rhapsody*'s sweeping theme.

> We're all living dangerously, there isn't any certainty anymore. There's just today and the hope of tomorrow. Oh, darling, please let's take all the happiness we can, while we can. Don't be afraid.[31]

The scene affirms this music's association with feeling and attachment in the midst of larger demands and uncertainties. The theme appears again, though, moments later when the film cuts to the final scene, with Lissa in Cornwall and aircraft flying overhead. The underscoring here suggests in part that Lissa and her music have contributed to the war effort after all by returning a fighter to the air. But the theme is also tellingly different: not only is it in the brass, it also cuts off after its stolid opening four notes, thus silencing the unstable and extravagant gesture that follows the theme's other appearances. It suggests both a new discipline and focus and something sacrificed or curtailed, something that was important to the identity of both the music and Lissa herself.

The film thus works through various models of music's potential contribution only to arrive at one compatible with melodramatic conventions—one that does not draw on music's social utility or even its ennobling qualities. Instead, it reclaims music's very association with the personal and the emotional, attempting to mobilize it on those grounds while limiting both women's and music's efforts to a supporting role in the service of fighting men.

[30] Antonia Lant, *Blackout: Reinventing Women for Wartime British Cinema* (Princeton: Princeton University Press, 1991), 39.

[31] *Love Story*, 1:47:00.

Men of Two Worlds

Men of Two Worlds is a much more ambitious film and, in some ways, all the more puzzling in its concern with music. The film follows the composer Kisenga as he returns to Tanganyika after fifteen years in London, to serve as Director of Education in his home district. But first, he is asked by the District Commissioner, Randall, to help with another task—convincing the people in his home village, the fictional Litu, to join in a mass relocation due to an infestation of the tsetse fly and a resulting epidemic of "sleeping sickness." The film goes on to dramatize a conflict between technocratic modernity and progress, on one hand, and the forces of resistance, on the other, casting this conflict mainly as an opposition between the British colonizers and the colonized. Progress is represented by Randall and the female medical doctor Munro, in collaboration with the researcher Gollner, a Viennese refugee, and Kisenga—who is held up by the Europeans as an ideal "new African," rather than a "carbon copy of a European."[32] Resistance is led by the witchdoctor Magole, an outsider who preys on local people's fear and ignorance to sustain his own power, in a clear nod to fascist politics closer to home. Returning to his village, Kisenga is caught between these forces and, indeed, between his European and African identities. Music becomes a way of both articulating and navigating this conflict and, ultimately, of mobilizing the village for progress.

Men of Two Worlds is one of the more spectacular failures of World War Two propaganda. It took three years to make, the director's insistence on Technicolor and two trips to Africa proving disastrous in wartime circumstances. Equipment was lost or damaged in military transport, shooting was further delayed by illness and weather, and much of the footage shot in Africa was lost due to delays in processing, meaning that the film had to be entirely reshot in a London studio in 1945.[33] The result was a complex

[32] *Men of Two Worlds*, 1:01:00; E. Fisher, *Men of Two Worlds: Adapted from the Two Cities Film* (London: World Film Publications, 1946), 45. In its use of this term, the film might recall the contemporary "New African movement," but that movement was more oriented toward decolonization. See Ntongela Masilela, "New African Modernity and the New African Movement," in *The Cambridge History of South African Literature*, ed. David Attwell and Derek Attridge (Cambridge: Cambridge University Press, 2012), 325–326.

[33] Dickinson describes these difficulties in Thorold Dickinson, "Making a Film in Tanganyika Territory," in *The British Film Yearbook 1947–48*, ed. Peter Noble (London: Skelton Robinson British Yearbooks, 1948), 53–58, and Peter Noble, *The Negro in Films* (London: Skelton Robinson, 1948), 133. The studio filming is described in some detail in John Huntley, *British Film Music* (London: Skelton Robinson, 1947), 85–86.

but confusing film that fell wide of its goal of box office success when it was finally released in 1946. Since then, it has largely disappeared from view as an embarrassing relic of late colonialism, only becoming publicly available in the past few years.[34] But its very failures are also telling, bespeaking a strain on wartime ideals of inclusion and mobilization as they come into contact with discourses of colonialism and Blackness. The film shows, moreover, how music was once again used to explore those ideals and test their limits.

Closely controlled by the Colonial Office and the MoI, *Men of Two Worlds* was designed both to convince domestic audiences of the need for continued colonial investment in wartime and to defend Britain's empire abroad. Its story of the struggle against the tsetse fly—based on real British projects in East Africa—had been identified since 1940 as a promising one for colonial propaganda (however optimistically).[35] Perhaps not coincidentally, the tsetse fly was also the subject of a 1943 Nazi film, *Germanin*, to which *Men of Two Worlds* might be seen as a rejoinder.[36] This piece of anti-British propaganda celebrated German development of a pharmaceutical cure for sleeping sickness in East Africa. Here, though, violent and self-interested British colonizers make it impossible to distribute this treatment, expelling a selfless German researcher and his female medical assistant (precursors of Gollner and Dr. Munro) and destroying their medical facility and supplies. Black characters are thoroughly dehumanized in this film, never conversing comprehensibly with White characters, let alone participating in their medical efforts. To play these Africans, moreover, three hundred Black POWs were transported to Italy and forced to work on set.[37]

Men of Two Worlds, by contrast, was a vehicle for promoting new policies of partnership and development: policies ensconced in the Colonial Development and Welfare Act of 1940 and applied particularly to Britain's remaining empire in Africa, but also extending British welfare efforts at

[34] When I first saw *Men of Two Worlds* in February 2017, it could only be viewed privately on 16 mm film at the BFI National Archive. Shortly afterward, the BFI made a digitized version available on its online Player, available in the UK only.

[35] Wendy Webster, *Englishness and Empire 1939–1965* (Oxford: Oxford University Press, 2005), 69.

[36] *Germanin: Die Geschichte einer kolonialen Tat*, dir. Max W. Kimmich, UFA, 1943 (International Historic Films, Chicago, 2012, DVD). On *Germanin*, see Willeke Sandler, *Empire in the Heimat* (New York: Oxford University Press, 2018), 261–262.

[37] Sandler, *Empire in the Heimat*, 262. Sandler notes the POWs were likely from the French army. Also see "Zwangsarbeit in den Studios," in "100 Jahre Babelsburg," a project directed by Jan Distelmeyer (https://www.filmportal.de/thema/zwangsarbeit-in-einem-filmstudio); and Bénédicte Savoy, *Museen: Eine Kindheitserinnerung und die Folge* (Cologne: Greven Verlag Köln, 2019), 58–63. I am indebted to Maria Fuchs for the latter reference and for bringing the film to my attention.

home.[38] These ideals had been explored in documentary film, as Marc Matera points out, but *Men of Two Worlds* was an attempt to bring them to wider attention, with the compelling force of melodrama.[39] The Colonial Office treated the film as a priority throughout its long and complex genesis, freeing up resources, monitoring progress, and facilitating transport. With the MoI, it commissioned a story on which to base the film, then found a studio willing to make it (Two Cities, which was responsible for a number of important wartime propaganda films, including *Henry V*); hired a director, Thorold Dickinson; and eventually settled on a screenwriter, Joyce Cary (a novelist and former colonial officer in Nigeria), after Dickinson read his pamphlet *The Case for African Freedom*. From the very beginnings, the official themes of partnership and development were central to the film.

The problem of how to represent this partnership was a little more complicated. The film, Dickinson wrote, "was not to be a spectacle of conquest or a documentary, but an intimate dramatic study of the two races working side by side."[40] As in colonial policy itself, though, partnership was imagined along distinctly paternalist lines: in the face of growing calls for independence, the British view was that Africans needed to be guided into readiness. Indeed, in *The Case for African Freedom*, Cary stated this view explicitly, arguing that European powers should take responsibility for development in Africa, which he relegated "a vast slum among the nations," with political emancipation only a distant goal.[41]

For Cary, "African freedom" was not independence; rather, freedom lay in the power to access and navigate a beneficial social order. In the expanded version of his pamphlet, published in 1944, he articulated a vision of freedom and colonial development grounded in the wartime state's concern with managing and mobilizing all aspects of life. Indeed, for one of his first concrete examples of freedom, he makes a surprising turn: to the wartime Council for the Encouragement of Music and the Arts (CEMA).

> C.E.M.A., for instance, which brings music and plays to remote [British] villages, at government expense, is actually, in the most literal sense of the

[38] Webster, *Englishness and Empire*, 68.

[39] Marc Matera, *Black London: The Imperial Metropolis and Decolonization in the Twentieth Century* (Berkeley: University of California Press, 2015), 301.

[40] Dickinson, "Making a Film in Tanganyika Territory," 53.

[41] Joyce Cary, "The Case for African Freedom (1944)," in *The Case for African Freedom and Other Writings on Africa* (Austin: University of Press, 1962), 130.

> word, increasing freedom. It has enabled thousands of people who were born with the love of good music, or dramatic sense, to enjoy it for the first time. Whereas they have said before, "I should like to hear a real orchestra, but I've never been able to find the time and money to go to town," now they have the power to listen to an orchestra or see a play, in their own neighborhood, at small cost. Government action has given them a new freedom which formerly they did not possess.[42]

It was in providing access to things that enriched life that the state could both empower its citizens and motivate them to be economically productive. In Cary's vision of the state, one of the great enemies is waste. The ideal state is "that which gives all its members the best chance of happiness and realization, and makes the best use of their different powers."[43] No state can afford to waste people, he says, calling on a central doctrine of total war. *Men of Two Worlds* reflects this abhorrence of waste; it represents a colonial logic that seeks to make everyone and everything productive.

Unsurprisingly, given the film's paternalistic stance, it met with some significant criticism. London's West African Student Union (WASU) called for extensive changes after seeing an early draft of the script. They mainly objected to the depiction of a witchdoctor and suggested that this character, Magole, be treated as a more equally weighted voice for independence and the legitimacy of African traditions.[44] The film also generated debate when it was released, prompting a lengthy correspondence in the *Times*. Here, the vice president of WASU took issue with the character of Kisenga as well, as a "type of African who only exists in the imagination of some people, a man of two worlds, who cannot fit into European or African society just because he has lived and studied in Britain."[45] At the same time, as Jordanna Bailkin has discussed, the issues of identity broached in *Men of Two Worlds* resonated with a broader concern about the psychiatric health of overseas—especially African—students in postwar Britain, on the part of both African and British researchers.[46] Indeed, its representation of Kisenga's crisis seems not so distant from the "inferiority complex" discussed by Frantz Fanon just

[42] Ibid., 25.
[43] Ibid., 131.
[44] Matera, *Black London*, 308–309.
[45] W. C. Peterside to *Times*, September 11, 1946, 5; also see Matera, *Black London*, 311.
[46] Jordanna Bailkin, *The Afterlife of Empire* (Berkeley: University of California Press, 2012), 119–125.

a few years later and diagnosed as the result of Black encounters with a White metropolis.[47]

Music might seem rather distant from these concerns, and indeed, it did not play a large part in the Colonial Office's original plans. In the story it commissioned, Kisenga was simply a teacher, not a musician. It was only when Dickinson became involved that music began to take a central role. First, he sought to represent African *traditional* music, deploying a conventional strategy to provide "authenticity" and appeal to audiences. It would also help create a contrast with Kisenga's "European" music. He wrote in 1947:

> Yet in our screen-play about Kisenga, the Europeanised composer who goes back to his Tanganyikan tribe, we needed local music for contrast, truly local, since we aimed at authenticity at all costs. And we also needed tribal dance music, to which popular audiences in the rest of the world could listen sympathetically. We were to make a film, not for the converted, the interested audience, but for the sympathetic and unsympathetic also.[48]

In Dar es Salaam, Dickinson had secured the services of Hans Cory—a colonial officer and amateur sociologist who studied the music and customs of local ethnic groups—to make recordings of local dances and songs on which to base the film's music and its ritual scenes.[49] He sent recordings to Bliss, who based two of the most obviously folk-like elements in the score on East African themes: the children's song discussed in the following section, and the cheerful group song that ends the film, as the Litu drive off to their new land.[50] In London, Dickinson went to great efforts to recreate some of these dances and rituals in the studio, bringing together performers from across London's Black diaspora. (These included the classically trained Jamaican dancer Berto Pasuka, who co-founded the Ballets Nègres—Europe's first Black ballet company—shortly afterward in 1946, drawing on some of the

[47] Frantz Fanon, *Black Skin, White Masks* (1952), trans. Charles Lam Markmann (London: Pluto Press, 1986), 13, 18–20.

[48] Thorold Dickinson, "Search for Music," in *The Penguin Film Review* 2 (London: Penguin, 1947), 9.

[49] Dickinson describes at length both Cory's participation and the reconstruction in London in "Search for Music," 9–15. Dickinson also reports being helped in Dar es Salaam by a young man named Daudi bin Amri who collected songs for him.

[50] Dickinson, "Search for Music," 15. Dickinson reports that the children's song "is developed from a war song of the Wangoni," while the finale "is a fishing song from Lake Victoria Nyanza."

dancers and musicians who participated in the film.[51]) This was all a relatively easy fit with other African-themed films.

More surprising were the idea of Kisenga as a composer and the decision to use his music as a central plot device, starting with the National Gallery scene. This was perhaps part of the attempt to push the film more compellingly into the territory of melodrama and away from the Colonial Office's sensibilities, rooted in documentary. The use of a piano concerto in particular brought the film in line with the current fashion for capsule concertos. And the concerto itself, *Baraza*, provided a useful marketing tool. Although only a few minutes of it are used in the film, Bliss composed a substantial three-movement work, lasting about eight minutes.[52] Exceptionally, it was premiered before the film, in a performance by Eileen Joyce at the Albert Hall, alongside Franck's *Variations Symphoniques*.[53] A recording by Joyce (who plays on the soundtrack) was immediately distributed as well—the first in Decca's series "Incidental Music from British Films."[54] Cinemas were strongly encouraged to emphasize *Baraza* in their publicity. As the distributor's pressbook put it, "the film itself can have no greater ambassador than this thrilling composition."[55] However, Kisenga's music fit less comfortably into the Colonial Office's goals than did the focus on traditional African music. Even for contemporary critics, it has seemed an unnecessary complication of the film's themes.[56] Critics at the time, too, tended to prefer the scenes of African dancing to what the *Spectator* called "the disastrous opening sequence purporting to depict a National Gallery concert."[57]

Kisenga's status as a musician—a highly regarded composer of "English" music at that—does complicate the film's representation of partnership,

[51] See Dickinson, "Search for Music," 13–14; Matera, *Black London*, 191–192.

[52] Arthur Bliss, *Baraza: Concert Piece for Piano and Orchestra, with Men's Voices ad lib., Arrangement for Two Pianos* (London: Novello, 1946).

[53] According to the program, it was performed on December 4, 1945 by the National Symphony Orchestra under Sidney Beer, and the concert also included Mendelssohn's *Hebrides Overture* and Schubert's Seventh Symphony (Eileen Joyce Collection, CAL0003, Box 1, Callaway Centre Archive, University of Western Australia).

[54] The Decca recording, made in 1946, was made with the same orchestra under Muir Mathieson (Huntley, *British Film Music*, 87).

[55] "Make the Most of Arthur Bliss's Music," in "*Men of Two Worlds*": *General Exploitation, Gaumont-British*, Box 9, Item 11, Thorold Dickinson Collection, BFI Special Collections.

[56] Jeffrey Richards writes that "The weakness of the film . . . perhaps lies partly in the fact that Kisenga is a composer at all, rather than the student originally intended," explaining that it unnecessarily distances him from audiences (Jeffrey Richards, *Thorold Dickinson and the British Cinema* [London: Scarecrow, 1997], 116).

[57] Basil Wright, "The Cinema," *The Spectator*, July 26, 1946, 87,

Figure 3.1 *Men of Two Worlds*, Kisenga and Randall try out Kisenga's new composition.

but it also inflects it in important ways. It works fundamentally to signal his achievement and his full acceptance and participation in British society, especially in the opening National Gallery scene. It also places him on somewhat equal terms with Randall, the representative of British colonialism, and allows the kind of intimate study of partnership that Dickinson envisioned. For instance, in one scene, Randall and Kisenga play a four-hands piano version of Kisenga's new composition—surely a rare interracial example of that powerful image of intimate partnership (Figure 3.1).[58] As an artist figure, Kisenga also becomes associated with a rich interiority and psychological depth. This was clearly a goal of Dickinson, who went so far as to have the character analyzed by a psychiatrist.[59]

But the idea of making Kisenga a composer—and the assumption of psychological complexity that went with it—generated some resistance

[58] See Philip Brett, "Piano Four-Hands: Schubert and the Performance of Gay Male Desire," *19th-Century Music* 21 (1997): 149–176; Adrian Daub, *Four-Handed Monsters* (New York: Oxford University Press, 2014).

[59] Richards, *Thorold Dickinson*, 102.

among officials in ways that suggest how it pushed at racial boundaries. Ian Dalrymple (formerly head of the Crown Film Unit [CFU]) advised the MoI that the idea of a Black artist figure was a hard sell.[60] Some figures within the MoI thought it was unrealistic for an African to become an established musician after three or five years of study in Europe, which led directly to his stay being extended to fifteen years in the final version.[61] Others found the very idea of an African composer hard to fathom. Gervas Huxley, head of the Empire Division of the MoI, objected to an early version of the screenplay on forthrightly racist grounds.

> I should doubt whether any East African native has yet progressed so far that he would either be a musician (apparently of some merit) or that his music would mean so much to him in psychological terms. In fact, I think that Kijana [Kisenga] is made to react emotionally as a European would react and not as an African would react. Even the most educated African, so far as I know, only reacts psychologically to much simpler things than any of the arts.[62]

The character of Kisenga might be seen as a progressive rejoinder to such views. But his status as an artist figure also renders him feminized and emotionally fragile in ways that can reinforce rather than undo racialized stereotypes, while his artistic crisis collapses into a crisis of racial identity.[63]

Another key to music's prominence in the film, though, is the theme of mobilization that underlies its more explicitly colonial themes of partnership and development. Through a story centered on the problem of literally moving a group from one place to another, it asks how Africans could contribute to colonial development projects. As Matera has observed, *Men of Two Worlds* depicts the "mobilization of the community's labor power for public works," as they are asked to build bridges and otherwise help in

[60] Ian Dalrymple to Jack Beddington, June 8, 1943, INF 1/218, The National Archives of the UK (hereafter National Archives).

[61] A note to a revised synopsis, dated October 31, 1944, reads: "The Empire Division were unhappy about the establishment of an African character as a front rank musician after 5 years' study over here. This criticism seems to have been met by increasing Kisenga's stay in Europe from 5 years to 15" (Memorandum from Winifred Winnell [?], INF 1/218, National Archives).

[62] Gervas Huxley to E. Arnot Robinson, June 15, 1943, INF 1/218, National Archives. Huxley's position is identified in Matera, *Black London*, 301. Kisenga was named Kijana in early scripts, but the name was changed due to "strong local opinion against name Kijana," which translates roughly as "boy" (Dickinson telegraph to John Sutro, January 21, 1944, INF 1/218B, National Archives).

[63] On the feminizing of Kisenga, also see Webster, *Englishness and Empire*, 71.

the move to new land chosen by the colonial authorities.[64] This sums up the film's notion of partnership. As Peter Swaab has pointed out, the resistant "Litu" people are depicted as indolent and lacking "initiative," while their land, too, is described as worn out and useless. The film depicts this population being "actively mobilized," Swaab suggests, adding, "This is a vision of the colonial power benignly facilitating active lives."[65] The logic is not so different from the mobilization involved in total war: all resources must be used toward the purposes of the larger social good. As the film progresses, it explores this problem through music, asking how the composer might harness African traditions to his European training but also giving the resultant music a pivotal role in mobilizing the whole community. It is finally a properly African music, rather than colonial technologies, that proves efficacious, suggesting both a mobilization of Africanness and a careful delimitation of its power.

Music and Inclusion at the National Gallery

The character of Kisenga seems to have been inspired by a number of Black musicians active in London, as Matera and Philip Zachernuk have discussed.[66] One was Paul Robeson, who had moved to London in 1928 for a long run of *Show Boat* and then starred in a number of British films in the 1930s, ending with *Proud Valley* in 1940. His film *Song of Freedom* (1936) bears some striking similarities to *Men of Two Worlds*, as noted even at the time.[67] It featured Robeson as a British dock worker turned opera singer in the early nineteenth century. (Despite the historical setting, Robeson sings in a distinctly folk-like style, and his signature role is in a new work called *The Black Emperor: A Negro Opera*, recalling his well-known role in 1930s revivals of Eugene O'Neill's play *The Emperor Jones*, as well as the 1933 film.) He finds he is the rightful heir to the

[64] Matera, *Black London*, 303.

[65] Peter Swaab, "Dickinson's Africa: *The High Command* and *Men of Two Worlds*," in *Thorold Dickinson: A World of Film*, ed. Philip Horne and Peter Swaab (Manchester: Manchester University Press, 2008), 185. Also see Matera, *Black London*, 303.

[66] The following three models for Kisenga's character have been discussed in Matera, *Black London*, 305–306; and Philip S. Zachernuk, "Who Needs a Witch Doctor? Refiguring British Colonial Cinema in the 1940s," in *Film and the End of Empire*, ed. Lee Grieveson and Colin MacCabe (London: Palgrave Macmillan), 101–102.

[67] *Song of Freedom*, dir. J. Elder Wills, Hammer Productions, 1936 (BFI Player). Dalrymple noted the resemblance as a potential problem already in 1943 (Ian Dalrymple to Jack Beddington, June 8, 1943, INF 1/218, National Archives), although he misremembers the title; on the relationship between these two films, also see Zachernuk, "Who Needs a Witch Doctor?" 97, 113.

throne of the African island kingdom of Cisenga (surely the source of Kisenga's name) and returns to help its people, bringing them Western medicine and rescuing them from the snares of a witchdoctor when he finally proves his identity by singing the king's ancestral song. Robeson's character thus marries African traditions and European technologies in the name of progress, in ways recalled by Kisenga's collaboration with Randall.

Another model for the character of Kisenga was perhaps the Nigerian composer Fela Sowande, who trained in London and drew on Nigerian themes in works such as his *African Suite* (1944). As the musical director of the Colonial Film Unit, he was familiar to many of the people involved in *Men of Two Worlds* and was mentioned in connection with the film by Dickinson.[68] A third model was the Guyanese clarinetist and journalist Rudolph Dunbar, who had settled in Britain by the early 1930s (after training at Juilliard and the Sorbonne) and started to make a name for himself as a conductor in the war years after appearing with the LPO in 1942. He was in fact chosen to play the role of Kisenga in *Men of Two Worlds*, until he was eventually replaced by the actor Robert Adams, also from British Guiana.[69] In addition to providing models for the film's hero, though, these figures reveal the limits on Black musicians and on how they were imagined in wartime London. Both Dunbar and Sowande, while classically trained, worked mainly in jazz and popular contexts, including the London and Paris Blackbird revues.[70] These contexts, where Black musicians were expected to excel (even if they were primarily trained as classical musicians), provided opportunities when the concert hall did not. Even when Dunbar was invited to conduct orchestras, it was often to perform American and jazz-influenced music, especially works by Black composers; he was particularly associated with William Grant Still's

[68] Dickinson mentioned Fela Sowande (referring to him as a performer rather than a composer though) in a letter to Arnot Robertson, June 30, 1943, INF 1/218, National Archives.

[69] It is unclear why Dunbar was replaced, and some historians have blamed a concern with his political and journalistic activities (Zachernuk, "Who Needs a Witch Doctor?" 114–115; Matera, *Black London*, 306). However, 1945 was the height of Dunbar's conducting career—he conducted a festival of American music in Paris and conducted the Berlin Philharmonic—so it is also possible his priorities had changed (The Foundation for Research in the Afro-American Creative Arts, "W. Rudolph Dunbar: Pioneering Orchestra Conductor," *The Black Perspective in Music* 9 [Autumn 1981]: 202–208).

[70] Dunbar also co-founded the Florence Mills Social Parlour, a nightclub in Soho named after the star of Blackbirds (Errol G. Hill and James V. Hatch, *A History of African American Theater* [Cambridge: Cambridge University Press, 2003], 278–279). Sowande, meanwhile, was closely associated with the American singer Adelaide Hall in the 1930s and early 1940s, accompanying her on organ (his main instrument) or with his band (John Cowley, "London is the Place: Caribbean Music in the Context of Empire 1900–1960," in *Black Music in Britain*, ed. Paul Oliver [Buckingham: Open University Press, 1990], 63).

Symphony No. 1 "Afro-American" (1930), which was featured in concerts he conducted with both the London Symphony Orchestra and the London Philharmonic in 1942 (as well as the Berlin Philharmonic in 1945).[71] The character of Kisenga both draws on these models and departs in many ways from the realities of London musical life for Black musicians. He is presented as more austerely high-cultural, and also more akin to the unstable male artist figures of films such as *Hangover Square* (1945) or *Deception* (1946).

As work on the film progressed, Kisenga's status as a musician steadily grew. At first, he was simply a promising student composer, the film opening with him attending an orchestral performance and afterward establishing a relationship of mutual respect with the conductor, to the bafflement of his patronizing friend.[72] In a later version of the script, he conducts his own music, now at the National Gallery—a "Suite of Dances for Small Orchestra," which is described in the script as completely lacking any African influence.[73] Finally, he ends up as the pianist in his own concerto, now a more ambitious and explicitly African-themed piece, *Baraza*.

The opening scene at the National Gallery works to establish Kisenga's status as a musician, but, most of all, as Wendy Webster suggests, it uses the iconic concerts and their association with the "people's war" to ensconce him in a diverse national community.[74] A basic strategy of the film is to create an opposition between British society as inclusive (hence modern and progressive) and African societies as closed, with Kisenga welcomed in the former and rejected in the latter. Even in Tanganyika, he is consistently supported by the representatives of British colonial governance, Randall and Munro, who act as quasi-parental figures, while he is ostracized by his own family and community. But it is most of all the opening scene at the National Gallery that works to place both Kisenga and his ostensibly African-influenced music at the heart of a site of national belonging.

The film opens by touching on all the familiar imagery attached to the National Gallery concerts in *Listen to Britain*: the scenes of Trafalgar Square, the poster outside announcing the concert—the name Kisenga and

[71] The Foundation for Research in the Afro-American Creative Arts, "W. Rudolph Dunbar," 198, 202. On Dunbar's Berlin performance, see Kira Thurman, *Singing Like Germans: Black Musicians in the Land of Bach, Beethoven, and Brahms* (Ithaca: Cornell University Press, 2021), 190–203.

[72] *Men of Two Worlds*, Third Treatment (March 3, 1943 to April 17, 1943), f.84, CO/875/17/5, National Archives.

[73] *Men of Two Worlds*, First Script (July 16, 1943 to August 13, 1943), f.84, CO/875/17/5, National Archives.

[74] Webster, *Englishness and Empire*, 70.

the title of his work *Baraza* standing out clearly—the sandbagged frames, the listeners in uniform, even the sandwiches.[75] But the National Gallery is treated as newly expansive, especially compared to the parallel scene in *Love Story*, with its solo performer and relatively small audience in tighter focus. Here, the Gallery is overflowing (Figure 3.2). A long tracking shot that opens the sequence both registers the crowd and follows ever more people as they pack into the space, standing in doorways and sitting on the tops of benches in an effort to see. The performance forces are huge—a men's chorus, large orchestra, and piano—crowding around Kisenga and overflowing the stage as well (Figure 3.3). This plenitude is perhaps partly what allows the scene to absorb some unusual signs of diversity, including a few Black audience members scattered among the crowd, Kisenga himself, and his concerto.

Musically, *Baraza* signals "Africanness" with syncopated rhythms and prominent percussion as well as modal elements and an incantatory men's chorus. These are the features highlighted in the film, which only includes about three minutes of the published work. In the complete work, these signs are deployed within a language that gestures to Rachmaninoff, Shostakovich (especially in the lyrical second movement), and even Chopin (in the heroic Polonaise rhythms of the long, virtuosic piano cadenza that ends the first movement). However, Kisenga's performance at the National Gallery begins at the syncopated second theme of the opening movement, significantly compresses the cadenza, and then cuts to the rambunctious, scherzo-like third movement, skipping the elegant second movement entirely. Of the complete recording, one music critic observed, "Mr. Bliss has met the problem of writing a Kisenga concerto by writing a typically Bliss one, with no noticeable modification of his Queen's Hall standard."[76] But the cut version on film leaves a rather different impression.

Baraza's specific references to East Africa are largely limited to the use of Swahili in the men's chorus and the title itself, also Swahili: Kisenga explains that it refers to a "council meeting, usually a heated discussion," associating it with unruliness and disruption.[77] Asked in 1974 whether the work was influenced by African music, Bliss responded,

[75] The single name "Kisenga" on the poster is obviously exoticizing, but also recalls the publicity practices of Solomon or Moiseiwitsch, popular British pianists of the period who similarly went by a single exoticizing name.

[76] William McNaught, "Gramophone Notes," *The Musical Times* 87, 1243 (1946): 272.

[77] The score also includes a note explaining "Baraza is a Swahili word meaning a discussion in council between an African chief and his headman" (Bliss, *Baraza*).

Figure 3.2 *Men of Two Worlds*, The National Gallery audience.

Figure 3.3 *Men of Two Worlds*, Kisenga at the National Gallery.

> Well, I can't say that it was. I was given various themes—they came from East Africa, I think. And I used, I think it's a Swahili word, the baraza, which means the gathering of the men. . . . And at the end of that, I have a male chorus declaiming African words to give it the right sort of feeling. We got over some African drummers but, of course, to try and imitate them is impossible. I mean, their rhythm is something the westerner doesn't know.[78]

Bliss's fetishization of African rhythm is typical of a long-standing tendency to reduce African music to an "essentially rhythmic phenomenon," as described by Kofi Agawu, and to treat this as a mark of difference.[79] This trope also shows up in the program note for the 1945 performance of *Baraza* at the Albert Hall, where the music was described as reflecting "the characteristics of a composer who belongs to two worlds—its strongly rhythmic features are associated with his African origin, while the harmonic style derives from his European training."[80] Within the National Gallery scene, *Baraza* functions mainly as a sonic sign of otherness and disruption, indexing Kisenga himself, to be absorbed and accepted. And the music *is* accepted, appearing to have the same solidarity-building powers as the Beethoven or Mozart normally featured at these concerts. The audience is attentive and enthusiastic, and adoring fans—again, an ostentatiously mixed group—immediately surround Kisenga after the concert. Signing autographs, he responds to eager questions about the piece. When it emerges that he is about to leave for Africa, they protest; Kisenga belongs in London, they suggest, and has a duty "to *English* music."

Even in the making of the film, the idealism of this scene bumped up against a different reality. The visual plenitude of the opening scene was enabled in part by the fact that it was filmed in a studio, not on location. Ironically, though, this was because the National Gallery refused permission to film there. In the 1970s, Dickinson recalled that "the director of the Gallery [Kenneth Clark] and the director of the concerts [Myra Hess] refused to believe that an African would be capable of composing a work worthy of their series."[81] Historians have offered an even more damning explanation, relying

[78] David Badder, Bob Baker, and Markku Salmi, "Interview with Sir Arthur Bliss," *Film Dope* 5 (July 1974): 3.

[79] Kofi Agawu, *Representing African Music: Postcolonial Notes, Queries, Positions* (London: Taylor & Francis, 2003), 125–149, here 130.

[80] Henry Coates, "Historical and Descriptive Notes," The National Symphony Orchestra, Royal Albert Hall, December 4, 1945 (Eileen Joyce Collection, CAL0003, Box 1, Callaway Centre Archive, University of Western Australia).

[81] Thorold Dickinson, "Some Notes on Film Music for Men of Two Worlds," October 1978, Thorold Dickinson Collection, BFI Special Collections.

on another statement by Dickinson: "She [Hess] had permitted no black man to play at any of the concerts, she said, and would not permit one to play for the film, even if it were for the government."[82] But Dickinson—particularly in the first statement quoted above—was perhaps conflating Hess's decision with some of the feedback received from the MoI and Colonial Office, which did run along these lines. Hess's problem seems to have been more specifically (if not unrelatedly) with Dunbar, who was then cast as Kisenga—at that point a conductor rather than a pianist. Kenneth Clark wrote to the head of the MoI Films Division, in 1943:

> You will know about the film which is apparently being made for the Colonial Office and which involves a negro conductor called Dunbar conducting an orchestra in the National Gallery. Dame Myra Hess is very much against this, as she does not think Mr. Dunbar a good conductor (this seems to be the general opinion) and she does not wish it to be thought that the National Gallery have employed him. As her word must be final in all matters concerning the National Gallery concerts, I am afraid that we cannot allow the Gallery to be used as a background for this scene.[83]

Whatever his qualities as a conductor—his London conducting debut was only the previous year— race was surely a factor both in the formation of this "general opinion" and in this attempt to distance the National Gallery concerts from Dunbar.[84]

Baraza itself might also be seen as evidence of how the realities of London musical life impinged on the idealism of the film. Its jazz-influenced style links more strongly to contemporary figures like Dunbar than to the character of Kisenga himself. Elsewhere in the film, Kisenga is depicted as utterly uninterested in jazz, popular music, or any sort of African influence. Indeed, the addition of *Baraza* late in the film's development significantly confuses the character and the film's musical logic. The work is never heard again after

[82] Richards, *Thorold Dickinson*, 109. The source of Richards's quote is unclear but is likely his own correspondence with Dickinson from around the same time. This explanation is repeated in Swaab, "Dickinson's Africa," 186; Matera, *Black London*, 299; and Stephen Bourne, *Black in the British Frame: The Black Experience in British Film and Television* (London: Continuum, 2001), 74.

[83] KC [Kenneth Clark] to Jack Beddington, July 23, 1943, INF 1/218, National Archives. Clark, then head of the National Gallery, was also Beddington's predecessor at the MoI.

[84] See, for example, the negative review of both Still's symphony and Dunbar's conducting in "Sunday Orchestral Concert: Afro-American Music," *Times*, April 28, 1942, 8. On the opposition Dunbar faced in Britain, especially from the BBC, see Wendy Webster, *Mixing It: Diversity in World War Two Britain* (Oxford: Oxford University Press, 2018), 109–112.

the opening scene and seems designed mainly as a stand-alone piece, useful for publicity purposes; it encapsulates some of the film's general themes of cultural hybridity while inflecting them with a touch of popular exoticism.

In previous versions of the script, this opening scene was meant to include music of a rather different kind. In the script approved by the MoI, the film opens with a "European Theme." This turns out to be Kisenga's "Suite of Dances for Small Orchestra," which he conducts at the National Gallery. This early script casts Kisenga as less touched by jazz or African influences, in ways that are presented as a problem. While the audience is enthusiastic, afterward Kisenga is brought to task by a Colonial Office official, who raises the question of his music's usefulness.

BRAND: "It's very nice of course—it's music of a sort—modern European. (using his hands) Well is that you—is it Africa—and if not what is it? . . . it's pretty but is it necessary?"

GILES [AGENT]: (quite shocked) "Necessary—you might ask is any music necessary?"

BRAND: "Yes, yes. What I'm asking is, is *this* music necessary—tinkle poop music. . . . Now I like music you can eat and drink."[85]

While casting music in familiar wartime terms of necessity and physical sustenance, Brand's statement more surprisingly makes music's usefulness dependent on its "authenticity," as defined by him. In the process, it presents a classic example of Blackness being "fixed" by the White gaze, as Fanon would put it a few years later.[86] And, in asking what Kisenga's music can do for him, he is also asking what Africanness can do for him, a question that animates the entire film.

This dialogue was eventually cut from the opening (and would make little sense as a response to *Baraza*), but the idea nonetheless continues to play out in the rest of the film. Randall, the District Commissioner, consistently encourages Kisenga to find ways of drawing on his African identity. Kisenga, meanwhile, seems both dismissive of African music and afraid of it. Apart from *Baraza*, his trajectory—which is articulated largely through music—is from a thoroughly Europeanized "Good African" to something slightly

[85] *Men of Two Worlds*, First Script (July 16, 1943 to August 13, 1943), f.84, CO/875/17/5, National Archives.
[86] Fanon, *Black Skin, White Masks*, 116.

different, a "New African" who accepts and uses African traditions. In the process, African music is mobilized for the larger goals of development.

Mobilizing African Music

From beginning to end, the film poses the question of what *kind* of music—and thus what kind of Africanness—is potentially most productive. As *Men of Two Worlds* unfolds, music is used to dramatize a conflict between a "bad" Africanness that stalls development and resists partnership and another kind of Africanness, which can be mobilized by colonial authorities for the purposes of progress and development. This tension plays out in a conflict between Magole and Kisenga, culminating in a bizarre musical showdown at the climax of the film. What emerges musically throughout the latter half of the film is that this usable Africanness is feminized and infantilized—it is literally the sound of women and children, and Kisenga himself becomes increasingly feminized and childlike—while the forces that must be defeated are masculine and aggressive. In some ways, the film thus echoes a tension that plays out in Paul Robeson's films and career, as described by Richard Dyer, between "folk" and "atavistic" images of Blackness, the latter associated especially with Africa and with "raw, violent, chaotic and 'primitive' emotions."[87] But if folk Blackness, as Dyer suggests, was often presented as a "radical alternative to materialistic, rationalistic, alienated white Western culture" (99) to be preserved untouched, *Men of Two Worlds* roundly rejects this view. Here, a folk Africanness partners effectively with a rationalized colonial technocracy and has a certain efficacy.

This tension between "folk" and "atavistic" images is presented musically already in the opening credits, as a conflict between a simple rhythmic pattern on the drums and a folklike melody sung by a solo female voice. This rhythmic pattern, it turns out, is closely associated with Magole, the witchdoctor, and with the malevolent forces he controls—forces presented as opposed to progress. Magole becomes a direct threat when Kisenga challenges him to prove his magical powers, insisting he is a "liar and a fraud." If Magole wins, Kisenga will die; if he is proved a fraud, the village will join the British project and move to safer territory. But Magole's powers are as much psychological as magical, and he succeeds in driving Kisenga into

[87] Richard Dyer, *Heavenly Bodies: Film Stars and Society* (London: Routledge, 2003), 85.

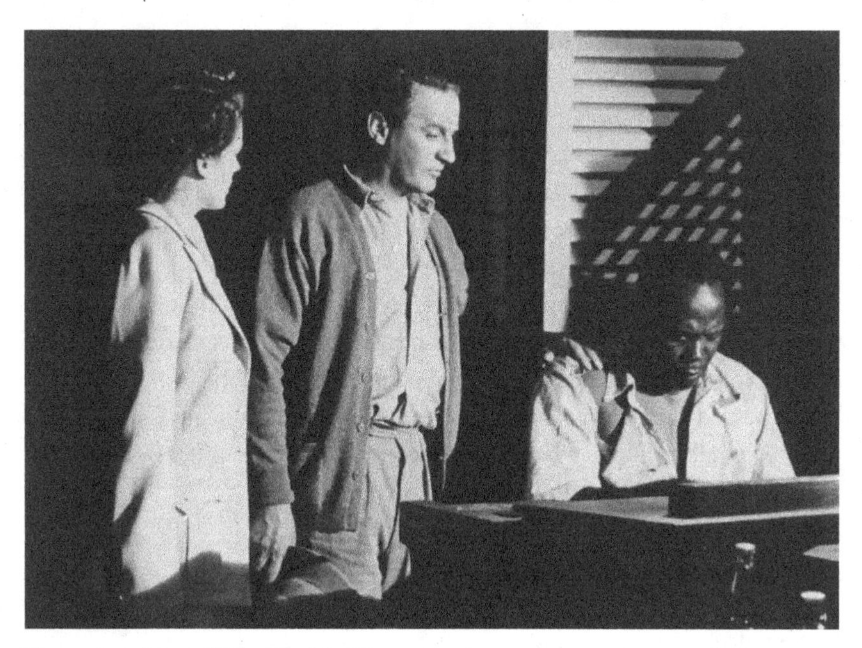

Figure 3.4 *Men of Two Worlds*, Kisenga undone.

a frenzy of fear and paranoia. As he does so, Magole's rhythmic pattern increasingly invades Kisenga's music. At one point after the challenge, Randall and Dr. Munro find Kisenga at Randall's headquarters in the middle of the night, half-crazed, his clothing torn (Figure 3.4). Sitting at the grand piano, he plays a series of loud, dissonant chords in the same, incessantly repeated rhythmic pattern—the rhythm of Magole's drums. He goes on to tell Randall about the invasive power of the drums, beating the rhythm on his thighs as he recalls his night-time encounter with ritual and dancing deep in the forest. "I am afraid," he says as the rhythm is echoed plaintively in the orchestral underscore. "It's not that kind of fear, fear of Magole. It's doubt of myself. I've failed!" Magole, then, exteriorizes a force that Kisenga fears is part of his own identity. What is fifteen years of European education, he asks, "against ten thousand years of Africa in my blood"?[88] Critics have pointed to the essentialism of this line as indicative of an essentialism that informs the film more generally.[89] Indeed, the whole episode recalls Robeson's similar undoing in the jungle in *The Emperor Jones*, which Dyer describes as "a classic

[88] *Men of Two Worlds*, 1:24:00.
[89] Webster, *Englishness and Empire*, 71.

statement of the atavistic idea in the black context—that . . . beneath a veneer of civilisation" there is "a chaos of primeval emotions that under stress will return, the raging repressed."[90] But *Men of Two Worlds* frames this atavistic sentiment as a product of Kisenga's paranoia and self-doubt. His emotional chaos, moreover—ostensibly associated with his Africanness—is expressed in his most dissonant, "modernist" music and thus becomes elided with the alienation of the modernist artist.

The true nature of the film's essentialism is laid bare a little later. In a repudiation of Kisenga's stark opposition between "European education" and African "blood," Randall suggests that some basic African "power" needs to be harnessed rather than feared. Here, when Kisenga again expresses his fears, Randall responds by encouraging him to draw on the music of Africa and his own (fictional) ethnic group, the Litu.

KISENGA: It's not Magole, it's something deeper. Africa.
RANDALL: Your music, you say you can't work. I thought Africa was giving you ideas.
KISENGA: Yes, it was, it was.
RANDALL: Of course. The quality, the power of your own race. Even I can feel that—I, a stranger.
KISENGA: But it's so remote, so primitive.
RANDALL: That's where your musical training comes in! An artist gains technique wherever he can find it, as you did in England. But the power, the quality comes from his own people. And he can't get that from anywhere else.
KISENGA: In Litu?
RANDALL: Why not? You say there's something frightening you. That is power if you like. Use it. Use your Africa. Go back and dominate it. Put a bit in its mouth and ride it. . . . There's nobody but you could do so much good for the Litu. Giving them back their convictions, their faith.[91]

Randall's language of exploitation and aggressive dominance is slightly jarring here, even if it does put Kisenga in the position of dominator. But, of course, it is ultimately Randall who is in charge. He seeks to mobilize

[90] Dyer, *Heavenly Bodies*, 92. Adams also played this role, on BBC television in 1938.
[91] *Men of Two Worlds*, 1:27:50.

Kisenga, who himself is rendered ever more childlike in the course of this scene. Through Kisenga, some quality of Africanness is musically mobilized. Randall even expresses this in a language that seems to have no other function than to invoke a wartime rhetoric of musical mobilization, calling especially on the ways music was said to help restore "courage and faith"[92] in the context of the National Gallery concerts. But, as the film plays out, this usable music comes to resemble Kisenga himself in being rendered increasingly childlike.

The musical conflict between a folk Africanness and something more aggressive comes to a head at the climax of the film, as Kisenga lies delirious and close to death, Magole's powers apparently having their effect. His rhythm is beating outside, slowly and incessantly. A hallucinated scene then stages a crisis of identity, as an orchestra beckons Kisenga on one side, while massed drummers, led by Magole, threaten him on the other, his arms at one point turning white to mark the crisis as a confusion of racial identity. But the music here stages this conflict in a slightly different way. Recalling the opening scene at the National Gallery, it similarly features piano and men's chorus, but this is a nightmare version of his *Baraza.*[93] Now pervaded by Magole's rhythm, it is frenzied and repetitive and occasionally overtaken by the sounds of the drums themselves. Musically, this scene is about a failure to harness or appropriately mobilize African culture, perhaps partly because of the very attempt at hybridity, but also because it is the "wrong" sort of Africanness. It takes a different music to defeat Magole and, once again, the enabling power of Randall himself.

As Kisenga seems about to die, the drums continuing relentlessly, Randall has the idea that his music might be able to help. Since his return to East Africa, Kisenga has been working on a piece for children's voices and orchestra. Near the beginning of his stay, still optimistic, he rehearses the village children—a choir accompanied by a group of traditional instruments—in a version of this piece. It is marked in the screenplay as "The African Theme"

[92] Kenneth Clark, "Music in Place of Pictures," in *Myra Hess by Her Friends*, ed. Denise Lassimonne and Howard Ferguson (London: Hamish Hamilton, 1966), 57.

[93] The literature on the film has consistently described this music as being from *Baraza*, but while the forces are the same, resulting in a broad similarity of sound, this music is never used in *Baraza* itself, and is stylistically quite different. It does appear in the opening credits, after the drum pattern and the folk theme, but there is a clear break (articulated by both silence and a set of chimes marking the time of the National Gallery concert) before *Baraza* begins. It seems important that this music represents a new development since Kisenga's return to Africa and not a return to a moment before.

and is based on the same folk-like melody heard in the opening credits.[94] As mentioned previously, this melody is based on an African tune, a "war song of the Wangoni [Ngoni]" according to Dickinson (somewhat ironically, for my argument).[95] This music is praised by Kisenga's ally, the local teacher Mr. Abrams, as "our music, African music" (in one of the film's many gestures to pan-Africanism—Abrams, like Kisenga's other ally in the village, is not Litu). Randall, too, approves, adding "That's what I like about it." But Kisenga is dismissive, saying it is "just to teach them some elements of music." Now, looking for a way of reviving Kisenga, Randall finds the ripped-up score and asks Mr. Abrams to get the children to sing it. A musical contest between Magole's drums and Kisenga's "African Theme" then begins. The children start to sing, drowning out the drums, but soon falter, threatened by Magole. Then Kisenga's sister takes up the melody, prompted by Dr. Munro. Soon, others in the village join in (with further encouragement from Munro), mobilized in a collective effort to help Kisenga. He survives the night, thus winning the challenge, and Magole is defeated, resulting in the relocation of the village in the next and final scene. Here, the villagers are shown on a set of modern trucks moving to their new home, singing another song based on an African tune.[96] Their collective mobilization by music is the crucial step, the turning point, in their mobilization toward the colonial goals of progress and development.

This musical ending provoked much consternation at the Colonial Office. When the MoI solicited feedback on the script—an earlier version in which Kisenga is saved by merely humming his music, rather than it being sung by the community as a whole—almost everyone commented on the ending as problematic. Dalrymple complained, "I really don't think that the final rescue of Kijana [Kisenga] from mumbo-jumbo by music is either convincing or effective. And this is presumably the plot-point of the whole motif of music."[97] The Deputy Director of the MoI Films Division wrote, "The ending is bad by any standard of judgment and must be radically changed. Kijana must be cured by Western medicine, not by some inexplicable process

[94] "First Script" (July 16, 1943 to August 13, 1943), f.134, CO 875/17/5, National Archives. While some elements of this script are different from the final film (especially the National Gallery scene), this scene is more or less unchanged.

[95] Dickinson, "Search for Music," 15.

[96] Ibid.

[97] Dalrymple to Beddington, June 8, 1943, INF 1/218, National Archives.

of abracadabra."[98] Another MoI official commented, "I am very doubtful whether the humming of Kijana's music has any propaganda significance. Surely the film should bring out quite clearly that the White Man's 'magic' is stronger than Magole's witchcraft."[99] Rather than following their advice, Dickinson responded by greatly expanding music's role in the scene, grounding it more clearly in the whole community and thus depicting a musical mobilization of the group that quickly translates into a physical mobilization. The confusion generated by the ending speaks to the strangeness of its basic move and to how the musical argument ran up against the official point of the film, which placed African traditions in more straightforward conflict with European science.

It is Kisenga's music, and his ability to draw on local tradition, that ultimately heals him and mobilizes his village. However, the film also insists on the enabling power of the two representatives of colonial rationality and progress, Munro and Randall. It is they who demand people perform his music when he is incapacitated. And, as Kisenga is increasingly infantilized in the scenes discussed above, they are cast in parental roles. His deathbed scene shows Munro and Randall hovering over him like a mother and father over their sick child, as Wendy Webster has observed.[100] Similarly, when Kisenga shows up at Randall's headquarters, they together put him to bed, tucking him in, while the paternalistic Randall even lays out fresh clothes for him the next morning. If the character of Kisenga had been younger, as originally planned, this might have seemed less odd, but these scenes are visually absurd with an older Kisenga played by Adams—in his mid-thirties and a former heavy-weight wrestling champion.[101] And, in both cases, they precede an attempt to convince him to take up a leading role by embracing and using his African identity, suggesting how his leadership is predicated on their authority. The film's heavily paternalistic approach to the idea of partnership, then, involves both a process of pacification and a push toward British ideas of what African identity might be—in this case, folklike, feminine, childlike. At the same time, the film insists on the usefulness of such

[98] Memorandum, R. Nunn May to Jack Beddington, May 31, 1943, INF 1/218, National Archives. The signature is barely legible, but the author is identified by Richards (*Thorold Dickinson*, 103).

[99] H. V. Usill (MoI) to Huxley (Empire Division), June 16, 1943, INF 1/218, National Archives.

[100] On this scene as an image of "White connectedness" and on Kisenga's breakdown, also see Wendy Webster, "Mumbo-Jumbo, Magic and Modernity: Africa in British Cinema, 1946–65," in *Film and the End of Empire*, ed. Lee Grieveson and Colin MacCabe (London: Palgrave Macmillan, 2011), 243, 240.

[101] Matera, *Black London*, 308.

Africanness in the world, endowing it with magical force and the power of solidarity.

The way *Men of Two Worlds* fixes Kisenga's musical identity, then, is deeply embedded in colonial logics, allowing him little authority to define this for himself. Nonetheless, *Men of Two Worlds* shares with *Love Story* a determination to use music to recover a certain notion of selfhood and to reintegrate aspects of the self that had been lost or denied. In both films, music thus enables a new sense of attachment to the world and to others, for characters who were alienated or adrift. What marks the films most of all, though, is their determination to make all aspects of the self usable—to mobilize this sense of attachment and selfhood, with the help of music.

4

Sounding Out Civilian Trauma

The Seventh Veil and *Brief Encounter*

Late Romantic piano concertos were a pervasive feature of wartime musical life, as expanding "middlebrow" audiences filled concert halls to see pianists such as Eileen Joyce perform Grieg, Tchaikovsky, and Rachmaninoff. In 1945, they emerged with force on the British screen as well. In *Brief Encounter*, Rachmaninoff's Second Piano Concerto (performed by Joyce) completely dominates the soundtrack, as the heroine recounts her recently ended affair.[1] That film was one of the biggest critical successes of the period, praised for its realism and restraint, and it still tops lists of the greatest British films ever made.[2] But there was also a much more popular 1945 film featuring the Rachmaninoff concerto performed by Joyce. *The Seventh Veil*, released a few weeks before *Brief Encounter*, was the British box office hit of the year.[3] It followed the development of a troubled young pianist and foregrounded music—by Grieg, Mozart, and Beethoven in addition to Rachmaninoff—in long scenes of performance and rehearsal. It also gave music a central role in her psychiatric treatment.

These two films make for a resonant pair.[4] Both rely on canonical works and treat them with reverence (never descending, for instance, to anything like the swing versions of Tchaikovsky heard in *The Great Lie*). Both are marked by concerns with "artistic quality" in a bid to differentiate themselves from Hollywood films and secure their middlebrow status; hence their focus on "authentic" classical music (rather than newly produced works like the *Warsaw Concerto* or *Cornish Rhapsody*) and touches of realism.[5] Both

[1] *Brief Encounter*, dir. David Lean, Cineguild, 1945 (Criterion Collection, 2016, DVD).

[2] On its critical reception and box office failure, see Antonia Lant, *Blackout: Reinventing Women for Wartime British Cinema* (Princeton: Princeton University Press, 1991), 163–164.

[3] *The Seventh Veil*, dir. Compton Bennett, Ortus Films, 1945 (Odeon Entertainment, 2009, DVD); "1945 Box Office Results," *Kinematograph Weekly*, December 20, 1945, 51.

[4] The resonances between these two films have also been discussed, more briefly, in Robert Murphy, *Realism and Tinsel: Cinema and Society in Britain 1939–49* (London: Routledge, 1989), 109–112.

[5] Pam Cook, *Screening the Past: Memory and Nostalgia in Cinema* (London: Routledge, 2004), 84–85.

Mobilizing Music in Wartime British Film. Heather Wiebe, Oxford University Press.
DOI: 10.1093/oso/9780197631713.003.0005

are woman's pictures—films orchestrated to appeal to women, observing the action primarily from the female lead's point of view.[6] Both begin with the heroine's suicide attempt and unfold through her subsequent flashback. And both were made in the last days of World War Two but are set slightly outside it (*Brief Encounter* in 1938, *The Seventh Veil* in some alternate present untouched by rationing, blackouts, or travel restrictions). While the films take remarkably different approaches to the music they present—to its cinematic function, its role in the lives of women, and its commodity status—they both seem obliquely concerned with issues of media and mechanical reproduction. Most of all, they both seem concerned with music in relation to traumatic experience. Indeed, they might be read as displaced reflections on the experience of the war itself, the conspicuous absence at the heart of both films.

Both Antonia Lant and Kent Puckett have discussed *Brief Encounter* as an attempt to process wartime experience. Set just eight years before its release, the film insistently establishes this recent past as distant from the present through details of mise-en-scène, as Lant has argued.[7] At the same time, she suggests, its preoccupations and techniques ("from adultery to the use of stroboscopic lighting") are distinctly of its postwar moment.[8] For Lant, *Brief Encounter* addresses a central problem for film at this postwar juncture, of how to organize time "in such a way as to close off the traumatic past of the war while also making sense of it."[9] Moreover, much of the film's narrative, which is cast as flashback, is concerned with just this process of working through and closing off a traumatic past. Writing more recently, Puckett suggests that *Brief Encounter*'s concern is very much with the "excluded middle" of the war itself.[10] Puckett has gone further to suggest that the heroine recalls the figure of the traumatized returning soldier, observing that the film itself might "be read as a sort of contrapuntal dream of war, an effort to

[6] Mary Ann Doane, *The Desire to Desire: The Woman's Films of the 1940s* (Bloomington: Indiana University Press, 1987), 13, 3. On British women's pictures specifically, also see Cook, *Screening the Past*, 73–90. On *Brief Encounter*'s relationship to melodrama, see especially Richard Dyer, *Brief Encounter* (London: BFI, 1993), 49. The standard British film trade magazine referred to both films as having an "irresistible feminine angle," calling *The Seventh Veil* "an ideal woman's film" and saying of *Brief Encounter*, "Women will revel in it" (*Kinematograph Weekly*, "Reviews for Showmen: The Seventh Veil," October 25, 1945, 26; *Kinematograph Weekly*, "Reviews for Showmen: Brief Encounter," November 15, 1945, 24).

[7] Lant, *Blackout*, 170.

[8] Ibid., 159.

[9] Ibid., 158.

[10] Kent Puckett, *War Pictures: Cinema, Violence, and Style in Britain, 1939–1945* (New York: Fordham University Press, 2017), 144.

cloak a latent story of violence and loss in the manifest garb of an 'ordinary' woman's brief affair."[11]

Similarly, *The Seventh Veil* erases wartime realities, taking place in a contemporary London that is realistically represented except for the conspicuous absence of any trace of war's effects. The film's concerns with trauma and psychotherapy can nonetheless be related even more directly to wartime experience, as a number of critics have pointed out. Sydney Box, who cowrote and produced the film with his wife Muriel Box, claimed that it arose from the making of a documentary film called *The Psychiatric Treatment of Battle Casualties*—a film I will come back to.[12] Berthold Hoeckner has used Box's intriguing claim as a prompt to explore the resonances between *The Seventh Veil* and World War Two treatments of battle trauma through hypnosis.[13] And while the heroine is the main victim of trauma, her violent guardian is also physically and emotionally damaged, as Tony Williams has observed, in ways that link him with the figure of the returning soldier described in contemporary guides to restoring postwar family life.[14] For Williams, *The Seventh Veil* is "a contemporary allegory about the necessity of returning wartime women to male control."[15]

Brief Encounter and *The Seventh Veil* were released in the context of a slew of British and American films that dealt much more obviously with issues of demobilization. Comedies such as *Demobbed* (1944) or *G.I. War Brides* (1946) dwelled on the problem of a return to ordinary employment or family life. But films also dealt more seriously with wartime trauma and postwar adjustment: the Hollywood film *The Best Years of Our Lives* (1946), for instance, or *Mine Own Executioner* (1947), about a traumatized former POW who undergoes psychiatric treatment after trying to kill his wife. In *Brief Encounter* and *The Seventh Veil*, such concerns are elaborately displaced, but the films are nonetheless preoccupied with familiar problems of female demobilization, returning women to the home, marriage, and the authority of men.

[11] Ibid., 183.
[12] Sydney Box, *The Lion That Lost Its Way*, ed. Andrew Spicer (Oxford: The Scarecrow Press, 2005), 49.
[13] Berthold Hoeckner, *Film, Music, Memory* (Chicago: University of Chicago Press, 2019), 165.
[14] Tony Williams, *Structures of Desire: British Cinema, 1939–1955* (Albany: State University of New York Press, 2000), 49–50. Also see Hoeckner, *Film, Music, Memory*), 168, and Andrew Spicer, *Sydney Box* (Manchester: Manchester University Press, 2011), 54.
[15] Williams, *Structures of Desire*, 50.

Considered as demobilization films, though, *Brief Encounter* and *The Seventh Veil* seem unusually concerned with female trauma—indeed, this concern perhaps helps explain their strategies of displacement. They address a war in which women's and civilians' experience diverged from deployed men's but was still traumatic, in ways for which there was little established discourse. Most obviously, this experience could include the air raid attacks that touched cities, towns, and villages across Britain. As Lucy Noakes has discussed, these attacks had a peculiar domestic intimacy, hard to assimilate to public commemoration and cloaked in familial silence.[16] Meanwhile, the less violent disruptions of ordinary life hardly registered in public discourse as trauma at all.

The heroines of these films, then, present a new figure of civilian trauma in total war. If this figure was represented through tropes associated with the demobilized soldier—rather than the conventional feminine model of the mourning mother or wife—those tropes were both newly applicable and palpably insufficient. In other words, these films explore a problem of representation, and of female inscrutability. The unknown nature of women's experience of total war is presented as a problem in need of solving because it creates a barrier to marriage and reconciliation, but, in many ways, these films seem more fundamentally concerned with the quality of unspeakability itself; hence the central role they give to music in filling the gaps of language and visual representation. In both films, music also works as a kind of treatment, allowing their heroines in different ways to work through trauma and reach a kind of catharsis. In the process, these films tell us much about the management of feeling in the wake of World War Two.

That's My Francesca

The heroine of The *Seventh Veil* is a troubled pianist, Francesca Cunningham (Ann Todd), who attempts suicide in the opening scene, convinced she will never play again. She is treated by a psychiatrist, and her progress from a young music student to a touring professional is followed in narcosis-induced flashback. The film capitalized on a perceived public interest in music, showcasing works by Beethoven, Mozart, and Chopin, as well as Grieg's

[16] Lucy Noakes, *Dying for the Nation: Death, Grief and Bereavement in Second World War Britain* (Manchester: Manchester University Press, 2020), 235–238, 246–249.

A minor Piano Concerto and Rachmaninoff's Second.[17] It also featured established musical institutions such as the London Symphony Orchestra, the Royal Albert Hall, and the Royal College of Music.[18] Throughout, this music is treated carefully and respectfully; it is represented as ensconced in the institutions of high culture and clearly demarcated from both popular music and Benjamin Frankel's score.

This carefulness seems connected with a broader concern with music as a tool and object of discipline. By focusing on the heroine's training, the film associates art music with work and sacrifice rather than pleasure or fantasy, selfhood or solidarity. Her life as a musician is cloistered, and she spends much of it practicing in her guardian's imposing house, filled with art and antiques. As a student at the Royal College of Music, Francesca focuses only on her work. Even her performances are pleasureless affairs, showing, as one review observed, the stress of "concerts which demand the highest standards of discipline and execution."[19] After one concert, she faints on stage in exhaustion and anxiety. Opposed to all of this is her affair with an American saxophonist, Peter, who is working his way through college as a dance band musician. He represents pleasure, freedom, and romance, all of which are aligned with popular culture. To make this opposition all the more clear, their romance comes to be associated with a sentimental waltz (written by Frankel, then known mostly as a dance music specialist). But Peter and his world are off limits. When she plays the waltz for her guardian, he reprimands her in the most severe terms, calling it "suburban shop girl trash." To break off her affair, he brings her to Paris to complete her training.

The force behind Francesca's music is ultimately this authoritarian guardian, Nicholas, a failed musician himself (played by James Mason, who also played a shell-shocked former pianist in the 1942 thriller *The Night Has Eyes*).[20] She is driven toward a musical career by Nicholas, and both she and

[17] For more on this and on Joyce's involvement in the film, see Heather Wiebe, "Music and the Good Life in Postwar Britain: The Phenomenon of Eileen Joyce," in *The Oxford Handbook to Music and the Middlebrow*, ed. Kate Guthrie and Christopher Chowrimootoo (Online ed, Oxford Academic, December 19, 2022), https://doi.org/10.1093/oxfordhb/9780197523933.013.6, accessed June 30, 2023.

[18] Hubert Clifford writes that musicians will be interested in "the personal appearances of some well-known performers. The London Symphony Orchestra figures prominently in some of the sequences, with George Stratton and John Moore looking completely photogenic" ("Music from the Films," *Tempo* 13 [December 1945]: 12).

[19] "The Seventh Veil," *The Monthly Film Bulletin* 12, no. 142, October 1945, 118.

[20] Ivan Raykoff, "Hollywood's Embattled Icon," in *Piano Roles: A New History of the Piano*, ed. James Parakilas (New Haven, CT: Yale University Press), 279. *The Night Has Eyes* was written and directed by Leslie Arliss, who also wrote and directed *Love Story*, discussed in Chapter 3.

her music are treated as his possession. When she threatens to leave him for an urbane German portrait painter, he crashes his cane down on her hands as she plays the second movement of Beethoven's "Pathétique," screaming "If you won't play for me, you won't play for anyone else ever again."[21] While she lives in fear and resentment of him, the climax of the film arrives when she realizes (after a therapeutic treatment involving the "Pathétique") that she has been in love with him all along and chooses him over both the saxophonist and the painter, to the consternation of many critics.[22] (As Andrew Spicer explains, this was actually one of three alternative endings prepared for the film, the first of which involved Francesca instead reuniting with the saxophonist; the choice of the final ending was based on audience votes at a sneak preview, and then the film was adjusted slightly around the chosen ending.[23]) Her playing of the "Pathétique" at the end of the film thus represents a return to music, but also a return, through music, to Nicholas's authority.

The Seventh Veil displays a set of postwar concerns with marriage and its breakdown, much like *Brief Encounter*. Nicholas's declared hatred of women and underlying trauma is rooted in his mother's divorce—a portrait of her hangs prominently in his house as a visual reminder of how she haunts his imagination. The concern with the breakdown of marriage emerges elsewhere as well. When Francesca finds Peter, the saxophonist, after returning from Parisian exile, he turns out to have been married and divorced since they last met. When she runs off with the German painter, she asks noncommittally if marriage is part of the plan—an idea, it seems, that had never occurred to him.

The film's focus on discipline emerges as a response to this disarray. But *The Seventh Veil* also represents discipline—associated here with both violence and music—as a *source* of trauma. As Francesca's treatment reveals, two canings (one by Nicholas and one at school) act as the source of her pathology. Psychiatry serves as a corrective to this misguided discipline, working instead to reveal women's deepest thoughts. "It dares to strip bare a woman's mind," as a publicity poster for *The Seventh Veil* titillatingly

[21] *The Seventh Veil*, 1:10:00.

[22] One critic observes, "precisely why she chooses him is not clear" ("The Seventh Veil," *Times*, October 22, 1945, *Seventh Veil*, press cuttings, British Film Institute Reubens Library [hereafter BFI]). Another suggests of the happy ending, "It only remains to cure him of an Oedipus complex, sadism, humourlessness and atrocious manners" ("The Seventh Veil," *Telegraph*, October 22, 1945, *Seventh Veil*, press cuttings, BFI).

[23] Spicer, *Sydney Box*, 53.

proclaimed. Psychiatry restores women to legibility, peeling off a last layer—the seventh veil—of self-protective secrecy. From the first moments of the film, when the nearly comatose Francesca is submitted to narcosis, she is in the hands of her psychiatrist, Dr. Larsen. In this initial treatment, she narrates some of the sources of her trauma, revealing an anxiety about her hands rooted in a childhood punishment that caused her to fail a music exam. If the initial trauma caused her to abandon music only to be restored to it by Nicholas, she now stands convinced once again of her inability to play due to damage to her hands. It is up to Dr. Larsen, in a series of treatments, to restore her to music.

These treatments are featured in two complex scenes, both of which play intriguingly on the relationship between psychiatry, media, and music, while also fixating on women as objects of male knowledge and control. In the first of these two scenes, Francesca is placed under hypnosis and, as she sits at the piano, is made to listen to one of her own recordings (of the slow movement of Beethoven's "Pathétique"). The idea is that she will unconsciously play along and then wake up to find she can play after all, her mental barrier broken. During this experiment, she is closely watched by a group of men, plus one female nurse who is almost completely obscured as she peers between the male faces squeezed claustrophobically into the image (Figure 4.1), as if her viewing is somehow mediated through them—an especially striking effect in a film explicitly directed at female viewers. As this audience watches and listens, Francesca's hands are placed on the keyboard by a pair of male hands (Figure 4.2), thus visually echoing the record stylus. With the doctor holding her wrists, she begins to play along, doubling herself. But the doctor has misjudged the piece. Instead of continuing to play, she relives the trauma of Nicholas attacking her while practicing this piece and breaks off abruptly. Far from being cured, she is even more trapped in her anxiety.

For Ivan Raykoff, this is a scene thematizing cinematic playback, where "the usually suppressed relationship between playing and playing-along becomes visible and audible too."[24] Indeed, in the reception of *The Seventh Veil*, the workings of playback were an especial source of fascination: critics commented repeatedly on the playing by the uncredited Joyce and on Ann Todd's convincing miming of performance.[25] More broadly, the scene

[24] Ivan Raykoff, *Dreams of Love: Playing the Romantic Pianist* (New York: Oxford University Press, 2014), 85. For another reading of this scene, as a reflection on the "cathartic method," see Hoeckner, *Film, Music, Memory*, 167.

[25] For example, C.A. Lejeune, "The Films," *Observer*, October 21, 1945, 2. For further discussion, see Wiebe, "Music and the Good Life in Postwar Britain."

Figure 4.1 *The Seventh Veil*, watching the first treatment.

Figure 4.2 *The Seventh Veil*, the first treatment: guiding Francesca's hands.

privileges looking—in its approach to both music and therapy—rather than listening, in a way that the final, more successful treatment will repudiate.

As Hoeckner points out, the scene also recalls an earlier episode in the film, where Nicholas, rather than the doctor, tries to trick Francesca into playing despite her refusal. In this earlier scene, soon after the young Francesca arrives at his house, Nicholas discovers her prior interest in music and tries to make her play the piano despite her resistance. He begins to play a Mozart sonata (K. 545), and she is visibly enthralled by the music. Approaching the piano as if compelled, she takes over from him and begins to play. Nicholas takes on a Svengali-like character here, as Hoeckner observes; indeed, reviews from the time also refer to Nicholas as a "modern Svengali," recalling the fictional musician with hypnotic power over his female prodigy.[26] In *The Seventh Veil*, this ability to control Francesca and her music is linked with an ability to *know* her—to render her transparent and legible—for both Nicholas and the psychiatrist.

This ability on Nicholas's part is thematized often in the film. At one point, for instance, Francesca refers to Nicholas as knowing her thoughts almost before she does and thus exercising a mysterious power over her. But it is at the end of the film, in the course of Francesca's final treatment, that this ability is put to the test. Her third and last treatment is very different from the others, partly because it denies the insistent scopophilia of the second treatment in particular, instead relying on a purely auditory gaze. This treatment is entirely hidden from view: Francesca and the doctor meet in an upper room, itself never seen, either by the film viewer or the other characters, who listen from downstairs. A gramophone record (this time of the sentimental waltz associated with the saxophonist) is brought upstairs and then heard a few moments later. The second movement of the "Pathétique" then begins, creating confusion about whether it is another recording or Francesca herself playing, which would signal her cure. As the music sounds, the image reveals only a group of men listening—her three competing lovers and her psychiatrist (Figure 4.3). "Is *she* playing?" Peter asks. Among the male listeners in the final scene, it is only the one revealed to "truly" love her—Nicholas—who recognizes the sound as hers. "That's my Francesca," he declares upon hearing her, in a statement that unites recognition and possession.

If Nicholas has a special insight into—and hence control of—Francesca and her music, the psychiatrist also acquires such knowledge, but in a

[26] *Kinematograph Weekly*, "The Seventh Veil," October 25, 1945, 26; Hoeckner, *Film, Music, Memory*, 167; also see Spicer, *Sydney Box*, 55.

Figure 4.3 *The Seventh Veil*, ending.

very different way. After the first failed treatment with the "Pathétique," he launches a kind of musical investigation. The piece becomes a clue to the mystery of Francesca's trauma, a mystery he must solve. He interviews Nicholas, playing the recording and asking him about the piece. Nicholas responds by violently smashing the record—definitely a clue. It seems the piece is key to more than one trauma. The psychiatrist then interviews Peter, the saxophonist, and asks him for a recording of the sentimental waltz associated with his romance with Francesca. His idea is to perform a "little experiment," as Nicholas puts it—the final treatment described above. The nature of this experiment is itself hidden, taking place beyond the sight of both the other characters and the cinema viewer, who can only hear the music that results. Indeed, the psychiatrist's ability to sonically penetrate mystery is perhaps what is being thematized in the strange absence from view of the main event in this final scene. Ultimately, music is his to manipulate and to restore.

Psychiatry, Mobilization, and the Management of Resources

Both Francesca's trauma and its musical treatment take on additional dimensions when we consider more closely the connection between *The Seventh Veil* and the wartime "documentary" Box remembered as *The Psychiatric Treatment of Battle Casualties.* A film by that title has proved elusive for scholars. What Box was surely recalling, though, from some years' distance, was *Field Psychiatry for the Medical Officer*, a training film made by his and Muriel Box's company Verity Films in 1944 for the War Office and the Directorate of Army Kinematography.[27] A substantial forty-three-minute reconstruction documentary, this was an important film in military psychiatry and was one of a few influential British training films used by the American military when it began to expand its use of psychiatry near the end of the war.[28] If *The Seventh Veil* "grew out of" this training film (as Box put it), it could be also seen as an *adaptation* in multiple senses—first, of the documentary training film as melodrama, and second, of military psychiatry for civilian use. As Michal Shapira points out, the latter posed a pressing challenge for wartime officials and psychiatrists, who were taxed with managing a population experiencing battle-type situations, but which included women and the elderly as well as people with histories of psychiatric problems—and without the tool of military discipline.[29] One 1941 study, discussed by Shapira, critiques official advice and recommends applying methods similar to those seen in *Field Psychiatry* to air raid victims suffering with "hysteria" and "psychoneuroses," some of whom exhibit symptoms much like Francesca's, including imagined damage to limbs.[30] According to this study, such a victim needed psychiatric treatment like that given to soldiers, not

[27] The film is archived at the Imperial War Museums, London, WOY 998 (https://www.iwm.org.uk/collections/item/object/1060019335) and is also available online from the Wellcome Collection (https://wellcomelibrary.org/item/b17270807#?c=0&m=0&s=0&cv=0). In archival catalogs, the film's producer is listed as the Directorate, which has made the film doubly elusive for anyone trying to follow up Box's reference, but Verity is listed in the credits in the film itself.

[28] Noah Tsika, *Traumatic Imprints: Cinema, Military Psychiatry, and the Aftermath of War* (Berkeley: University of California Press, 2018), 67–68. On the British military's comparatively early preparation for "psychiatric casualties," also see Alison Winter, *Memory: Fragments of a Modern History* (Chicago: University of Chicago Press, 2012), 55, 58.

[29] Michal Shapira, *The War Inside: Psychoanalysis, Total War, and the Making of the Democratic Self in Postwar Britain* (Cambridge: Cambridge University Press, 2013), 41.

[30] This fascinating—and quite moving—study, by a young psychiatrist in London is Felix Brown, "Civilian Psychiatric Air-Raid Casualties," *Lancet* 237 (May 31, 1941): 686–691.

just to be told to "relax, pull himself together, and go home" as official advice directed.[31]

Field Psychiatry uses actors to play out the story of a fictional private Wragge, paralyzed by fear and anxiety after a few days of mortar fire. A medical officer (MO) treats Wragge and recalls related cases and their treatments. The film thus provides basic training for nonspecialists in battle situations, as well as advice for officers in how to handle stricken soldiers—by listening to them and getting them medical attention, rather than simply disciplining them or sending them back into battle. In other words, *Field Psychiatry* is much more concerned with psychiatry in relation to questions of the proper exercise of military discipline than is apparent from Box's short description. Much like the psychiatric discourse on noise discussed in Chapter 1, the film identifies the central problem in all cases as anxiety, which can affect anyone, the film insists, and which manifests in a range of forms, including depression or confusion. The case on which *The Seventh Veil* clearly draws is its most severe: a case of "hysterical conversion," which the MO explains as "when a man develops an hysterical condition, to blot out his anxiety." In the case described by the MO, anxiety has become so severe "that the mind can only deal with it by shutting out everything," and the soldier goes into a stupor. The treatment, which takes place in a psychiatric hospital, is to place him under narcosis—narcotics-induced hypnosis—and ask him to recall the source of trauma, in this case a battle. "Under narcosis, they get it all out," the MO explains.

The Seventh Veil draws most directly on this scene in its opening, where Francesca is in a similar stupor and is treated by narcosis. Images of Francesca even echo the striking image of the prone, corpselike soldier, his face and bedding glowingly illuminated against a shadowed background (Figure 4.4). But the *Seventh Veil* has other resonances with *Field Psychiatry*. One is the use of sound in the soldier's treatment, as the muted rattle of mortar fire helps prompt his memory. As Alison Winter mentions, this was an established technique in World War Two narcosis treatments.[32] Another has to do with the ways the soldiers themselves are presented: as helpless objects of experts' control. Passed around from officer to officer, Wragge is eventually placed in a "Core Exhaustion Centre," which involves treating the soldiers as if they are in a state of regression: for two days they are treated as babies,

[31] Brown, "Civilian Psychiatric Air-Raid Casualties," 687.
[32] Winter, *Memory*, 65.

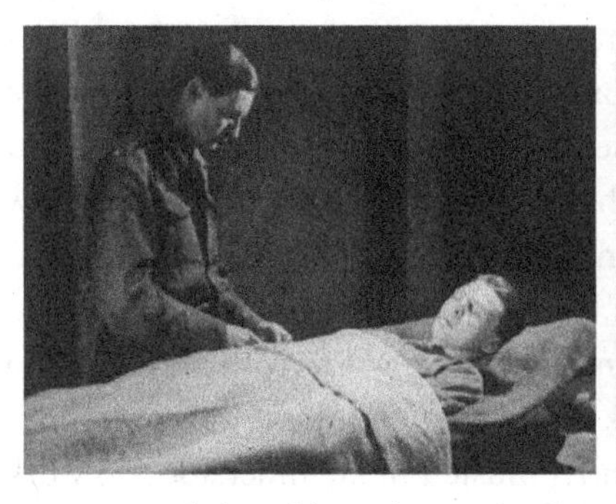
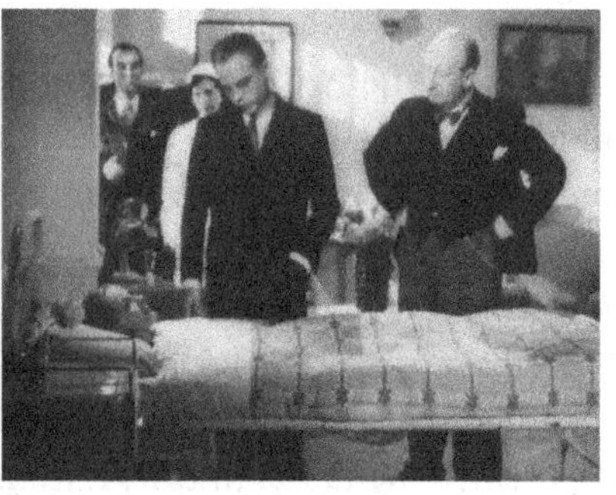

Figure 4.4 (A) *Field Psychiatry for the Medical Officer*, soldier's hysterical conversion. (B) *The Seventh Veil*, Francesca's hysterical conversion.

given hot food and sedated; then they are treated like children and do crafts and games; finally they practice being soldiers again before being sent back to their posts. The point of psychiatric treatment, moreover, is to return these soldiers to service as quickly as possible—to make them useful again after they had ceased to serve their function. In this sense, it is part of a process of mobilization. More broadly, psychiatry is presented as an essential part of an apparatus of discipline and control. This is typical of World War Two psychiatry, which "conformed effortlessly to the military demands of rationalization, standardization, and hierarchical discipline," as Joanna Bourke has observed.[33] But here, as in *The Seventh Veil*, psychiatry corrects a misguided, insensitive use of discipline that only contributes to the malfunctioning it seeks to address. Reading *The Seventh Veil* through *Psychiatric Treatment*, Francesca—rather than Nicholas—emerges as a civilian translation of the traumatized soldier, subject to an apparatus of scrutiny and control aimed at restoring her usefulness. Music is mobilized in the service of psychiatry to make her a legible object of discipline. In this scheme, music itself also serves as the sign of her usefulness: the purpose of psychiatric treatment is to restore Francesca to her calling as a musician—to make her play again, just as a soldier returns to battle or a traumatized civilian returns to productive life.

This all makes for a somewhat odd relationship between music—specifically, a Late Romanticism marked as hyper-expressive—and feeling.

[33] Joanna Bourke, "Disciplining the Emotions: Fear, Psychiatry and the Second World War," in *War, Medicine and Modernity*, ed. Roger Cooter, Mark Harrison, and Steve Sturdy (London: Sutton, 1998), 225–238, here 232.

Feelings are above all things to be managed in *The Seventh Veil*, and not by oneself, but by others. Music becomes a way of thinking about how the hidden feelings of women can become knowable to and managed by men—men who have special insight into the secrets of music itself. This is how trauma is surmounted, reconciliation achieved, and the past set aside. At the same time, Francesca herself has little agency in her music-making, in ways that are elaborately thematized in the film's concerns with playback and recordings. It is this that really sets the film apart from earlier concerto films, especially *Love Story*. In *Brief Encounter*, music can be understood to work similarly as a kind of treatment. But here the heroine exerts even less agency in this music, while the film's concerns are less with issues of control or legibility, and more with music as a cathartic force that allows trauma to remain unspoken.

Thank You for Coming Back to Me

Brief Encounter has no overt relationship with either psychiatry or trauma. And yet both seem major concerns in this film, if carefully displaced. One emblem of those concerns is the foregrounding of Rachmaninoff's Piano Concerto No. 2 in C minor (1901). Rachmaninoff's Second was famously dedicated to the composer's psychologist, Nikolai Dahl, with whom he underwent hypnosis therapy—this was often noted in the wartime discourse about Rachmaninoff.[34] In 1943, the *Times* suggested that the concerto represented "some sort of catharsis" for Rachmaninoff, after what it calls "the crisis of his manhood."[35] Another link to psychiatry comes by way of Trevor Howard, who co-stars in *Brief Encounter*, and, oddly, had only previously appeared in films related to military psychiatry. Indeed, one of his first screen roles was in *Field Psychiatry for the Medical Officer*, discussed above.[36] His first credited role, moreover, was in Carol Reed's *The Way Ahead* (1944), which was based on another major psychiatric training film made by the Army Kinematograph Service, *The New Lot* (1943). Howard also had a

[34] Ralph Hill's notes for Eileen Joyce's performance with the National Symphony Orchestra mention this, for instance (May 20, 1944, Albert Hall, Nottingham), as do Edwin Evans's for the London Philharmonic Orchestra (October 29, 1944, Royal Albert Hall), both held in the Eileen Joyce Collection, Callaway Centre Archive, University of Western Australia.

[35] "Rachmaninoff's Trilemma: Imagery and Ideas," *Times*, April 2, 1943, 6.

[36] Howard is uncredited but appears as a commanding officer near the end of the film.

more personal and traumatic connection with military psychiatry, having been discharged in 1943 on the grounds of a "psychopathic personality."[37] As many scholars have pointed out, the American military commonly used this diagnosis in the early 1940s to screen out gay service members (and others suspected of "immoral" behavior).[38] Given the close relationship between British and American military psychiatry at this time, Howard's puzzling discharge might have been for similar reasons. Meanwhile, he allowed stories to circulate of his heroic military service, including reports that he received a Military Cross. This background is difficult to separate from standard queer readings of the film's repressed affair, and from its pervasive concerns with shame and deception.[39] However, it is not with the experience of Howard's character that *Brief Encounter* is primarily concerned. Instead, it turns to the hidden experience of its heroine, and to an affair that reads as trauma.

In *Brief Encounter*, adapted from Noël Coward's play *Still Life* (1936), Rachmaninoff's concerto provides an accompaniment to the inner thoughts of the heroine, Laura Jesson (Celia Johnson), as she recalls in flashback an affair that has just come to an end.[40] Laura is a comfortably middle-class woman, married with two children; her most defined trait, we are repeatedly told, is complete ordinariness. Her affair, with a similarly ordinary doctor named Alec (Howard), is unglamorous in many ways, taking place during her weekly shopping trips into the nearest town. It nevertheless has an emotionally violent, disruptive force—a force underlined by the turbulent concerto that accompanies it. The affair's ending is even more traumatic, as Alec decides to move to South Africa, promising never to contact her again. After they part at the train station for the last time, Laura, in despair, nearly throws herself in front of a train. The film begins at this moment of despair before following Laura home, where her flashback begins. As she and her husband Fred listen to the Rachmaninoff concerto on the radio, she recalls the affair, addressing herself to Fred but never actually speaking out loud. The concerto thus stands in for all the things she cannot say and for aspects of her experience that are hidden from him. In this sense, *Brief Encounter* shares *The Seventh Veil*'s concern with the opacity of female experience, but,

[37] Terence Pettigrew, *Trevor Howard: A Personal Biography* (London: Peter Owen, 2001), 154.

[38] Allan Bérubé, *Coming Out Under Fire: The History of Gay Men and Women in World War Two* (New York: The Free Press, 1990), 12.

[39] See Andy Medhurst, "That Special Thrill: *Brief Encounter*, Homosexuality and Authorship," *Screen* 32, no. 2 (1991): 197–208. Also see Dyer, *Brief Encounter*, 10–11.

[40] Johnson herself was mainly associated with wartime propaganda (*In Which We Serve*, *This Happy Breed*) and the figure of the suffering wartime woman; see Puckett, *War Pictures*, 188.

instead of attempting to render women legible—to strip their minds bare—it seeks reconciliation without exposure, as direct communication is displaced by music. Finally, and despite the absence of overt gestures to psychiatry, music seems to serve a cathartic function here. In this sense, listening to Rachmaninoff acts as a kind of treatment in itself.

Throughout the film, the concerto is associated with passion, fantasy, restlessness, and mobility, mapping onto the spaces of the trains and anonymous station where Laura's affair takes place. But it is also, almost inseparably, associated with anxiety and loss. All of this is established quickly in the very opening of the film. Before the credits even begin, the first chords of the concerto sound as a train hurtles past, the music emerging out of the rattling of the tracks. After the credits, as the orchestral introduction reaches its climax, they merge back into the sounds of the train's steam whistle. As Puckett has suggested, that whistle works often in the film as a sudden release of passion or feelings under the pressure of restraint; it acts "both to index and to produce anxiety."[41] We might also understand it as a cathartic release or, like Puckett, as an "externalization of hysteria." In its link with the train whistle in these opening moments, the concerto takes on many of these associations as well.

While the concerto is clearly associated with excessive feeling, though, it is also both an object and a tool of containment. *Brief Encounter*, after all, is a film largely about restraint in the face of strong feeling. This is made clear in the narrative, of course, but it also emerges in other ways. One is a kind of temporal discipline—the film is obsessively concerned with time, timetables, and lateness.[42] Another is through a temporal compression, as suggested by the title itself. As Lant has pointed out, the film reduces the time span of the original play, and its events take place over five consecutive Thursdays. It could even, she adds, be understood as taking place in the single afternoon during which Laura's flashback occurs. To this, the concerto adds a further level of compression. Beginning with its first chords in the opening credits and ending with the final movement's conclusion, the film in some sense takes place within the space of the concerto itself. If Laura's flashback frames and contains most of the film's narrative, in other words, the concerto works even more completely to contain the film.[43]

[41] Puckett, *War Pictures*, 156.

[42] See Lant, *Blackout*, 171–172.

[43] Lant makes a related point about the concerto being used to "seal off the experience" (*Blackout*, 176–177).

The concerto is itself also contained in various ways, in a process that unfolds as Laura returns home. After the opening credits, where the concerto emerges from the sound of the train, the next time we hear it is on Laura's train journey home, after her near suicide. This is the first time it appears as the underscore of her interior monologue, even before her flashback begins. Here it is plainly associated with longing, the first movement's melancholy second theme (in solo horn) accompanying a voice-over recital of dissatisfaction ending with the words "I wish, I wish. . . ."[44] But as Laura arrives home, the film abandons the concerto's links with the mobility of trains and its free-floating acousmatic status, relocating it in her library and, furthermore, in the boxlike apparatus of the radio. Here, as Laura's husband works on a crossword puzzle, she turns on the radio and twists the knob from station to station, finding first some dance music, which proves unsatisfactory, and then a performance of Rachmaninoff's Second: the middle of the recapitulation in the first movement. As she sits and listens, the camera closes in on her face, the solo horn and clarinet statements of the second theme echoing the visual image of isolation, and she begins to reflect on her emotional turmoil. "I've fallen in love!" she muses silently. "I'm an ordinary woman—I didn't think such violent things could happen to ordinary people."[45] It is the same theme heard earlier, but, as she listens now, sunk deep in her overstuffed chair, all impulse to longing and movement seems reversed.

I want to dwell on this scene more closely, in order to suggest how it reads as an elaborately displaced representation of hypnosis therapy—one that casts the concerto itself as treatment. As Alison Winter has argued, cinematic flashback is strongly linked with psychiatry in the 1940s.[46] Those associations are played on here, not least through the choice of the Rachmaninoff concerto so strongly foregrounded in this scene, with its link to hypnosis. Visually, there are more cues to psychiatric treatment. Laura sits dazed and immobilized while her husband sits across from her, pen and paper (his folded-up crossword puzzle looking much like a notepad) in hand. As she reflects on the past, the screen around her face begins to go dark (Figure 4.5A), just as it does when Francesca enters a state of narcosis in *The Seventh Veil* (Figure 4.5B). As the image dissolves to the scene she is recalling, moreover, she seems

[44] Noël Coward, *Brief Encounter*, in *Masterworks of the British Cinema* (London: Faber, 1990), 126.
[45] Coward, *Brief Encounter*, 132.
[46] Winter, *Memory*, 64. Also see Hoeckner, *Film, Music, Memory*, 173–174.

Figure 4.5 (A) *Brief Encounter*, musical "narcosis." (B) *The Seventh Veil*, narcosis treatment.

Figure 4.6 (A) *Brief Encounter*, Laura watching herself. (B) *The Seventh Veil*, Francesca watching herself.

to watch it herself, as if on a screen (Figure 4.6A). (Again, a similar effect occurs when Francesca's narcosis-induced flashback begins and she is briefly doubled on screen, but her gaze is not directed at the image [Figure 4.6B].) As Puckett has observed, the lighting is key here: the image of Laura sitting at home briefly persists in the foreground, "the back of her head cast in shadow and her face apparently illuminated by the reflected light of the remembered past."[47] For Puckett, this is an example of the film's preoccupations with cinematic technique; however, it also recalls established ways of figuring hypnosis in relation to trauma. Hoeckner writes (in his discussion of *The Seventh Veil*) of the early twentieth-century psychoanalyst Ernst Simmel,

> Simmel noted how the hypermnesia that a patient "commanded" during hypnosis made it possible to repeat an experience, like a film that was made

[47] Puckett, *War Pictures*, 139.

"to roll once again; the patient dreams the whole thing one more time, the sensitized subconscious releases the affect, which in turn discharges in an adequate emotional expression, and the patient is cured."[48]

In *Brief Encounter*, it is music rather than hypnosis that enables the hypermnesia (heightened memory), but Laura's "treatment" otherwise plays out much as Simmel imagines. As we will see, it is only by the end of her flashback—her unhappy "dream," as her husband Fred calls it—that she is able to fully assimilate the emotional trauma of her experience.[49]

The film returns to the scene of Laura's library twice more, both scenes further elaborating the idea of music as treatment. Almost exactly midway through her flashback, it is interrupted by Fred protesting that the music is too loud. It is the beginning of the recapitulation in the first movement, emerging out of the sound of the train tracks just after Laura and Alec kiss for the first time. It is a moment in her narrative, in other words, when feeling overwhelms restraint. As Laura is jarred out of her recollection, the same odd dissolve happens in reverse; she is shown in her chair watching herself and Alec in the station while Fred's voice calls her name (Figure 4.7), and the scene in front of her suddenly shifts to the here and now, as if he has called her temporarily out of her trance. Fred turns the music down a notch, and Laura begins her account again in a more distanced mode. Fred, then, has some power to intervene in Laura's recall, acting like a therapist to guide and moderate it, even though he is only privy to it through the music.

We return to the library again at the end of the film when Laura reaches the end of her flashback, her voice-over falling silent after she recounts the moment when she nearly jumps in front of a train. As she turns away from the edge of the track, the Rachmaninoff concerto picks up from the sound of the train's whistle and the rattling of the tracks, echoing in reverse the very opening of the film. Then the film cuts to Laura in her living room (no dissolve this time), the concerto bridging the two scenes. She continues to stare into space as Fred, watching her silently, sets aside his paper and walks over to her. He leans over her as she sits, in an image that closely recalls *The Seventh Veil*'s scenes of narcosis (Figure 4.8). Saying her name, he brings her back to the present, and says, "Whatever your dream was, it wasn't a very happy one, was it." "No," she agrees. He replies, in the film's closing words,

[48] Hoeckner, *Film, Music, Memory*, 174, quoting Ernst Simmel, *Kriegs-Neurosen und "Psychisches Trauma"* (Munich & Leipzig: Otto Nemnich, 1918).
[49] Coward, *Brief Encounter*, 188.

Figure 4.7 *Brief Encounter*, interrupted narcosis.

Figure 4.8 *Brief Encounter*, coming out of "narcosis."

"You've been a long way away. Thank you for coming back to me."[50] Now Laura dissolves into tears, embracing him as the C-major closing statement of the movement's second theme sounds out. The moment represents cathartic release, reconciliation, and finally closure, as the episode is sealed off in the past. The Rachmaninoff treatment is a success.

If music does much to provide this sense of closure here, though, it also reveals that closure as forced and hence slightly false or unstable. The ending of the concerto—in a triumphant C major—is perhaps a little false itself in its exuberance, but Rachmaninoff's original ending is also manipulated here to create a more secure sense of closure. It is worth looking more closely at how this works. The scene begins with the second theme from the recapitulation section of the third movement, in D-flat major (although heavily inflected by minor). As Raykoff observes, this is the concerto's "love theme," and it is associated for much of the film with Laura and Alec, accompanying their passionate kiss in one earlier scene.[51] Here, the theme bridges the two scenes as the film cuts to Laura's library, the piano statement beginning as Laura settles back into her chair. Unlike in previous scenes in the library, the concerto clearly acts as underscore rather than emanating from the radio—the radio is never highlighted, and the music fades slightly as Fred begins to speak. But the strangest moment occurs in the last moments of the film, at the end of its final line, "Thank you for coming back to me." Here the concerto suddenly cuts from the end of the second theme—left hanging oddly on the dominant seventh of D-flat—to the C-major statement of the theme at the *Maestoso* section seventy-five measures (and a piano cadenza) later, with its big opening C-major chord. As Raykoff points out, this is the one spot where the theme is stated by the piano and orchestra together; the "love theme" is thus not only transferred to Fred, but also suggests a new stage of reconciliation—a musical homecoming in multiple ways.[52] What does it mean, though, that this large shift is so sudden in the film's edited version of the concerto? One explanation has to do with the status of Laura's flashback as therapy and the sudden catharsis she experiences as she breaks into sobs, just before the *Maestoso* theme sounds out. At a more straightforward narrative level, though, it reads as abrupt and unmotivated. The film ends, moreover, after a few measures of this, midway through the theme, by simply replacing Rachmaninoff's more

[50] Coward, *Brief Encounter*, 188.
[51] Ivan Raykoff, "Concerto con Amore," *Echo* 2, no. 1 (2000), https://echo.humspace.ucla.edu/issues/concerto-con-amore/, accessed September 30, 2020.
[52] Ibid.

evasive dominant-function chord with a final C major chord, as "The End" appears on the screen. The result is a closing gesture, descending down the scale from G to C, which sounds impressively stolid but also suddenly cuts off the already familiar winding theme. The film uses the concerto to contain and seal off trauma, then, but its efforts to do so become audibly strained here, the pressures on closure and reconciliation forcibly set aside.

Listening to Rachmaninoff and the Luxury of Grief

Brief Encounter is unusual among concerto films in featuring a heroine who is a listener and not a producer of music. The music, moreover, is never visually attached to a performer or to a scene of live performance. This sets it apart even from other listener-centric concerto films like *Humoresque* (1946) or *Deception* (1946), both of which feature women listening to (and conspicuously watching) male musicians who act as objects of desire. One effect of Laura's status as radio listener is to cast her as a passive consumer of music. *Brief Encounter* is a film visually obsessed with commodities, as Pam Cook has pointed out. Its prewar setting allowed for the tantalizing display of goods that were largely unavailable to British viewers in 1945: Laura's stockings, cosmetics, conspicuous furs, and imported Cona coffee machine.[53] Laura is insistently figured as a consumer, and the connection between her experience of feeling and her stance as a consumer is strong. She conducts her affair while on her weekly shopping expeditions (when she also attends the cinema), and it begins after a particularly extravagant purchase. There is a sense, then, in which her romantic escapades are merely an extension of her consumerist escape. Something similar is suggested by her act of listening to Rachmaninoff's Second. While its expression of feeling is clearly meant to compensate for her own silence and restraint, it is at the same time vicarious, mediated, standardized. If the Rachmaninoff concerto is an object of consumption here, moreover, the film situates it specifically within the middlebrow world of "women's culture."[54] The Rachmaninoff concerto is represented as the sort of music Laura might listen to, of a piece with the films she watches every week and the books she reads: "a particular kind

[53] Cook, *Screening the Past*, 101

[54] On women's culture as middlebrow, see Lauren Berlant, *The Female Complaint: The Unfinished Business of Sentimentality in American Culture* (Durham, NC: Duke University Press, 2005), 285.

of middlebrow fiction aimed at middle-class women," as Richard Dyer has observed.[55] Indeed, Coward himself suggested much the same thing when he insisted on using the Rachmaninoff concerto rather than a newly composed work because it fit Laura's middlebrow patterns of consumption: "She listens to Rachmaninoff on the radio, she borrows her books from the Boot's library and she eats at the Kardomah," Coward declared.[56]

Meanwhile, women as producers of music are presented as comical, even grotesque. There are only two scenes featuring musicians in the film. In one, a women's trio performs at a lunchtime café (the Kardomah), to the amusement of Laura and Alec.[57] When they attend the cinema, one of the same women appears playing a Schubert *Marche Militaire* on the Wurlitzer, prompting more laughter. Laura herself is not a musician. She is "too sane—and uncomplicated" to be that, Alec teasingly suggests.[58]

This is just one of the ways in which music is subtly distanced in the film. Another is an interaction that immediately precedes Laura's musically induced flashback. Her husband, working on his crossword, is looking for a missing word in a quotation from Keats. The word is "romance," Laura replies after a moment, referring him to the *Oxford Book of English Verse*. For Fred, such sentiments have become the object of word games. ("Romance" fits in with "delirium" and "Baluchistan," he replies, further associating it with fantasy and the exotic, not of a wholly pleasant kind.[59]) Like "romance," music and the emotion it engenders have a circumscribed place within the colloquial realities of English middle-class life, the film suggests.

A number of film critics found the use of Rachmaninoff in *Brief Encounter* slightly confusing. John Huntley, a film historian who wrote extensively about music, thought the concerto too substantial a work to be used as underscore, complaining that he could not "follow a first-class film at the same time which is largely unrelated in any way to the music." As a result, he also felt it was not an effective way of introducing "serious music to the public via the screen."[60] (By contrast, he thought *The Seventh Veil* was an "outstanding success in bringing music to a wider audience in an artistically satisfying,

[55] Dyer, *Brief Encounter*, 37.

[56] Coward, quoted in Barry Day, "Introduction to *Brief Encounter*," in *Noel Coward Screenplays*, ed. Barry Day (London: Bloomsbury, 2015), 216–217. Kardomah cafes were an early twentieth-century chain that catered largely to women and featured live music.

[57] Coward's screenplay calls for a "Ladies Orchestra" (Coward, *Brief Encounter*, 146).

[58] Ibid., 146.

[59] Ibid., 131.

[60] John Huntley, *British Film Music* (London: Skelton Robinson, 1947), 82.

technically pleasing . . . manner."[61]) One American film critic found the music too high-cultural for the film: he wrote that the film "may be set to Rachmaninov's Concerto No. 2, but it is keyed to daydreaming, the Dodie Smith of 'Call it a Day', and women's glossy magazines."[62] If the rest of the film was about "women's culture," in other words, he did not recognize the Rachmaninoff concerto as fitting into that world.

Within the discourse of music criticism, though, this use of Rachmaninoff made more sense.[63] For Mellers, as seen in Chapter 2, music—including Rachmaninoff concertos—was valued by middlebrow audiences precisely for "the daydreams it gives rise to."[64] And if Mellers was concerned about listeners' preference for "feeling which is mushy and inexact" or their propensity to use music for the purposes of "self-dramatization," Laura's appropriation of Rachmaninoff could have illustrated his case. Traces of Adorno's critique of Late Romanticism might also be seen in *Brief Encounter*'s use of Rachmaninoff. Discussing a Tchaikovsky symphony *as* cinema and the public taste for what he called "standardized Slav melancholy," he wrote,

> Most people listen emotionally: everything is heard in terms of the categories of late Romanticism and of the commodities derived from it, which are already tailored to emotional listening. Their listening is the more abstract the more emotional it is: music really only enables them to have a good cry.[65]

Music like the Rachmaninoff concerto always was a commodity, in other words, tailored for the purposes to which it is put in *Brief Encounter*. Adorno's discussion of "emotional listening," moreover, is clearly gendered, with references to the listening practices of shop girls and elderly mothers. In short, *Brief Encounter* echoed such high-cultural critiques of Rachmaninoff's music and of the middlebrow listening with which it was associated, much as it critiqued melodrama and women's pictures themselves.

[61] Ibid., 78.

[62] John Mason Brown, "Seeing Things, The Midas Touch," *Saturday Review of Literature*, October 12, 1946, 36, quoted in Lant, *Blackout*, 184.

[63] Peter Franklin points similarly to the distance between Huntley's assessment of Rachmaninoff and the disdain felt in music-critical circles: *Seeing Through Music: Gender and Modernism in Classic Hollywood Film Scores* (New York: Oxford University Press, 2011), 32–33.

[64] Wilfrid Mellers, *Music and Society: England and the European Tradition* (London: Dennis Dobson, 1946), 13.

[65] T. W. Adorno, "Commodity Music Analyzed" (1934–40), in *Quasi una Fantasia*, tr. Rodney Livingstone (New York: Verso, 1992), 50. Franklin also notes the Adornian resonances of *Brief*

Brief Encounter also reflected high-cultural tendencies to associate Rachmaninoff's music with luxury and indulgence, endowing this music with commodity status. The *Times* described the First Piano Concerto as displaying the "luxuriance of pathetic sentiment and the lyrical self-pity which is characteristic of the composer's melody and defines his kinship with Tchaikovsky,"[66] and elsewhere referred to the Second Piano Concerto as "luscious."[67] In an article marking Rachmaninoff's death in 1943, the *Times* tackled the idea of emotional luxury head-on: "His music has no tonic properties for the remedy of life's ills, but only a narcotic to numb its pain. If the realms of art and morals were coextensive we might even prohibit, or at any rate ration, the luxury of his grief."[68] To ration Rachmaninoff: it is a remarkable idea, suggesting a wartime economy of feeling shadowing the more practical measures of austerity. Even more curious here, perhaps, is the idea of *grief* specifically as the luxury offered by Rachmaninoff.

Increasingly, critics have begun to see *Brief Encounter* as less about desire than about grief, less about falling in love than about processing loss.[69] Grief is something that comes up surprisingly little in wartime discourse, which is dominated instead by discussions of fear and anxiety—from the noise-prompted anxiety discussed in Chapter 1 to the anxiety placed at the center of all trauma in *Field Psychiatry for the Medical Officer*.[70] In the immediate postwar years even mourning had to be mobilized, as Lucy Noakes has suggested; memorials were often utilitarian in character, while grief was seen "as pointless and as selfish, as working against the collective aims of the war."[71] Grief, in this context, seems even more illicit than desire (which, like anxiety, is at least future-oriented) and hence more elaborately displaced in *Brief Encounter*. In addition to the basic trajectory of Laura's tale—toward the

Encounter (referencing a different essay, "On the Fetish Character in Music and the Regression of Listening") in *Seeing Through Music*, 32.

[66] "The Gramophone: Rachmaninoff's Piano Concertos," *Times*, January 13, 1941, 6. The Second Piano Concerto, the review admits, "seems to justify its popularity, because it is the most deeply felt."

[67] "Red Cross Concerto," *Times*, August 9, 1940, 7.

[68] "Rachmaninoff's Trilemma: Imagery and Ideas," *Times*, April 2, 1943, 6. Not long before this, in summer 1942, the BBC did attempt to ban popular music deemed overly sentimental, suggesting it was unsuitable in wartime. See Baade, *Victory Through Harmony*, 131–152; Guthrie, "Vera Lynn on Screen," 252–253.

[69] See Puckett, *War Pictures*, 183; Noakes, *Dying for the Nation*, 230–231, 258.

[70] On the centrality of fear and anxiety in wartime psychiatric discourse, also see Bourke, "Disciplining the Emotions," 225–226.

[71] Noakes, *Dying for the Nation*, 252–256, 232. On the marginalization of postwar discussions of grief, see also 231–232, 258.

loss of Alec and her own devastation—there are a number of striking gestures to death, grief, and remembrance in *Brief Encounter*. One is the Keats poem referenced in Laura's and Fred's conversation immediately before her reverie, which is essentially about the fear of death and ends with the lines "then on the shore / Of the wide world I stand alone, and think / Till Love and Fame to nothingness do sink."[72] Another is in the couple's parting conversation at the train station, when Laura says starkly ("without emotion"), "I want to die—if only I could die." Alec responds, a little selfishly perhaps, "If you died you'd forget me—I want to be remembered."[73] And there is the pivotal scene shortly before, which shares the same music: the theme from the second movement. Here, Laura runs away from Alec and wanders the streets in despair, realizing the affair must end. She finds herself at a World War One memorial, which is strongly featured and is described in the screenplay in detail. It reads: "The foreground of the shot is composed of part of the war memorial statue: a soldier's hand gripping a bayoneted service rifle. Beyond it Laura is seen as a tiny figure walking toward a seat near the base of the memorial."[74] Indeed, the memorial—with its suggestion of violence as well as loss—looms over Laura, dwarfing her as she sits miserable and lost. If, as Lant and Puckett suggest, *Brief Encounter* works to close off wartime trauma, the experience of loss and grief seems to be part of that trauma in ways that are even more completely unspoken. At the same time, this scene powerfully suggests how female civilian trauma is overshadowed by representations of battlefield experience. When Laura is chased away by a vigilant policeman and made to feel guilty and suspect in the process, the legitimacy of her experience is even further called into question.

For postwar audiences, at least of a certain kind, *Brief Encounter* often released a flood of emotions. This emerges, though, in ways that both mirror Adorno's observations about emotional listening and seem elaborately caught up in shame. In August 1950, Mass Observation (the polling body co-founded by Humphrey Jennings) included this question in its monthly questionnaire: "Do you ever cry in the pictures? Which films, if any, have made you cry, how much, and—if you remember—which part of the film? How

[72] John Keats, "When I Have Fears That I May Cease To Be," in *Oxford Book of English Verse 1250–1900*, ed. A.T. Quiller-Couch (Oxford: Clarendon Press, 1900), 743.
[73] Coward, *Brief Encounter*, 186.
[74] Coward, *Brief Encounter*, 179.

far, if at all, do you feel ashamed on such occasions?"[75] Despite never having been a box office success, *Brief Encounter* was the film that topped the list, appearing most often in the 318 responses, according to an analysis by Sue Harper and Vincent Porter.[76] As they have discussed, the question prompted unusually lengthy and heated answers from participants (all of which can now be viewed online, in their original handwriting);[77] in some cases, they observe, these responses read "like a personal catharsis."[78] Respondents identified music as a major factor in *Brief Encounter*'s effect, with one woman writing, for instance, "the music was responsible for a good deal here. I would have wept without it, but with that and the story to contend with, there was no hope."[79] They also commented in particular on its ending. One twenty-eight-year-old man wrote that an "emotionally supercharged film, such as *Brief Encounter*, made me cry most of the way through, but most of all at the end."[80] This is a response shared by other viewers beyond those who wrote in to Mass Observation. Ronald Neame, who worked on the film, recalled how, even on repeated viewings, it always left him in tears, especially the ending, to his own "great embarrassment."[81] In his history of weeping in Britain, Thomas Dixon suggests the particular postwar resonance of the film's closing line:

> It was a film that could connect with the countless men and women who, after six years of sacrifices, separations, and real or imagined infidelities, had their own reasons for saying "Thank you for coming back to me" in 1945. That poignant closing line spoke to the hearts of *Brief Encounter*'s

[75] Mass Observation Online, August 1950 Directive, https://0-www-massobservation-amdigital-co-uk.catalogue.libraries.london.ac.uk/Documents/Images/DirectiveQuestionnaire-1950aug/0, accessed September 30, 2020.

[76] Sue Harper and Vincent Porter, "Moved to Tears: Weeping at the Cinema in Postwar Britain," *Screen* 37 no. 2 (Summer 1996): 152, 159.

[77] Mass Observation Online, August 1950 Directive, https://0-www-massobservation-amdigital-co-uk.catalogue.libraries.london.ac.uk/Documents/Details/DirectiveQuestionnaire-1950aug, accessed September 30, 2020.

[78] Sue Harper and Vincent Porter, "Moved to Tears: Weeping at the Cinema in Postwar Britain," *Screen* 37 no. 2 (Summer 1996): 153.

[79] Mass Observation Archive, University of Sussex, August 1950 Directive, quoted in Harper and Porter, "Moved to Tears," 167.

[80] Mass Observation Archive, University of Sussex, August 1950 Directive, participant index no. 1008, quoted in Thomas Dixon, *Weeping Britannia: Portrait of a Nation in Tears* (Oxford: Oxford University Press, 2015), 235.

[81] "Ronald Neame on *Brief Encounter*'s Ending," The Criterion Collection, March 29, 2012 (https://www.criterion.com/current/posts/2227-ronald-neame-on-brief-encounter-s-ending, accessed 30 September 2020), quoted in Dixon, *Weeping Britannia*, 241.

first audiences, expressing on the screen their often secret feelings of guilt, loss, gratitude, relief, or disappointment.[82]

Perhaps, though, viewers were responding less to the line and more to Laura's moment of emotional release immediately before it, sharing in her experience of music-induced catharsis.

As Harper and Porter point out, the fact that Mass Observation respondents turned so frequently to music in their discussion of cinematic emotion might be explained in part by an earlier question in that August questionnaire.[83] This question reads "What particular bits of music, if any, give rise to strong emotions in you? Describe your feelings when you hear the music in question."[84] This question, too, prompted long, emotionally heated responses. Porter and Harper also suggest that it was partly the nature of the music in *Brief Encounter* that allowed audiences to admit its emotional effect, a point that brings us back to the middlebrow status of the film and its music. Porter and Harper observe something odd about the responses to *Brief Encounter*: both men and women identify it as moving, but they all appear to be middle-class. (Respondents identified their occupation—as well as their sex, age, and marital status—from which their class identification was extrapolated.) Working-class and lower-middle-class respondents, they report, tended to identify more explicitly war-related films such as *Morning Departure* or *The Best Years of Our Lives*. Moreover, the other film these middle-class respondents most often identified as moving was *Bicycle Thieves*, the Italian neorealist film with a lush score by Alessandro Cicognini. The films have in common their middlebrow status and non-Hollywood origin, as well as their realism. With *Bicycle Thieves*, too, respondents pointed in particular to the *music* as prompting tears. Porter and Harper, themselves echoing the discourse of emotional listening as luxury, observe, "A forty-year-old woman from this group luxuriated in the emotional impact of the soundtrack. She recalled, 'I wept through *Bicycle Thieves*, the music was so wonderful, minor key, it made me feel the hopelessness of it all.'"[85] Indeed, Porter and Harper go so far as to suggest that only middle-class respondents

[82] Dixon, *Weeping Britannia*, 242.
[83] Harper and Porter, "Moved to Tears," 153.
[84] Mass Observation Online, August 1950 Directive, https://0-www-massobservation-amdigital-co-uk.catalogue.libraries.london.ac.uk/Documents/Images/DirectiveQuestionnaire-1950aug/0, accessed September 30, 2020.
[85] Harper and Porter, "Moved to Tears," 167.

noted the emotional impact of music when asked about crying at the cinema. For them, one possible explanation has to do with differences in education and cultural knowledge, but another is more likely: "the Rachmaninov score of *Brief Encounter* and the quasi-classical music of *Bicycle Thieves* permitted middle-class respondents to address the intense feelings prompted by music, but in an intellectually respectable context which conferred some status."[86] Laura herself, similarly, with her middlebrow tastes and elaborate sense of propriety, finds an appropriate outlet in the Rachmaninoff concerto. This is in part what makes it effective as treatment, helping her to process and assimilate her experience. This is music that enabled people to "have a good cry," as Adorno put it. But what allowed this was not just its power to manipulate emotion, but its ability to do so in a respectable manner, much like psychiatry itself.

Brief Encounter and *Love Story* share a preoccupation with the hiddenness of women's trauma. But they suggest different ways in which music might treat that trauma and promote reconciliation, which is imagined in both films as a return to traditional gender and marital roles. In many ways, trauma in both films reads as connected to the experience of war. It seems all the more striking, then, that these films also seem so elaborately committed to displacing wartime experience. Their commitment to music reads as related to this sense of displacement. In *Brief Encounter* in particular, music was endowed with the power to access hidden experience while preserving some basic silence. It was a way of processing trauma without ever having to say anything. But music was also framed and contained, suggesting that dwelling on the past was a luxury—one not to be indulged in for long.

[86] Ibid., 168.

5

Possessed by Music

The Glass Mountain and *The Red Shoes*

> I think that the real reason why *The Red Shoes* was such a success was that we had all been told for ten years to go out and die for freedom and democracy, for this and for that, and now that the war was over, *The Red Shoes* told us to go out and die for art.
>
> —Michael Powell, *A Life in Movies*

> The music is all that matters, and nothing but the music.
>
> —Lermontov in *The Red Shoes*

The wartime concerto film tradition arguably reaches its endpoint in *While I Live* (1947), with its tabloid concerto—Charles Williams's *The Dream of Olwen*—its female composer-pianist, and its Cornish setting.[1] But this little demobilization melodrama marks some telling turns in the discourse of musical efficacy established in wartime. In *While I Live*, the composer Olwen Trevelyan is long dead, apparently killed by her own uncompleted concerto. It haunted her dreams and eventually drove her to fall off a cliff in a trance. This concerto, *The Dream of Olwen*, goes on to haunt the postwar present, serving to disrupt not one, but two young marriages. First, it exerts a strange power over a young woman who is working on a magazine story about the composer. When she hears the concerto on the radio, in her coldly modern London flat, she is suddenly possessed by the ghost of the composer and

[1] *While I Live*, dir. John Harlow, Edward Dryhurst Productions, 1947 (Renown Pictures, 2009, DVD). On some later examples of the tabloid concerto, though, see K. J. Donnelly, *British Film Music and Film Musicals* (Basingstoke: Palgrave Macmillan, 2007), 24.

Mobilizing Music in Wartime British Film. Heather Wiebe, Oxford University Press. © Oxford University Press 2024.
DOI: 10.1093/oso/9780197631713.003.0006

goes in a trance to Olwen's family home in Cornwall, where she immediately sits down and plays *The Dream of Olwen*.[2] Ensconcing herself as the reincarnation of Olwen, she abandons her husband, who comes looking for her, and also manages to trouble the young couple staying in the house—a newly demobilized soldier and his wife trying to establish their married life after the end of the war. Finally, she is nearly driven to death herself, heading toward the cliffs just as Olwen did, the concerto's theme playing in the underscore moments before. It is up to the old servant Nehemiah—with his special access to the mysteries of Cornish magic and folklore, clearly set apart from urban English modernity—to sort out what has happened and set things right.

If concertos on the radio offered a therapeutic catharsis in *Brief Encounter*, here they are a destructive force of possession. And while the music of Rachmaninoff seems at odds with the suburban English settings in *Brief Encounter*, it works to animate the film's grim colloquial spaces with an emotional plenitude; in *While I Live*, by contrast, music is completely incompatible with the couple's London flat. A comparison to *Love Story* (discussed in Chapter 3), which it clearly recalls with its Cornish setting and female composer, presents some even more conspicuous reversals. There, music was a force for good, restoring life and enabling marriage. And while music was similarly a product of Cornwall, set against the exhaustion and emotional depletion of urban England, its life-giving force could be brought back home in transformative ways. In *While I Live*, the concerto is a force of disruption and destruction. It is ultimately something to be dispelled if normal life—however disenchanted—is to continue.

The turn toward music as a destructive force of possession is unusually foregrounded in *While I Live*. But the same concerns can be seen to animate two later music-centered films of the 1940s, Henry Cass's *The Glass Mountain* (1949) and Michael Powell and Emeric Pressburger's *The Red Shoes* (1948), one of the most internationally successful British films of the period.[3] In these films, there is a striking fixation on the idea of music and art as a force of enchantment—a force with the power to possess people and drive them to their deaths. Music is somehow opposed to life. More specifically, music

[2] On a wider British preoccupation with ghosts and spiritualism in World War Two, as well as official attempts to quash it, see Patrick Deer, *Culture in Camouflage: War, Empire, and Modern British Literature* (New York: Oxford University Press, 2016), 153–191.

[3] *The Glass Mountain*, dir. Henry Cass, Renown Pictures, 1949 (VCI Entertainment, 2007, DVD); *The Red Shoes*, dir. Michael Powell and Emeric Pressburger, The Archers, 1948 (Criterion Collection, 2010, DVD).

becomes incompatible with marriage and domesticity and, indeed, to some extent with England as a larger figure of "home." It is to be renounced if normal life is to continue. These ideas about music are linked more or less explicitly with postwar demobilization, as they are in *While I Live*. *The Glass Mountain* deals directly with the theme of settling into domestic married life after the return from war, while *The Red Shoes* addresses its postwar moment more obliquely. On the one hand, it appears as if music itself is being released from its wartime duties and realigned with excess and enchantment. On the other hand, there is something about the totalizing demands and destructive force of music in these films that seems to act as a remnant of the *feeling* of total war, now displaced from England and normal life. War's affective world exerts a strong attraction, while domestic normality appears evacuated of meaning and intensity, even as the films insist that such normality is key to life.

The Glass Mountain and the Renunciation of Musical Plenitude

Both *The Red Shoes* and *The Glass Mountain* place the genesis and performance of a fantastical music-dramatic work at their core, the themes of which then pervade the rest of the film. In *The Glass Mountain* it is an opera, performed at Venice's Teatro La Fenice and starring Tito Gobbi (playing himself). The opera, like the rest of the score, was composed by Nino Rota, who recycled material from a wartime Italian film on very similar themes, *La donna della montagna* (1943).[4] In *The Glass Mountain*'s publicity, the opera was treated much like the tabloid concertos of earlier films. Rota even produced a version for piano solo, called *The Legend of the Glass Mountain*.[5] This was also arranged for orchestra and recorded by a number of light music orchestras, while other parts of the score were published and widely recorded as well (see Figure 5.1).[6] As the star of the film Michael Denison

[4] See Richard Dyer, *Nino Rota: Music, Film and Feeling* (London: BFI Publishing, 2010), 14–15. Dyer notes that he also used this music in a 1947 non-cinematic work, the *Sinfonia sopra una canzone d'amore*.

[5] Nino Rota, *The Legend of the Glass Mountain* (London: Keith Prowse & Co., 1949); *The Legend of the Glass Mountain: From the Music of the Film "The Glass Mountain," Arranged for Orchestra by Arthur Wilkinson* (London: Keith Prowse & Co., 1949). Also see Dyer, *Nino Rota*, 19.

[6] Mantovani and His Orchestra, *Mantovani Concert*, London Records, LPB.127 (1949); The Melachrino Orchestra, HMV B.9765 (1949), https://www.discogs.com/The-Melachrino-Orchestra-The-Legend-Of-The-Glass-Mountain-Song-Of-The-Mountains-La-Montanara/release/2486803.

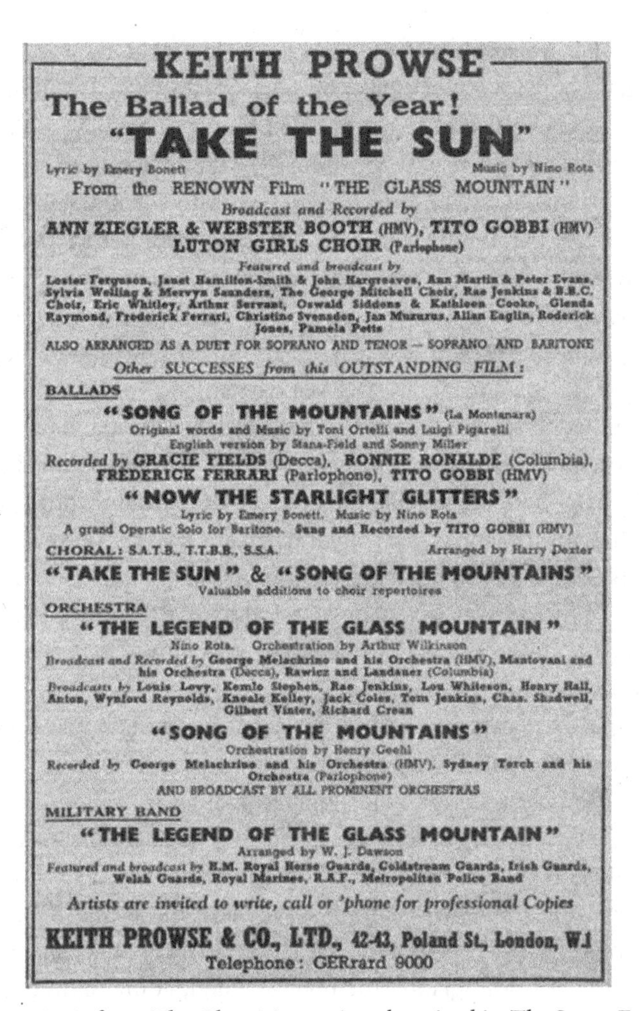

Figure 5.1 Music from *The Glass Mountain*, advertised in *The Stage*, February 1, 1951, p. 5.

observed, *The Legend of the Glass Mountain* was the *Warsaw Concerto* of the moment.[7]

But the film also reveals a clear set of anxieties about music, which once again serves to disrupt a happy marriage in its association with the fantastical and the ghostly. The hero of *The Glass Mountain* is an English composer,

[7] Michael Denison, *Overture and Beginners: The Story of Dulcie Gray and Michael Denison* (London: Gollancz, 1973), 221.

Richard, who enlists as a RAF pilot (recalling Radetzky in *Dangerous Moonlight*). Shot down over Italy, he is trapped in the Dolomites with a group of Italian resistance fighters, fortuitously including Gobbi. While there, Richard falls in love with the beautiful Alida (Valentina Cortese, in her first English-language role), who had rescued him when his plane was shot down. It is from her that he learns the legend of the Glass Mountain, which is in many ways a tale of death's sonic allure: a woman betrayed by her betrothed disappears on the mountain, and her ghost calls to her former lover, beckoning him to his own death. The legend continues to haunt Richard when the war ends and he returns to London, and to his formerly happy domestic life with his wife Anne. Restless and dissatisfied, he works on an opera based on the tale, ignoring his wife and eventually returning to Italy and to his inspiration, Alida, to complete the opera. Anne, however, finally pursues Richard to Venice, and, when her plane crashes on the Dolomites, echoing his earlier crash, he abandons his opera's premiere at La Fenice to rescue her. In the end, opera and passion (which are displaced to Italy) must be sacrificed as inimical to life, while home and spousal loyalty are revealed as the ultimate values.

One of the problems with the film, though, is that it never manages to make those values very compelling. For one thing, Italy exerts *too* much attraction. The evacuation of meaning in the film's representation of both England and marriage—which clearly function as extensions of each other—was so stark that a number of critics commented on it at the time. The scenes shot in Venice and the Dolomites were "enchanting," according to the *Guardian*: "It must, however, be regretfully recorded that 'The Glass Mountain' also contains a number of scenes in England," the review added, going on to describe the tiresomeness of these scenes and of the married couple on which they focused.[8] Another review reports: "The film divides its time and attention between England and Italy, and Italy, it must be confessed, comes off the better at all points." Again, the couple itself is part of the problem with England in this "uninspired variation on the overworked theme of the difficulties the returned soldier finds in settling down."[9]

Throughout the film, Richard and Anne's marriage is characterized by a cozy domesticity and associated not so much with duty as with the acceptance of a comfortable and commodity-filled ordinariness. This association

[8] "New Films in London," *Manchester Guardian*, February 5, 1949, 3.
[9] "The Glass Mountain," *Times*, February 4, 1949, 7.

is reinforced by the image of the actors who play the pair, the real-life couple Dulcie Gray and Michael Denison. As Hollie Price has discussed, they had already established themselves as paragons of ordinary married life, with the publicity for the 1948 film, *My Brother Jonathan*—a film in which Gray similarly played the sensible, slightly dull choice of wife for a more torn Denison.[10] Price shows how the couple's image was used in advertising for armchairs and magazine features in ways that linked them with an increasingly consumerist postwar vision of the home, after years of austerity, and also with a model of companionate marriage, widely seen as "the ideal way to re-establish relationships in peacetime."[11] These visions of home and married life are central to *The Glass Mountain*, but the film also presents them as emotionally impoverished.

Even at the end of the film, home and marriage appear compromised and are never endowed with the richness of feeling associated with Italy and Richard's opera. This difference is communicated above all musically. The central love story of the film—between the composer and his wife—is symbolized not by Rota's lush "Glass Mountain" music, but by a self-consciously commercial tune. It is a sentimental folklike ballad called "Wayfarer," which Richard wrote just before the war. As he explains it himself, it was composed in an attempt to make some money and "buy a decent home for his wife."[12] While its success may have bought a "dream house" and domestic happiness—swiftly cut off by the war—the song is clearly presented as a compromise of the composer's artistic goals. This is a kind of compromise he is newly loath to make after the war. ("All I want to do right now is get this 'Glass Mountain' out of my system," he says. "Nothing else matters—not success, not even happiness."[13]) A conventional resolution would seem to require a coming together of Richard's marriage and his "Glass Mountain" music, reassigning his passion to the rightful object and endowing marriage with meaning (much as happens at the end of *Brief Encounter*).[14] However, when Richard reunites with his wife at the end of the film, rescuing her on the mountain top, it is the insipid "Wayfarer" tune that plays out, entirely

[10] Hollie Price, *Picturing Home: Domestic Life and Modernity in 1940s British Film* (Manchester: Manchester University Press, 2021), 254. Also see Denison, *Overture and Beginners*, 223.

[11] Price, *Picturing Home*, 255.

[12] *Glass Mountain*, 0:08:00.

[13] Ibid., 0:33:00.

[14] Indeed, some scholars have seen such a conventional ending in the film. Price suggests that "Richard's opera, the myth of the Glass Mountain and its romance . . . become wrapped up in the ordinary, homely companionship between husband and wife" (Price, *Picturing Home*, 264).

displacing the "Glass Mountain" music in the underscore. The association between domesticity and Richard's frankly profit-driven little song makes its relationship with consumerism and compromise explicit. It is Italy, Alida, and Richard's opera that hold all the power of attraction.

At the same time, the "Glass Mountain" opera is presented as frightening in its all-consuming power. As Richard works on the opera, unable to complete it (recalling the unfinished concerto in *While I Live*), he becomes increasingly unhappy and alienated from his wife. Finally, he decides to give it up, prompting a strikingly out-of-character discussion between Anne and Richard about the idea of art as possession and as an impediment to life:

ANNE: It's the most important piece of work you've ever done. You believed in it. You were *possessed* by it.
RICHARD: I don't want to be possessed by anything. I want to possess myself.
ANNE: Isn't to be utterly possessed the best way to write real music?
RICHARD: Perhaps it is, but it's not the way to live. My life with you has been shortened by six years already. Ever since I started this work, I don't taste the food I eat, I don't enjoy the air I breathe. There are whole days together I don't really look at my wife. It's maybe being a genius, but it isn't being alive. It's got to stop.
ANNE: Can you stop something that's got such a grip on you?
RICHARD: I've got to break that grip. Find you again. Find me again.[15]

As Richard's brief reference to the disruption of war helps to signal here, the hold his opera has on him is also caught up in his memories of war itself—memories of an emotionally richer life, perhaps in part because of its proximity to death—and the difficulty of returning to an emptier normality. Indeed, the main theme of Richard's opera—the theme on which he most obsessively works—is about music that calls one away from life. Here, the ghost of the abandoned woman calls to the man she will lure to his death: "And though you stop your ears / To my insistent call / I shall not sleep my love / Nor rest till the day you come." Richard himself associates these words with both the allure of Alida and that of the opera itself, at one point reciting them, obsessed by his unfinished composition, as he sees her spectral face in his English surroundings.[16]

[15] *Glass Mountain*, 0:45:30.
[16] Ibid., 0:42:40.

The source of musical attraction, I would suggest, also goes beyond Alida, to a broader sense of communal plenitude attached to wartime in this film. Indeed, what Alida represents is not so much a more passionate romantic alternative to Anne, but a sense of social belonging alternative to marriage itself. This is suggested in part by the fact that Richard and Alida are rarely alone, interacting instead in the context of village life and convivial groups, in scenes often filled with music and singing. It is in one rare scene on their own that Alida tells Richard the story of the Glass Mountain, but when he suggests climbing it together, she refuses—"there is too much danger, too much enchantment," she says. At this moment, the possibility for intimacy is further cut off by the sound of bells announcing the end of the war, which works to return the lovers to their social world. The war's end is a moment especially saturated with sound and music: triumphant bell-ringing in the mountain village of San Felice ("I wonder if the bells in London sound half so clear as they do here in San Felice," Richard wonders), singing in the church, and a train full of Italian soldiers singing together.[17] These moments of sonic plenitude are also moments of social plenitude and belonging as people crowd into the church or the village square, almost overflowing the screen.

Indeed, it is the music associated with these images of communal plenitude—not with Alida or the Glass Mountain—that haunts Richard on his return to normal married life. The final shot of him leaving the Italian mountains is accompanied by the sound of other soldiers on his train singing the nostalgic folklike song "La Montanara."[18] This song follows Richard into the next scene in England, where he sits at his grand piano and tries to pick out the same tune. But here, back in his "dreamhouse," his solitude stands in stark contrast to the song's origins in the previous scene, teeming with life. Surrounded by the objects with which he has filled his home, he is a figure of isolation. And it is the communal singing of "La Montanara"—not Alida—that first haunts him. Even in happier times, Richard and Anne are a strikingly atomized unit with little relationship to a larger society, their only friend an eccentric old Scottish poet whom they meet in Richard's quest to write a hit song. When Richard returns to Italy, what is emphasized is not so much his relationship with Alida—who is a distant figure, clearly belonging to the operatic tradition of "alpine virgins" identified by Emanuele Senici

[17] Ibid., 0:27:00–0:32:00.

[18] "La Montanara" is not by Rota and is attributed to Antonio Ortelli and Luigi Pigarelli in the credits. On the song's use and origins, see Dyer, *Nino Rota*, 18.

and very much out of place in Venice—but rather his participation in the collaborative activities required to put on his opera.[19]

In the film's association of music and emotional plenitude with community life rather than marriage, it palpably recalls the closing scene of *Millions Like Us* (which shares the same music director, Louis Levy), where the recently widowed heroine finds comfort and connection in communal singing (as discussed in Chapter 1). But it is as if *The Glass Mountain* needs to reverse the meaning of the earlier film—to retract the promise of fullness associated (especially through music) with larger solidarities and to restore the centrality of marriage and a consumption-driven domesticity. That it fails compellingly to do so, insisting instead on the danger of a single-minded commitment associated with music, shows the power and continued draw of those older models of musical plenitude. Music's power of possession, then, seems aligned with a model of musical plenitude actively promoted in wartime, but now represented as dangerous and destructive to life.

Making Music the Master: *The Red Shoes*

Many of these themes and strategies in *The Glass Mountain* echo another more complicated film, *The Red Shoes*, released the previous year. It, too, ends with a composer abandoning his opera's premiere to find his wife—in this case, not so much to rescue her as to reclaim her. And it is even more committed to the incompatibility between art and domestic happiness. *The Red Shoes* similarly places a musical work—in this case a ballet—at its center and positions it as the object of unhealthy obsession.[20] It also figures music and art as a force of enchantment and possession and situates them largely beyond England, casting this model of art as somehow incompatible with ordinary English life. The scholarship on *The Red Shoes* has tended to focus on the ballet itself, the film's connections with contemporary ballet culture (both in Britain and the United States), and the odd love triangle in which

[19] Emanuele Senici, *The Alpine Virgin: Landscape and Gender in Italian Opera* (Cambridge: Cambridge University Press, 2005). The choice of La Fenice for the opera's premiere seems telling. As Harriet Boyd Bennett has pointed out, Venice was remarkable for being largely untouched by war (much like the Dolomites), with La Fenice in particular functioning as a site of continuity and renewal due to continued Fascist investment in wartime; see Harriet Boyd-Bennett, *Opera in Postwar Venice: Cultural Politics and the Avant-Garde* (Cambridge: Cambridge University Press, 2018), 2, 26.

[20] The ballet was also published in a version for piano solo: Brian Easdale, *The "Red Shoes" ballet*, arranged for piano solo (London: Chappell, 1950).

the heroine is caught.[21] But reading the film alongside *The Glass Mountain* brings into relief some additional concerns: first, with how to manage the residual energies and commitments of wartime in a postwar world, and second, with music itself as something closely associated with the all-consuming demands of total war.

Powell and Pressburger's *The Red Shoes* is centrally concerned with art as a site of enchantment, even of a kind of sexualized ecstasy. It focuses on the Ballet Lermontov, clearly modeled on the Ballets Russes, as it moves from London to Paris to Monte Carlo. The fifteen-minute ballet at its heart is based on the Hans Christian Anderson tale about a magical pair of shoes that forces its wearer to dance without stopping. This tale imbues the rest of the film, which plays out a related story of a young dancer, Vicky Page, obsessed by her art and torn between the demands of the impresario Boris Lermontov—a Diaghilev-like figure memorably played by Anton Walbrook (the pianist in *Dangerous Moonlight*)—and her eventual husband, the young composer Julian Craster. The former represents a total sacrifice to art, which offers life at its most intense and ecstatic; the latter represents a more compromised state of domestic ordinariness in England.[22] In the end Vicky is destroyed, as the magical red shoes—and arguably the music of the ballet—take over her body and force her to her death.

The Red Shoes is one of a set of postwar films by Powell and Pressburger that place music at their core while also dealing with issues of female ambition and desire.[23] In their fantastical extravagance and female-centricity, these films mark a shift from Powell and Pressburger's wartime films, but they also pick up on those earlier films' concerns in some surprising ways. With *49th Parallel* (1941), *One of Our Aircraft Is Missing* (1942), *The Life and Death of Colonel Blimp* (1943), and *A Canterbury Tale* (1944), Powell and Pressburger developed an idiosyncratic cinematic propaganda that blended realism with extravagant touches of magic, fantasy, or surrealism; in the

[21] For detailed readings of the film, see especially Andrew Moor, *Powell and Pressburger: A Cinema of Magic Spaces* (London: I. B. Tauris, 2012), 197–218; Adrienne L. McLean, *Dying Swans and Madmen: Ballet, The Body, and Narrative Cinema* (New Brunswick: Rutgers University Press, 2008), 133–171; Mark Connelly, *The Red Shoes* (London: I. B. Tauris, 2005).

[22] This is a "hysterical scenario" typical of Powell and Pressburger's postwar melodramas, in which the heroine is trapped between "two equally unacceptable positions" (Moor, *Powell and Pressburger*, 185).

[23] On the focus on women in Powell's postwar films, see Natacha Thiéry, "That Obscure Subject of Desire: Powell's Women, 1945–1950," in *The Cinema of Michael Powell: International Perspective on an English Film-Maker*, ed. Ian Christie and Andrew Moor (London: British Film Institute, 2005), 224–238.

process, they also offered complex meditations on the demands of total war. Kent Puckett has argued that *Colonel Blimp* in particular thematizes a central paradox, wherein total war required a complete commitment that was itself a betrayal of English values, however necessary.[24] For him, it serves as an exemplar of how British war films allowed audiences to confront "the disturbing, paradoxical, and maybe self-defeating possibility that a commitment to a total war against totalitarianism was perhaps also a commitment to totalitarianism."[25] As if in reaction to the end of such totalitarian demands, but also to the peculiar sense of purpose and the habits of mind they engendered, Powell and Pressburger's postwar films turn to female characters obsessed with new commitments of their own choosing: Anglican nuns establishing a convent in the Himalayas in *Black Narcissus* (1947) and a young dancer pursuing artistic greatness in *The Red Shoes*. Powell himself framed the latter as a rerouting of wartime thinking, reflecting that "we had all been told for ten years to go out and die for freedom and democracy, for this and for that, and now that the war was over, *The Red Shoes* told us to go out and die for art."[26] In both films, these aspirations also involve communities that pose a clear alternative to marriage and family—the convent or the ballet company—recalling the communities of wartime, as did *The Glass Mountain*. Shot through with an intense eroticism and a disturbing morbidity, these films also take their characters far beyond the confines of England to more colorful, fantastical lands beyond, as if to suggest the continuing allure of a fanaticism marked as antithetical to Englishness. As Andrew Moor suggests, each of these films "marks a desire for plenitude which will be quashed . . . as though faith in the utopianism once articulated in the various propagandist nuggets of rhetoric in the war films . . . can no longer be maintained."[27]

Music plays a central role in articulating this plenitude, even as it becomes linked with totalizing demands at the level of both narrative and form. In this regard, Powell and Pressburger's postwar films pick up on another aspect of their wartime work—their experimentation with music and sound—while pushing it in new directions.[28] A number of their wartime propaganda films

[24] Kent Puckett, *War Pictures: Cinema, Violence, and Style in Britain 1949–1945* (New York: Fordham University Press, 2017), 20, 34. As Puckett notes, Powell discussed these themes explicitly in notes to the Ministry of Information.

[25] Ibid., 2.

[26] Michael Powell, *A Life in Movies: An Autobiography by Michael Powell* (London: Faber and Faber, 1986), 653.

[27] Moor, *Powell and Pressburger*, 71–72.

[28] Anita Jorge, "Liminal Soundscapes in Powell & Pressburger's Wartime Films," *Studies in European Cinema* 14, no. 1 (2017): 22–23.

explore distinctive approaches to the soundtrack: the spare use of music by Ralph Vaughan Williams in *49th Parallel*, the limitation to diegetic sound in *One of Our Aircraft Is Missing*, or the historical soundscapes mysteriously emanating from contemporary scenes in *A Canterbury Tale*.[29] In some of these films, too, music has a magical efficacy, just as it does in other wartime films discussed in previous chapters. *One of Our Aircraft Is Missing*, as Jorge has discussed, includes pivotal moments where the playing and communal singing of the forbidden Dutch national anthem has the power to dispel Nazi forces.[30] In *A Canterbury Tale*, music is strongly connected with the film's preoccupations with blessings and miracles, and it facilitates the magical collapse of past and present.[31] In the postwar films, however, Powell and Pressburger explore this idea of efficacy in new ways, which have much more to do with control. By 1946, Powell wanted to create a kind of film, he later said, "where music was the master."[32] This involved abandoning his usual composer, Allan Gray, to find someone who "thought operatically." Eventually he settled on Brian Easdale.[33] An accomplished young composer who had indeed written a couple of operas, Easdale had worked mainly in documentary and propaganda film.[34] His first film with Powell was *Black Narcissus*, followed by *The Red Shoes*. Both experiment with what Powell called "composed film," which involved giving music a more leading role by shooting scenes to pre-composed music.[35]

Powell first experimented with this idea of filming to playback in a sequence at the climax of *Black Narcissus*.[36] In that film, Powell said, "I started out almost as a documentary director and ended up as a producer of opera." The twelve-minute scene, which includes almost no speech, "was opera in

[29] Jorge, "Liminal Soundscapes," 23–24. The latter two films in particular seem in close dialogue with Humphrey Jennings's sonic experiments in *Listen to Britain*. *One of Our Aircraft Is Missing* also bears a close relationship with the sonic effects in Jennings's *The Silent Village*. On sound, music, and *Listen to Britain* in *A Canterbury Tale*, see Moor, *Powell and Pressburger*, 110, 115–118, and Jorge, "Liminal Soundscapes," 27. Victor Burgin's 2001 video installation *Listen to Britain* also explores a relationship between *A Canterbury Tale* and Jennings's film, and both Burgin's video and Jennings's film are included in the Criterion DVD of *A Canterbury Tale* (CRRN1639DVD, 2006).

[30] Jorge, "Liminal Soundscapes," 26.

[31] For further discussion of music and sound in *A Canterbury Tale*, see Jorge, "Liminal Soundscapes," 24, and Moor, *Powell and Pressburger*, 115–118.

[32] Powell, *A Life in Movies*, 583.

[33] Ibid., 581.

[34] Easdale worked with the GPO, the Crown Film Unit, and Information Films of India; his films included the innovative Crown narrative documentary *Ferry Pilot* (1941) and Jennings's first wartime propaganda film *Spring Offensive*. See Steve Foxon, "Spring Offensive (1940)," *BFI Screenonline* (http://www.screenonline.org.uk/film/id/1364871/index.html), accessed July 30, 2021.

[35] Powell, *A Life in Movies*, 582.

[36] *Black Narcissus*, dir. Michael Powell and Emeric Pressburger, The Archers, 1947.

Figure 5.2 *Black Narcissus*, Sister Ruth possessed.

the sense that music, emotion, image and voices all blended together into a new and splendid whole."[37] In this sequence, a young nun, deranged by desire, attempts to kill her mother superior. With her deathly pallor and eyes ringed in red, Sister Ruth appears as if possessed (Figure 5.2). The way in which music is used in this scene, moreover—as an unseen force controlling the action—points to music itself as a force of possession. As Moor suggests, one of the effects of the technique of pre-composition "is to suggest that human elements are guided according to exterior forces."[38] Powell himself emphasized the ways in which music could act as a force of precise control and how that control then extended to him as a director. "For the first time," he said of his experiment in *Black Narcissus*, "I felt I had control of the film with the authority of the music."[39] After this experiment, Powell launched on *The Red Shoes* with the aim of exploring the technique further in the film's ballet sequence. He finally made a fully composed film with *The Tales of Hoffmann* in 1951—a version of Offenbach's operetta, in which all the parts

[37] Powell, *A Life in Movies*, 583.
[38] Moor, *Powell and Pressburger*, 215.
[39] Powell, *A Life in Movies*, 583.

are doubled by dancers.[40] If *Hoffmann* involves an overt fascination with male control of female bodies, though, *The Red Shoes* explores murkier areas of overlap between music as a mysterious force of enchantment, an emanation of one's own radical desires, and a tool of control manipulated by others.

In *The Red Shoes*, there is a stark opposition between the intensity offered by art, as an object of total sacrifice, and the world of love, marriage, domesticity, and, to some extent, England. For women in particular, the film suggests, the latter was a world of compromise inimical to intensity; only a single-minded devotion to art could produce ecstasy. For critics at the time, this stark opposition was nonsensical in conventional or realistic terms: as one pointed out, many great dancers, including Pavlova, were married.[41] But their bafflement is a clue, perhaps, that the film's concerns are not really with marriage but rather with something more abstract: the allure of sacrifice to totalizing demands and the idea of art—not love—as the site of greatest intensity.

Vicky is linked with the music of the "Red Shoes" ballet throughout the film. Opposed to this is the music of her husband Julian's opera, *Cupid and Psyche*. Her music—also composed by Julian, but commissioned by Lermontov and clearly derived from the Stravinskian world of the Ballets Russes—is brilliant and kinetic, strongly linked to the visual sphere. Julian's opera, on the other hand, is lyrical and richly expressive, and dominated by the soprano voice. Most strikingly, this voice is always disembodied. Julian's music is entirely detached from the world of vision occupied by ballet and, indeed, from the notion of cinematic spectacle embraced by the film itself. Even when it premieres at Covent Garden at the end of the film, it is only heard over the radio. These two musics come into direct conflict at a number of crucial moments in the film, where the opera is strongly associated with marriage and also with England—in short with the demands of Julian himself. But there are also ways in which both musics act together as powerful and dangerous forces of possession, used by men as tools of control but ultimately controlling them as well, and jointly driving Vicky to her death.

Both this opposition between the two musics and their similarly possessive power can be seen in the central scene depicting the composition of the opera, which takes place in Vicky and Julian's cavernous London bedroom,

[40] On some of these issues, see Marissa Fenley, "When the Puppets Get Together: Looking Like a Subject in The Archers' *The Tales of Hoffmann*," *The Opera Quarterly* 35 (2019): 276–296.

[41] "New Films in London," *Manchester Guardian*, July 24, 1948, 3. A similar point is made in C. A. Lejeune, "In Love with the Ballet," *The Observer*, July 25, 1948.

at night—the film's only representation of their domestic married life. As the couple lie awake—in conspicuously tiny beds, placed very far apart—Vicky recalls the music of "The Red Shoes," while Julian hears a distant female voice, singing a haunting melody. He gets up and goes to the grand piano in the next room, picking out the melody and gradually filling in the harmonies. Meanwhile, Vicky goes to a set of drawers and opens them to caress her red ballet shoes as the playful theme of the ballet sounds, reduced to a single tentative flute. As a number of scholars have noted, the red shoes are endowed with a sexualized intensity;[42] here, that intensity offered by art is set against marriage itself as fundamentally chaste. But Julian's music, too, draws him away from the bedroom and seems in some ways to control his actions. As he picks out the melody for his opera, moreover, there is a sense that he is transmitting music he hears, which exists apart from him. This impression is reinforced by the odd way in which the scene's sound was recorded: rather than using playback, Powell insisted that Easdale play the piano off-camera as the scene was filmed, to the consternation of his sound department. There was "something special," Powell said, "about a scene rehearsed and recorded this way, in which the piano would be an extra voice."[43] This music is external to Julian and has power over him in much the same way that the shoes come to control Vicky.

This impression is reinforced by the mysterious appearance of a similar disembodied operatic voice earlier in the film, before Julian has even decided to write an opera. This is in a dreamlike scene at Lermontov's villa in the French Riviera, where Vicky's starring role in the "Red Shoes" ballet is announced and its music is first heard. Vicky arrives at the gates of the villa's wild garden, elaborately dressed in fairy-like gown and crown. As she stops at the gate, one of the film's many thresholds between real and magical worlds, an operatic tenor voice quietly emerges and she enters to climb up a seemingly endless staircase, accompanied by the increasingly rapturous singing (Figure 5.3).[44] The magical quality of this voice, which seems to beckon Vicky toward the villa, is suggested in part by its confused status: it might appear diegetic, growing louder as she approaches the villa, but it turns out to be pure acousmêtre, and, while it belongs musically to the world of

[42] See, for instance, Linda Ruth Williams, "The Shock of *The Red Shoes*," *New Review of Film and Television Studies* 15 (2017): 9–23, especially 19–20.

[43] Powell, *A Life in Movies*, 656–657.

[44] On these thresholds, see Henning Engelke and Tobias Hochscherf, "Colour Magic at Pinewood: Hein Heckroth, The Archers and Avant-Garde Production Design in *The Red Shoes* (1948)," *Journal of Design History* 28 (2015): 48–66 (62).

Figure 5.3 *The Red Shoes*, a voice beckons Vicky up the staircase.

Julian's opera, he has not yet begun to compose it. Moor has suggested that the scene also resonates with the story of Cupid and Psyche on which Julian's opera is based, recalling the episode in which the human Psyche makes her way through a grove to Cupid's magical palace.[45] Moor is more concerned with other aspects of the tale, but the story as originally told by Apuleius is also strangely preoccupied with acousmatic sound, in ways that seem crucial for this scene. In Apuleius's story, Cupid's palace is filled with disembodied voices—of the unidentified Cupid himself, but also of servants and musicians (including a choir), all invisible to Psyche: "She could see no living soul, and merely heard words emerging from thin air."[46] In *The Red Shoes*, the tenor voice emerging from the landscape perhaps suggests the "unidentified voice" of Psyche's divine lover, which "consoled her loneliness," but it also recalls the palace's enchanted world of disembodied sound more generally.[47] If the voice draws Vicky up the staircase, what it leads her to is the

[45] Moor, *Powell and Pressburger*, 212.
[46] Apuleius, *The Golden Ass*, trans. P. G. Walsh (New York: Oxford University Press, 1994), 81.
[47] Ibid., 82.

root of her dilemma: Julian, whom she sees first, and then Lermontov and the "Red Shoes" ballet itself. Indeed, the music here could be seen to root itself in both Vicky and Julian. In the course of the film, the disembodied voice seems to become increasingly embodied, always in proximity to the "Red Shoes" music: Julian later hears and transcribes a similar operatic voice, then it manifests in a real operatic performance (over the radio), and finally it seems to take root in Vicky's body.

In the climactic scene of the film, Julian's opera once again threatens to immobilize Vicky and, in the end, seems to drive her to her death. The opera is having its premiere at Covent Garden while Vicky is in her dressing room in Monte Carlo, secretly about to dance "The Red Shoes." She is listening to the premiere on the radio when it is announced that Julian is not there to conduct, and he suddenly shows up in her room, confronting her as his music continues. His arrival sets up a dramatic battle for control between Julian and Lermontov, who demands complete devotion to art, ridiculing the idea of Vicky as a "faithful housewife" with "a crowd of screaming children." Julian makes a case for love and marriage, pointing out that he has sacrificed his music—leaving his own first night—while she will not make a similar sacrifice. Vicky, meanwhile, is caught between them, increasingly incapacitated.

While Vicky is most obviously trapped between the demands of Julian and Lermontov, the forces acting on her in this scene are also musical, as Julian's opera continues to play loudly on the radio. As the scene progresses and the opera's overture gives way to a soprano aria (all semblance of a realistic progression of the opera now being forgot), the music becomes increasingly foregrounded, structuring the scene. The voice enters at the moment Vicky is finally forced to make a decision, and slowly rises to a climax as Julian gives up on Vicky and leaves. There is something deeply confusing about the aria's status in this scene, as Moor attests when he suggests that it is "effectively Vicky's own voice, appropriated by Julian, filtered through him."[48] While it reads more as vocalise than as intelligible text, the aria speaks in elaborate ways to Vicky's suspension between two opposing forces. In the 1960s, Easdale described how this aria had been composed earlier and then used in the film and was imagined as part of his own potential opera on the subject of Cupid and Psyche. He writes, "Psyche's place in the drama at the time of the Aria was between the two worlds of my—it seems—perennial theme. She was 'alone' between the worlds of God and Man. Thus she sings this coloratura

[48] Moor, *Powell and Pressburger*, 218.

passage on the word, 'alone.'"[49] In this sense, this aria, like Vicky herself, is poised between the music of Julian (the opera overture) and Lermontov (the ballet overture). But the disembodied voice might be seen to *act upon* her—and indeed on Julian—rather than originating from either one of them.

This impression is created in part by how the aria is cued by Lermontov, whose exclamation "Wait!" effectively pauses the cinematic action until it begins.[50] This idea of the voice as an external controlling force becomes even clearer moments later, when the soprano aria shifts to the haunting modal melody heard in the bedroom scene. This shift again seems to be prompted by Lermontov, as he pushes Vicky toward the magical, deathlike world of dance: "There it is, all waiting for you," he says, the new music beginning as he gestures to the stage, as if conjuring this world beyond. "Sorrow will pass, believe me. Life is so unimportant. And from now on you will *dance*, like nobody ever before."[51] Vicky, handed her ballet shoes and led toward the stage, is suddenly stopped in her tracks—visually, by the red shoes taking control of her feet, but also sonically, as the soprano's rising melody becomes stuck on its apogee, to be overtaken by the orchestral music of the "Red Shoes" overture. Possessed by forces beyond her control, she turns and runs down the theater steps, finally throwing herself off a balcony to fall crumpled to the tracks below, directly in the path of an oncoming train.

Scholars have often commented on the strangeness of this dressing room scene, with its sudden shift into hyper-theatrical melodrama.[52] Part of its strangeness, I would suggest, is that it functions covertly like another of Powell's "composed" scenes, although he never identified it as such. The moment Julian enters is when the scene suddenly departs from reality, most obviously because his appearance—with the slicked-back hair, black leather coat, and cold stare of a Weimar villain—is so uncharacteristic (Figure 5.4). But this is also the moment the *music* enters, as the overture begins with a dramatic gesture just as Julian appears (from behind a theatrical curtain that covers the door). This diegetic music plays continuously (almost a full five minutes) until the moment Vicky crosses the opera house threshold—another of those thresholds between ordinary and enchanted worlds in

[49] Brian Easdale, "The Composition of Opera" (1962), p. 5, Michael Powell Collection MLP-1-21-2-2-1, British Film Institute Special Collections (hereafter BFI Special Collections). Also see Moor, *Powell and Pressburger*, 212.

[50] *The Red Shoes*, 2:05:00.

[51] Ibid., 2:06:00.

[52] Moor, *Powell and Pressburger*, 218; Ian Christie, *Arrows of Desire: The Films of Michael Powell and Emeric Pressburger*, 2nd ed. (London: Faber and Faber, 1994), 67.

Figure 5.4 *The Red Shoes*, Julian enters.

The Red Shoes—and the film switches to a more realist, outdoor world. The dressing room scene thus functions much like the "Red Shoes" ballet itself and even more like the climactic scene of *Black Narcissus*, which similarly involves a woman possessed who falls over a precipice to her death. Powell, recall, described that scene as an "opera." Here, at the end of *The Red Shoes*, the operatic tendencies of his "composed film" are fully realized, and music's power to control is centrally at issue.

This theme of control is most apparent in Lermontov's strange ability to cue the music. Moor has pointed out that he is "stage-managing" this scene, as elsewhere in the film.[53] However, it is more fundamentally *the music* than the stage that he seems to manage. He is like Powell's description of the film director of composed scenes, controlling the action "with the authority of the music."[54] Indeed, with his white tie and cueing gestures, Lermontov looks more and more like a *conductor*. Even his odd final gesture as Vicky departs for the stage, where "he suddenly lets his arms fly in an ecstatic

[53] Moor, *Powell and Pressburger*, 218.
[54] Powell, *A Life in Movies*, 583.

Figure 5.5 *The Red Shoes*, Lermontov as conductor (ending).

eruption" according to Moor, can be explained as the motion of a conductor (Figure 5.5).[55] The idea of Lermontov vying with Julian for the conductor's role—or even secretly occupying it—has already been established in the film, in the "Red Shoes" ballet itself, where the image of Lermontov, arms raised just as in the dressing room scene, briefly replaces the conductor Julian in Vicky's hysterical vision (Figure 5.6). Now that Julian has literally vacated his role as conductor of his own opera—leaving its Covent Garden premiere—Lermontov takes over completely. If Julian is able to sacrifice the enchantment of music and step away from his position of control, this only gives Lermontov more power. Now he can co-opt even Julian's more sincere, expressive music (not just the ballet music that he commissioned) for his own purposes. What makes music especially insidious here is that it is not just a mysterious force of the beyond, but also something wielded by men; they either resist its power (like Julian) or use it to control, recalling the dictators and demagogues of the recent war.

[55] Moor, *Powell and Pressburger*, 218.

Figure 5.6 *The Red Shoes*, Lermontov as conductor ("Red Shoes" ballet).

Ultimately, however, music is revealed in *The Red Shoes* as a dangerous force of possession beyond men's control, which they unleash at their own peril. While Lermontov seems to magically wield music's power in his conductorly role, he then *loses* control when Vicky leaves his presence, at the moment the shoes—and the music—fully possess her and she plummets to her death. Moreover, music's power of possession extends to Lermontov himself. When he emerges on stage moments later to announce her death, he is no longer a conductor or a puppeteer. He is revealed as a puppet himself—Powell describes Walbrook playing this scene "like a marionette," with a voice "like that of a ventriloquist's dummy."[56] He is a broken figure, his animating force having deserted him. As in *The Glass Mountain*, but with more devastating effects, music is a dangerous force of possession. Associated with totalizing demands and affective intensity, it is incompatible with ordinary life—or indeed life itself. But if *The Glass Mountain* insisted on life and normality, however unconvincingly, *The Red Shoes* is more ambivalent, showing

[56] Powell, *A Life in Movies*, 639.

the attractions of totalizing commitments, as well as their dangers, while thematizing their incompatibility with modern English life.

What does all of this have to do with war? It is especially in light of the larger turn toward music as a force of possession in postwar British film that *The Red Shoes*' themes can be tied to the retrospective allure of wartime commitment—an allure registered well beyond this eccentric film. This larger turn gives new resonance to Powell's own comments linking a postwar impulse to die for art with wartime demands to die for democracy, and to Powell's new interest in music as a controlling authority in his postwar films. Seen in this light, *The Red Shoes* offers a meditation on how the affective intensity of total war continued to haunt the present, with music serving as a central figure of this haunting. It also shows how the efficacy and power with which music was endowed in wartime became an object of suspicion or danger when loosed from its wartime goals.

There are also two slightly more fanciful ways of reading war into *The Red Shoes*. One has to do with that villa on the French Riviera, where the music that eventually destroys the film's characters is first heard and which seems haunted in particular by the acousmatic tenor voice. In choosing locations for this and other Riviera scenes, Powell relied on his intimate prewar knowledge of the area, where he had spent his holidays from boyhood through the 1930s, and had also lived for three years in the 1920s. For *The Red Shoes*, he describes in his autobiography, "we had to find villas like private palaces, untouched by war."[57] Indeed, in *The Red Shoes*, the Riviera can seem a place outside of war. But this is not always the case in Powell's account. He describes, for instance, his ambivalence about returning to France to film *The Red Shoes*—his first visit since the war and since "those of us who loved France," as he put it, "realised there was a France we didn't know" (637). And when he describes the villa in this scene, Villa La Leopolda, he dwells in particular on the garden, "neglected since the war" and overgrown with weeds (638). His remark resonates with another story he tells, about his friend Bussell, the "head gardener and agent" at a nearby villa, Maryland, who also looked after surrounding villas (perhaps including La Leopolda).[58] Bussell, he reports in his biography (twice), was arrested near the end of the war and died in a Vichy camp (637). Powell included a scene shot at Maryland in *The Red Shoes* as a "dedication to Bussell's memory," he said (103). But the

[57] Ibid., 637.
[58] Ibid., 103.

overgrown garden in the Leopolda scene, where Vicky ascends the magical and seemingly never-ending staircase as a mysterious voice sounds, might be a more haunting testament to this loss, giving new resonance to this scene as the site of music's originary haunting in the film.

The other link with wartime has to do with the film's reflection on the status of the arts themselves in postwar London. It is to this aspect of the film that I turn now, as a way of bringing both this chapter and *Mobilizing Music* to a close.

Conclusion: The Enchantment of "War Time"

If *The Red Shoes* presents ballet and music as having the power to possess, this is mainly the case outside England. Both the enchantment and the danger of music are displaced to Europe, in this most European of British films, much as they are in *The Glass Mountain*. Meanwhile, in postwar London, ballet is an empty and somewhat threadbare luxury. What is at issue, I would argue, is not only geography, but a temporal relationship with war. For while *The Red Shoes* is set very clearly in a postwar moment, it also illustrates how the before, during, and after of war linger and intermingle in the experience of postwar life. If ballet generally thrives elsewhere in *The Red Shoes*, the film does find a domestic location for art's flourishing—one superior to any of its postwar homes beyond England—in a retrospective vision of the war culture described throughout this book. Indeed, *The Red Shoes* might be seen as the story of an attempt to recapture this state of "ecstasy," an attempt that goes inevitably wrong.

Pressburger first wrote the script for *The Red Shoes* in 1937, and then heavily revised it in 1946, making this another film split between the before and after of war.[59] And yet, few films could be so firmly embedded in the postwar reawakening of London's cultural scene. It is caught up most of all in the reopening of the Royal Opera House (ROH), a locus of official cultural renewal in the immediate postwar period. In 1946, the year Powell and Pressburger began work on the film, the ROH was established as the new national home of opera and ballet, incorporating the Sadler's Wells ballet and

[59] Moor, *Powell and Pressburger*, 200; Powell, *A Life in Movies*, 611–618. An early treatment of the film, written by G. B. Stern, had an entirely different plot from the postwar film, one focused explicitly on the Ballets Russes, with no supernatural themes ("A pair of red shoes, by G. B. Stern, property of Korda (treatment)," Michael Powell Collection MLP 1-1-59-1-1, BFI Special Collections).

building a new opera company from scratch. It was the only institution to be directly controlled by the newly founded Arts Council of Great Britain, and it received by far the biggest chunk of its funding in what seemed to signal a shift away from the more modest and participatory wartime vision of the democratization of high culture.[60] The first performance at the reopened ROH would be Tchaikovsky's ballet *Sleeping Beauty*. As Kate Guthrie observes, it was a topical choice, resonating with the theater's magical transformation, its awakening from a long and grim night.[61]

It is at this postwar ROH that *The Red Shoes* begins as an eager young crowd rushes the doors, excited to see a new work by the Ballet Lermontov. If the gesture to the Ballets Russes belongs to the 1930s, in other ways the setting has realist specificity.[62] The poster highlighted in the opening moments, for instance, carefully replicates the design for ROH's current productions, including the one for that 1946 *Sleeping Beauty*. Moreover, the whole making of the film is embedded in the developments at Covent Garden and in British ballet culture more generally. Its star was Moira Shearer, a dancer with the Sadler's Wells ballet who appeared in that 1946 production of *Sleeping Beauty* (first in a secondary role and then as Princess Aurora in spring 1947). Powell first saw her in a revival of the new Sadler's Wells ballet *Miracle in the Gorbals* (1944), choreographed by Robert Helpmann (with music by Arthur Bliss).[63] Helpmann, a principal dancer at Covent Garden, was the main choreographer of *The Red Shoes* and plays a dancer in the film, as does Léonide Massine, a former fixture of the Ballets Russes. Marie Rambert, one of the two doyennes of British ballet, also makes an appearance, in a scene depicting her company at the Mercury Theatre, its prewar home. And the distinctive look of the film is the work of the designer Heins Heckroth, who had worked with the Ballets Jooss, another important presence in Britain's wartime dance scene.

[60] See Heather Wiebe, *Britten's Unquiet Pasts: Sound and Memory in Postwar Reconstruction* (Cambridge: Cambridge University Press, 2012), 29. As Kate Guthrie argues, the postwar revival of ballet at Covent Garden was still very much driven by populist concerns, in tension with ballet's historic association with luxury and elite culture. See Kate Guthrie, "Awakening 'Sleeping Beauty': The Creation of National Ballet in Britain," *Music & Letters* 96 (2015): 418–448, especially 420–421.

[61] Guthrie, "Awakening 'Sleeping Beauty,'" 419.

[62] On the visually realist approach in the opening Royal Opera House scenes, also see Nanette Aldred, "Hein Heckroth and The Archers," in *The Cinema of Michael Powell: International Perspective on an English Film-Maker*, ed. Ian Christie and Andrew Moor (London: British Film Institute, 2005), 192–193. As Aldred notes, the Royal Opera House scenes were filmed in an elaborate reconstruction at Pinewood studios.

[63] Powell, *A Life in Movies*, 618–619.

Given its rootedness in British ballet culture, it seems strange how insistent *The Red Shoes* is on locating ballet elsewhere, much as *The Glass Mountain* locates opera in Italy. Like music, ballet in Britain had a long history of being exoticized, but the goal of many of the figures and institutions highlighted in *The Red Shoes* was to develop a homegrown art.[64] *The Red Shoes*' tendency to locate the enchantment of art outside Britain seems especially striking when compared to Powell and Pressburger's wartime films, which more often display the opposite tendency. *A Canterbury Tale*, for instance, works powerfully to enchant the English landscape, which it renders magically animated with music and sound.

In The Red Shoes ballet clearly becomes more magical and more divorced from life as the film progresses, and especially as it moves further and further away from England. While the Covent Garden scenes render dance as labor and back-stage politics, the next stop is Paris, where the company rehearses *Giselle* (with its ghostly maidens dancing men to death) in the opulent Foyer de la danse of the Paris Opéra. But it is when the Ballet Lermontov arrives in Monte Carlo and the French Riviera that the magic of ballet comes into full force. This is where *The Red Shoes* is conceived and performed. By the time the ballet is staged, at the Salle Garnier in Monte Carlo, the ballet has completely taken over real life. In this fifteen-minute sequence, all sense of the theater as a real place disappears, and the ballet is situated instead in a kind of fantasy space. Its characters, moreover, merge with and take over the cinematic characters who play them, just as the red shoes themselves take over their wearer. Life has become absorbed in art. This is also, of course, the central "composed" section of the film, where every detail is ultimately controlled by music itself. From here, the film becomes almost entirely absorbed in theater. All we see of the world tour that follows is a montage of performances, elaborately staged and all about magic and animation: *Coppélia* and Massine's own *La Boutique Fantasque*—both about animated dolls—as well as *La Sylphide*, with its airy spirits. Back-stage scenes of rehearsal recede, as indeed does the audience, which is never shown during these performances, giving them a newly absorptive effect.

In the first quarter of the film, though, set in England, art and quotidian reality have a more contested relationship. When *The Red Shoes* begins at Covent Garden, it is with a performance of a new ballet called *Heart of Fire*, by an English composer. Like the other ballets in the film, this one has some

[64] Guthrie, "Awakening 'Sleeping Beauty,'" 432–436.

element of myth or magic. The program, highlighted briefly, tells us that it is based on a "Scythian legend"—recalling early staples of the Ballets Russes such as *The Rite of Spring* or *Firebird*—and features a phoenix and a warrior as well as "spirits of the ruined town" (perhaps all gestures to London's postwar recovery amid the memory and traces of war). But from the little of the performance shown, in a long shot, the sets look shoddy—a few cardboard columns strewn about—and the costumes are cheap, depending on some painted streaks and clumsy headgear to suggest the uncanny nature of the spirits. It is hard to believe this is the same Ballet Lermontov seen later in the film. Indeed, the scene seems to reflect a resistance to glamor and spectacle that Guthrie has described as characteristic of British ballet, and of Sadler's Wells in particular, and which was self-consciously used to set it apart from the Ballets Russes.[65] In addition to the flimsy costumes and sets, the dancing here is dull and unremarkable, and the music is self-consciously insipid, lacking the brilliance of "The Red Shoes."

If the ballet lacks glamor, though, there is plenty to be found in the hall. Whereas the audience is almost entirely absent outside England, here it provides most of the spectacle, as the dancing itself is largely lost in high-society intrigues. The film thematizes this idea with a shot of the conductor's score reading "curtains up," followed by a shot not of the stage, but of the curtained boxes: Lady Nestor, Vicky's aunt, is trying to entice Lermontov to her post-performance party by way of the ballet's composer. Only Vicky is completely absorbed in the ballet, looking through her opera glasses and ignoring everything else around her, transfixed. It is only after alighting on Vicky that the camera turns to the ballet performance, as if directed to it by her gaze. Meanwhile, the gallery is filled with a mob of excited students, jostling for seats, fighting over programs, eating sandwiches, reading newspapers, and spotting recognizable figures in the circle. In this opening scene, then, ballet is not particularly magical or enchanting. The excitement comes from the audience: from the postwar restoration of a lively young intelligentsia freed of wartime concerns, and of a glittering high society after years of austerity. The party scene immediately after the performance reinforces this focus on the audience while offering an even clearer critique of art as luxury entertainment for high society.

However, there is an alternative English space for ballet in *The Red Shoes*, where its relationship with enchantment and ordinary life is slightly

[65] Ibid., 434–436.

different. One scene in the first section of the film briefly abandons Covent Garden to feature a performance by the Ballet Rambert at the tiny Mercury Theatre in Notting Hill, with Vicky in the lead role. This is a curiously outlying scene, one that has never garnered much critical attention. But it is also pivotal, as the moment when Lermontov first sees balletic greatness in Vicky, and when ballet itself suddenly seems magical.

At the Mercury, Vicky is dancing the lead in a scene from *Swan Lake*: Act II, Dances of the Swans. When she begins a solo set of turns across the stage, the music picks up in tempo slightly, building to a climax as she becomes increasingly exhilarated. Close-ups of her face are interspersed with point-of-view shots of the hall, everything around her transformed into a dizzying blur as she turns and turns. When she pauses, she sees Lermontov in the audience, gazing at her, and, for a moment, it is unclear who is mesmerizing whom. (Indeed, in earlier versions of the screenplay, it is unclear if Lermontov is there at all or is a figment of Vicky's imagination.[66]) She gazes back (Figure 5.7), in a close-up that anticipates later shots of Vicky in various states of possession: in the "Red Shoes" ballet as her character realizes she is possessed by the dancing shoes (Figure 5.8) and, at the end of the film, as the real Vicky loses control to the shoes and runs to her death (Figure 5.9). The Mercury Theatre scene develops the theme of Lermontov as a magician figure—another Svengali like the hero of *The Seventh Veil*—who demands complete devotion to art and who seems, like art itself, to exert some sort of mesmeric force on Vicky. These themes are echoed in the ballet itself, in which Vicky dances the role of Odette, the woman turned into a swan by an evil magician. But the scene more broadly thematizes the power of total devotion to art, under the right circumstances, and the state of ecstasy that devotion can produce, even in the midst of ordinariness. When Vicky later dances "The Red Shoes" for the first time, Lermontov recalls this moment at the Mercury, saying: "I want you to dance tonight with the same ecstasy I've seen in you only once before. . . . Yes, at the Mercury Theatre in London on a wet Saturday afternoon."[67]

It is perhaps the only wet afternoon in *The Red Shoes*. But this alone is not enough to explain the scene's remarkable visual difference from the rest of the film. This difference is signaled instantly by the opening shot, of a grim

[66] "Red Shoes: A Screenplay by Emeric Pressburger & Keith Winter," Michael Powell Collection MLP 1-1-59-1-2, BFI Special Collections.

[67] *Red Shoes*, 1:05:00.

Figure 5.7 *The Red Shoes*, Vicky possessed (*Swan Lake*).

Figure 5.8 *The Red Shoes*, Vicky possessed ("Red Shoes" ballet).

Figure 5.9 *The Red Shoes*, Vicky possessed (ending).

urban street in the pouring rain, filled with grayish-beige buildings and figures (Figure 5.10). The film color, normally supersaturated, is suddenly washed out, especially compared to the previous shots outside the ROH, with their bright colors and brilliant sunshine (Figure 5.11). The Mercury Theatre scene, I would argue, serves in part as a window onto a wartime history of ballet, despite its postwar setting (and the postwar repertory announced on the poster outside). More broadly, it suggests an imaginative shift into a kind of "war time." The scene's visual difference from the rest of the film—its reversion to the gray world of austerity—is one sign of this displacement. Another is the setting at the Mercury, a simple theater that looks more like a church and was indeed formerly used as a church hall. Ballet Rambert had been based there in the 1930s, but it had outgrown the tiny theater by the end of the war and rarely performed there by the time *The Red Shoes* was made. In wartime, it had presented lunchtime performances—much like Myra Hess's concerts and indeed inspired by them, according to one of the dancers—at the Arts Theatre Club, a few blocks away from the

Figure 5.10 *The Red Shoes*, a wet afternoon at the Mercury Theatre.

Figure 5.11 *The Red Shoes*, outside the Royal Opera House.

National Gallery, eventually adding later afternoon performances as well.[68] From 1943, it toured extensively with the Council for the Encouragement of the Arts, performing at hostels, factory canteens, and other improvised venues. A Ministry of Information newsreel shows one such performance at a factory canteen; here, the dancers rehearse and prepare in makeshift spaces, hanging stockings on rafters, and eventually perform a light work, *Peter and the Wolf*, for their lunchtime audience.[69]

These sorts of conditions are clearly evoked in *The Red Shoes*. As the sound of pouring rain outside the Mercury gives way to the sound of music, the scene shifts to the matinée performance inside the theater. *Swan Lake* is the definition of ballet as an enchanted world, but, aside from the dancing itself, everything is shabby and makeshift. As the opening shots reveal, the music comes from a gramophone and a speaker perched in the rafters of the ugly little hall. Later, the gramophones—two of them, operated by spare dancers—malfunction slightly, creating a glitch in the music and pained flinches all round, including from Rambert herself, crouching in the back. The stage is tiny, the waiting dancers clearly visible in the wings. The set is nothing but a painted backdrop. In all of this, the scene recalls the halls and theaters of wartime tours, as well as the grander but similarly improvised surroundings of the National Gallery concerts. The audience, meanwhile, is transfixed. Shot from the front and shown as a collective mass, their upturned faces display variations on the same earnest, attentive gaze (Figure 5.12). In this respect, the shot palpably recalls images of the National Gallery audience in Humphrey Jennings's 1946 documentary *A Diary for Timothy* (discussed in Chapter 1), transformed by music (see Figure 1.5). Still and silent, they could not be more different from the rambunctious crowd at Covent Garden. And unlike even the attentive Vicky in that scene—who watched the dancing carefully from afar, with the mediation of opera glasses—this audience is intimately connected to the performance, the faces in the first few rows bathed in the light of the stage.

[68] Ballet Rambert merged with the London Ballet in 1940, as the Rambert-London Ballet. It was dissolved in 1941, then reinstated under the auspices of CEMA in 1943 (https://www.rambert.org.uk/performance-database/timeline/ accessed November 12, 2020). Mary Clarke, *Dancers of Mercury: The Story of Ballet Rambert* (London: Adam and Charles Black, 1962), 124 (on Hess) and 117–146 (for a detailed wartime history of the company).

[69] The film is *Worker and War-Front Magazine Issue no. 10*, held at the Imperial War Museums, and viewable online: https://www.iwm.org.uk/collections/item/object/1060005141 (November 12, 2020). Clarke describes *Peter and the Wolf* (chor. Frank Staff, 1940) as epitomizing Ballet Rambert's aesthetic (*Dancers of Mercury*, 122–123).

Figure 5.12 *The Red Shoes*, the audience at the Mercury Theatre.

Here, as in the discourse around the National Gallery concerts, art offers beauty and sustenance in the midst of grimness. The conditions of wartime—conditions replicated in this scene—are conducive to total devotion. But these are also the conditions that give birth to the dangerous forces unleashed in the rest of the film. In *The Red Shoes*, moreover—and in the other two postwar films considered in this chapter—it is as if the ultimately violent, life-destroying purposes for which music was mobilized were finally unveiled.

If postwar musicians and administrators were busily building on a wartime discourse of music's utility, postwar cinema registers a stronger set of anxieties about the powers that accrued to music in total war, and about the demands for productivity and efficacy placed on it. At the same time, music served as a medium—in all the senses of that word—for the lingering affects of wartime, capable of reanimating them in ways that were both invigorating and dangerous.

Filmography

Battle for Music: The London Philharmonic Orchestra at War. Directed by Donald Taylor. Strand Film Company, 1943.
Black Narcissus. Directed by Michael Powell and Emeric Pressburger. The Archers, 1947.
Brief Encounter. Directed by David Lean. Cineguild, 1945.
A Canterbury Tale. Directed by Michael Powell and Emeric Pressburger. The Archers, 1944.
Dangerous Moonlight. Directed by Brian Desmond Hurst. RKO Radio Pictures, 1941.
A Diary For Timothy. Directed by Humphrey Jennings. Crown Film Unit, 1946.
Field Psychiatry for the Medical Officer. Verity Films for the War Office and the Directorate of Army Kinematography, 1944.
Germanin: Die Geschichte einer kolonialen Tat. Directed by Max W. Kimmich. UFA, 1943.
The Glass Mountain. Directed by Henry Cass. Renown Pictures, 1949.
Listen to Britain. Directed by Humphrey Jennings. Crown Film Unit, 1942.
London Can Take It. Directed by Harry Watt and Humphrey Jennings. Crown Film Unit, 1940.
Love Story. Directed by Leslie Arliss. Gainsborough Pictures, 1944.
Men of Two Worlds. Directed by Thorold Dickinson. Two Cities, 1946.
Millions Like Us. Directed by Sidney Gilliat and Frank Launder. Gainsborough Pictures, 1943.
The Red Shoes. Directed by Michael Powell and Emeric Pressburger. The Archers, 1948.
The Seventh Veil. Directed by Compton Bennett. Ortus Films, 1945.
Spare Time. Directed by Humphrey Jennings. GPO Film Unit, 1939.
While I Live. Directed by John Harlow. Edward Dryhurst Productions, 1947.

Bibliography

Archives

British Film Institute National Archive, London, UK.
British Film Institute Reubens Library, London, UK.
British Film Institute Special Collections, London & Berkshire, UK.
Eileen Joyce Collection, Callaway Centre Archive, University of Western Australia, Crawley, Australia.
The National Archives of the UK, Kew, UK.

Selected Primary Sources

Adorno, T. W. "Commodity Music Analyzed" (1934–40). In *Quasi una Fantasia*, tr. Rodney Livingstone. New York: Verso, 1992.

Brook, Donald. *Masters of the Keyboard*. London: Rockliff, 1946.

Brown, Felix. "Civilian Psychiatric Air-Raid Casualties." *Lancet* 237 (May 31, 1941): 686–691.

Cary, Joyce. *The Case for African Freedom and Other Writings on Africa*. Austin: University of Texas Press, 1962.

Clark, Kenneth. "Concerts in the National Gallery." *The Listener* 22 (November 2, 1939): 884.

Clarke, Mary. *Dancers of Mercury: The Story of Ballet Rambert*. London: Adam and Charles Black, 1962.

Coward, Noël. *Brief Encounter*. In *Masterworks of the British Cinema*. London: Faber, 1990.

Dean, Basil. *The Theatre at War*. London: George G. Harrap and Co., 1956.

Dickinson, Thorold. "Making a Film in Tanganyika Territory." In *The British Film Yearbook 1947–48*, edited by Peter Noble, 53–58. London: Skelton Robinson British Yearbooks, 1948.

Dickinson, Thorold. "Search for Music." In *The Penguin Film Review* 2, 9–15. London: Penguin, 1947.

Falls, Cyril. *The Nature of Modern Warfare*. London: Methuen, 1941.

Fisher, E. *Men of Two Worlds: Adapted from the Two Cities Film*. London: World Film Publications, 1946.

Gibbon, Monk. *The Red Shoes Ballet: A Critical Study*. London: Saturn Press, 1948.

Hardy, Forsyth. "The British Documentary Film." In *Twenty Years of British Film 1925–1945*, edited by Michael Balcon et al., 45–80. London: Falcon Press, 1947.

Hill, Ralph. "New Books About Music." In *Music 1951*, 159–172. London: Penguin, 1951.

Huntley, John. *British Film Music*. London: Skelton Robinson, 1947.

Lassimonne, Denise, and Howard Ferguson, eds. *Myra Hess by Her Friends*. London: Hamish Hamilton, 1966.

Mackerness, Eric David. *A Social History of English Music*. London: Routledge & Kegan Paul: 1964.

Mayer, J. P. *British Cinemas and Their Audiences: Sociological Studies*. London: Dennis Dobson, 1948.

McNaught, W. "Music." In *The Annual Register: A Review of Public Events at Home and Abroad for the Year 1943*, edited by M. Epstein, 346–351. London: Longmans, Green & Co., 1944.

Mellers, Wilfrid. *Music and Society: England and the European Tradition*. London: Dennis Dobson, 1946.

National Gallery Concerts in Aid of the Musicians Benevolent Fund, 10th October 1939–10th October 1944. London: National Gallery, 1944.
Noble, Peter, ed. *The British Film Yearbook 1947–48.* London: Skelton Robinson, 1948.
Noble, Peter. *The Negro in Films.* London: Skelton Robinson, 1948.
Powell, Michael. *A Life in Movies: An Autobiography by Michael Powell.* London: Faber and Faber, 1986.
Sullivan, Harry Stack. "Psychiatric Aspects of Morale." *American Journal of Sociology* 47, no. 3 (1941): 277–301.
Weisgall, Hugo. "English Musical Life: A Symposium, IV." *Tempo* 12 (September 1945): 8–10.

Selected Secondary Sources

Agawu, Kofi. *Representing African Music: Postcolonial Notes, Queries, Positions.* London: Taylor & Francis, 2003.
Aldgate, Anthony, and Jeffrey Richards. *Britain Can Take It: British Cinema in the Second World War.* London: I. B. Tauris, 2007.
Anderson, Ben. "Modulating the Excess of Affect: Morale in a State of 'Total War.'" In *The Affect Theory Reader,* edited by Melissa Gregg and Gregory J. Seigworth, 161–186. Durham, NC: Duke University Press, 2010.
Anderson, Ben. *Encountering Affect: Capacities, Apparatuses, Conditions.* Farnham: Ashgate, 2014.
Baade, Christina. "Radio Symphonies: The BBC, Everyday Listening and the Popular Classics Debate During the People's War' Baade." In *Ubiquitous Musics: The Everyday Sounds That We Don't Always Notice,* edited by Marta García Quiñones, Anahid Kassabian, and Elena Boschi, 49–71. London: Routledge, 2013.
Baade, Christina. *Victory Through Harmony: The BBC and Popular Music in World War II.* New York: Oxford University Press, 2011.
Bailkin, Jordanna. *The Afterlife of Empire.* Berkeley: University of California Press, 2012.
Beattie, Keith. *Humphrey Jennings.* Manchester: Manchester University Press, 2010.
Berlant, Lauren. *The Female Complaint: The Unfinished Business of Sentimentality in American Culture.* Durham, NC: Duke University Press, 2005.
Bérubé, Allan. *Coming Out Under Fire: The History of Gay Men and Women in World War Two.* New York: The Free Press, 1990.
Binkley, Sam. "Kitsch as a Repetitive System." *Journal of Material Culture* 5, no. 2 (2000): 131–152.
Bourke, Joanna. "Disciplining the Emotions: Fear, Psychiatry and the Second World War." In *War, Medicine and Modernity,* edited by Roger Cooter, Mark Harrison, and Steve Sturdy, 225–238. London: Sutton, 1998.
Bourne, Stephen. *Under Fire: Black Britain in Wartime 1939–45.* Cheltenham: The History Press, 2020.
Brooks, Peter. *The Melodramatic Imagination: Balzac, Henry James, Melodrama, and the Mode of Excess.* New Haven, CT: Yale University Press, 1976.
Calder, Angus. *The Myth of the Blitz.* London: John Cape, 1991.
Chapman, James. *The British at War: Cinema, State and Propaganda, 1939–1945.* London: I. B. Tauris, 1998.
Christie, Ian. *Arrows of Desire: The Films of Michael Powell and Emeric Pressburger.* 2nd ed. London: Faber and Faber, 1994.
Christie, Ian, and Andrew Moor, eds. *The Cinema of Michael Powell: International Perspective on an English Film-Maker.* London: British Film Institute, 2005.
Cook, Pam. *Screening the Past: Memory and Nostalgia in Cinema.* New York: Routledge, 2005.
Daughtry, Martin. *Listening to War: Sound, Music, Trauma, and Survival in Wartime Iraq.* New York: Oxford University Press, 2015.

Daughtry, Martin. "Thanatosonics: Ontologies of Acoustic Violence." *Social Text* 32 (2014): 25–51.

Davis, Richard. *Eileen Joyce: A Portrait.* Fremantle, Australia: Fremantle Arts Centre Press, 2001.

Deer, Patrick. *Culture in Camouflage: War, Empire, and Modern British Literature.* New York: Oxford University Press, 2009.

DeNora, Tia. "The Concerto and Society." In *The Cambridge Companion to the Concerto*, edited by Simon Keefe, 19–32. Cambridge: Cambridge University Press, 2005.

Dixon, Thomas. *Weeping Britannia: Portrait of a Nation in Tears.* Oxford: Oxford University Press, 2015.

Doane, Mary Ann. *The Desire to Desire: The Woman's Films of the 1940s.* Bloomington: Indiana University Press, 1987.

Donnelly, K. J. *British Film Music and Film Musicals.* Basingstoke: Palgrave Macmillan, 2007.

Douglas, Susan. *Listening In: Radio and the American Imagination.* Minneapolis: University of Minnesota Press, 2004.

Dyer, Richard. *Brief Encounter.* London: BFI, 1993.

Dyer, Richard. *Heavenly Bodies: Film Stars and Society.* London: Routledge, 2003.

Dyer, Richard. *Nino Rota: Music, Film and Feeling.* London: BFI, 2010.

Dyer, Richard. *Only Entertainment.* London: Routledge, 1992.

Dyer, Richard. *Stars*, 2nd ed. London: BFI, 1998.

Ellis, Katherine. "Female Pianists and Their Male Critics in Nineteenth-Century Paris." *Journal of the American Musicological Society* 50 (1997): 353–385.

Fairclough, Pauline. "The 'Old Shostakovich': Reception in the British Press." *Music and Letters* 88 (2007): 266–296.

Fauser, Annegret. *Sounds of War: Music in the United States During World War II.* New York: Oxford University Press, 2013.

Favret, Mary A. *War at a Distance: Romanticism and the Making of Modern Wartime.* Princeton: Princeton University Press, 2009.

Fleeger, Jennifer. *Mismatched Women: The Siren's Song Through the Machine.* New York: Oxford University Press, 2014.

Fox, Jo. *Film Propaganda in Britain and Nazi Germany: World War II Cinema.* New York: Berg, 2007.

Franklin, Peter. "Modernism, Deception, and Musical Others." In *Western Music and Its Others: Difference, Representation, and Appropriation in Music*, edited by Georgina Born and David Hesmondhalgh. Berkeley: University of California Press, 2000.

Franklin, Peter. *Seeing Through Music: Gender and Modernism in Classic Hollywood Film.* Oxford: Oxford University Press, 2011.

Fry, Andy. *Paris Blues: African American Music and French Popular Culture*, 1920–1960. Chicago: Chicago University Press, 2014.

Fussell, Paul. *Wartime: Understanding and Behavior in the Second World War.* New York: Oxford University Press, 1989.

Gledhill, Christine, and Gillian Swanson, eds. *Nationalising Femininity: Culture, Sexuality and British Cinema in the Second World War.* Manchester: Manchester University Press, 1996.

Goodman, Jordan. *Paul Robeson: A Watched Man.* New York: Verso, 2013.

Goodman, Steve. *Sonic Warfare: Sound, Affect, and the Ecology of Fear.* Cambridge, MA: MIT Press, 2012.

Guerreri, Matthew. *The First Four Notes: Beethoven's Fifth and the Human Imagination.* New York: Knopf, 2012.

Guthrie, Kate. *The Art of Appreciation: Music and Middlebrow Culture in Modern Britain.* Berkeley: University of California Press, 2021.

Guthrie, Kate. "Awakening 'Sleeping Beauty': The Creation of National Ballet in Britain." *Music & Letters* 96 (2015): 418–448.

Guthrie, Kate. "Democratizing Art: Music Education in Postwar Britain." *Musical Quarterly* 97 (2015): 575–615.

Guthrie, Kate. "Soundtracks to the 'People's War.'" *Music & Letters* 94 (2013): 324–333.

Guthrie, Kate. "Vera Lynn on Screen: Popular Music and the 'People's War.'" *Twentieth-Century Music* 14 (2017): 245–270.

Guynn, William. *A Cinema of Nonfiction*. Rutherford, NJ: Fairleigh Dickinson University Press, 1990.

Hansen, Miriam. "The Mass Production of the Senses: Classical Cinema as Vernacular Modernism." *Modernism/Modernity* 6, no. 2 (1999): 59–77.

Harper, Sue, and Vincent Porter. "Moved to Tears: Weeping at the Cinema in Postwar Britain." *Screen* 37 no. 2 (Summer 1996): 152–173.

Hayes, Nick, and Jeff Hill, eds. *"Millions Like Us"? British Culture in the Second World War*. Liverpool: Liverpool University Press, 1999.

Hesmondhalgh, David. *Why Music Matters*. Chichester: Wiley Blackwell, 2013.

Highmore, Ben. *Cultural Feelings: Mood, Mediation and Cultural Politics*. London: Routledge, 2017.

Higson, Andrew. *Waving the Flag: Constructing a National Cinema in Britain*. Oxford: Clarendon Press, 1995.

Hodgkinson, Anthony W., and Rodney E. Sheratsky. *Humphrey Jennings: More Than a Maker of Films*. Hanover and London: University Press of New England, 1982.

Hoeckner, Berthold. *Film, Music, Memory*. Chicago: University of Chicago Press, 2020.

Hunter, Jefferson. *English Filming, English Writing*. Bloomington: Indiana University Press, 2010.

Jackson, Kevin. *Humphrey Jennings*. London: Picador, 2004.

Jackson, Kevin, ed. *The Humphrey Jennings Film Reader*. Manchester: Carcanet, 1993.

Jorge, Anita. "Liminal Soundscapes in Powell & Pressburger's Wartime Films." *Studies in European Cinema* 14, no. 1 (2017): 22–32.

Jorge, Anita. "A 'Symphony of Britain at War' or the 'Rhythm of Workaday Britain'? Len Lye's When the Pie Was Opened (1941) and the Musicalisation of Warfare." In *Soundings: Documentary Film and the Listening Experience*, edited by Geoffrey Cox et al., 220–239. Huddersfield: University of Huddersfield Press, 2018.

Killingray, David. *Fighting for Britain: African Soldiers in the Second World War*. Woodbridge: Boydell & Brewer, 2010.

Laing, Heather. *The Gendered Score: Music in 1940s Melodrama and the Woman's Film*. London: Routledge, 2007.

Lant, Antonia. *Blackout: Reinventing Women for Wartime British Cinema*. Princeton: Princeton University Press, 1991.

Leach, Jim. "The Poetics of Propaganda: Humphrey Jennings and *Listen to Britain*." In *Documenting the Documentary: Close Readings of Documentary Film and Video*, edited by Barry Keith Grant and Jeannette Sloniowski. Detroit: Wayne State University Press, 2013.

LeMahieu, D. L. *A Culture for Democracy: Mass Communication and the Cultural Mind in Britain Between the Wars*. Oxford: Clarendon, 1988.

Leventhal, F. M. "CEMA and the Arts in Wartime: 'The Best for the Most.'" *20th-Century British History* 1 (1990): 289–317.

Mansell, James. *The Age of Noise in Britain: Hearing Modernity*. Urbana: University of Illinois Press, 2017.

Manvell, Roger. *Films and the Second World War*. London: Dent, 1974.

Marzola, Alessandra. "Negotiating the Memory of the 'People's War': *Hamlet* and the Ghosts of Welfare in *A Diary for Timothy* by Humphrey Jennings (1944–45)." In *Shakespeare and Conflict: A European Perspective*, edited by C. Dente and S. Soncini, 132–144. Houndmills: Palgrave Macmillan, 2013.

Masilela, Ntongela. "New African Modernity and the New African Movement." In *The Cambridge History of South African Literature*, edited by David Attwell and Derek Attridge, 325–338. Cambridge: Cambridge University Press, 2012.

Matera, Marc. *Black London: The Imperial Metropolis and Decolonization in the Twentieth Century*. Berkeley: University of California Press, 2015.

McLean, Adrienne L. *Dying Swans and Madmen: Ballet, The Body, and Narrative Cinema*. New Brunswick: Rutgers University Press, 2008.

McVeigh, Simon. "A Free Trade in Music: London During the Long 19th Century in a European Perspective." *Journal of Modern European History* 5 (2007): 67–94.

Medhurst, Andy. "That Special Thrill: *Brief Encounter*, Homosexuality and Authorship." *Screen* 32, no. 2 (1991): 197–208.

Moor, Andrew. *Powell and Pressburger: A Cinema of Magic Spaces*. London: I. B. Tauris, 2012.

Morris, John. *Culture and Propaganda in World War II: Music, Film and the Battle for National Identity*. London: I. B. Tauris, 2014.

Murphy, Robert. *Realism and Tinsel: Cinema and Society in Britain 1939–49*. London: Routledge, 1989.

Napper, Lawrence. "Time and the Middlebrow in 1940s British Cinema." In *Middlebrow Cinema*, edited by Sally Faulkner, 71–87. London: Routledge, 2016.

Ngai, Sianne. *Ugly Feelings*. Cambridge, MA: Harvard University Press, 2005.

Noakes, Lucy. *Dying for the Nation: Death, Grief and Bereavement in Second World War Britain*. Manchester: Manchester University Press, 2020.

Overy, Richard. *Blood and Ruins: The Great Imperial War 1931–1945*. London: Allen Lane, 2021.

Pasler, Jann. *Composing the Citizen: Music as Public Utility in Third Republic France*. Berkeley: University of California Press, 2009.

Potter, Pamela M., Christina L. Baade, and Roberta Montemorra Marvin, eds. *Music in World War II: Coping with Wartime in Europe and the United States*. Bloomington: Indiana University Press, 2020.

Price, Hollie. *Picturing Home: Domestic Life and Modernity in 1940s British Film*. Manchester: Manchester University Press, 2021.

Pronay, Nicholas, and D. W. Spring, eds. *Propaganda, Politics and Film, 1918–45*. London: Macmillan, 1982.

Puckett, Kent. *War Pictures: Cinema, Violence, and Style in Britain, 1939–1945*. New York: Fordham University Press, 2017.

Rancière, Jacques. *Film Fables*. Translated by Emiliano Battista. Oxford: Berg, 2006.

Raykoff, Ivan. "Concerto con Amore." *Echo* 2, no. 1 (2000), https://echo.humspace.ucla.edu/issues/concerto-con-amore/

Raykoff, Ivan. *Dreams of Love: Playing the Romantic Pianist*. New York: Oxford University Press, 2014.

Raykoff, Ivan. "Hollywood's Embattled Icon." In *Piano Roles: A New History of the Piano*, edited by James Parakilas. New Haven, CT: Yale University Press, 2002.

Richards, Jeffrey. *Thorold Dickinson and the British Cinema*. London: Scarecrow, 1997.

Robbins, Christopher. *The Empress of Ireland: A Chronicle of an Unusual Friendship*. London: Scribner, 2004.

Rose, Sonya O. *Which People's War: National Identity and Citizenship in Wartime Britain, 1939–1945*. New York: Oxford University Press, 2003.

Rosen, David. "The Sounds of Music and War: Humphrey Jennings's and Stewart McAllister's *Listen to Britain* (1942)." In *"Coll'astuzia, col giudizio": Essays in Honor of Neal Zaslaw*, edited by Cliff Eisen, 390–428. Ann Arbor, MI: Steglein, 2009.

Russell, Dave. *Popular Music in England: A Social History*, 2nd ed. Manchester: Manchester University Press, 1997.

Saint-Amour, Paul K. *Tense Future: Modernism, Total War, Encyclopedic Form*. New York: Oxford University Press, 2015.

Sandler, Willeke. *Empire in the Heimat*. New York: Oxford University Press, 2018.

Savran, David. *A Queer Sort of Materialism: Recontextualizing American Theater*. Ann Arbor: University of Michigan Press, 2003.

Scarry, Elaine. *The Body in Pain: The Making and Unmaking of the World*. Oxford: Oxford University Press, 1985.

Scranton, Roy. *Total Mobilization: World War II and American Literature*. Chicago: University of Chicago Press, 2019.

Self, Geoffrey. *Light Music in Britain Since 1870: A Survey*. Aldershot: Ashgate, 2001.

Shapira, Michal. *The War Inside: Psychoanalysis, Total War, and the Making of the Democratic Self in Postwar Britain*. Cambridge: Cambridge University Press, 2013.

Spicer, Andrew. *Sydney Box*. British Film-Makers. Manchester: Manchester University Press, 2006.

Stansky, Peter, and William Abrahams. *London's Burning: Life, Death and Art in the Second World War*. London: Constable, 1994.

Stokes, Martin. "The Musical Citizen." *Etnomüzikoloji Dergisi/Ethnomusicology Journal* 1 (2018): 15–30.

Swaab, Peter. "Dickinson's Africa: *The High Command* and *Men of Two Worlds*." In *Thorold Dickinson: A World of Film*, edited by Philip Horne and Peter Swaab. Manchester: Manchester University Press, 2008.

Sweet, Matthew. *The West End Front: The Wartime Secrets of London's Grand Hotels*. London: Faber & Faber, 2011.

Swynnoe, Jan G. *The Best Years of British Film Music, 1936–1958*. Woodbridge: Boydell, 2002.

Sykes, Jim. "Ontologies of Acoustic Endurance: Rethinking Wartime Sound and Listening." *Sound Studies* 4 (2018): 35–60.

Thumim, Janet. "The Female Audience: Mobile Women and Married Ladies." In *Nationalising Femininity: Culture, Sexuality and the British Cinema in the Second World War*, edited by Christine Gledhill and Gillian Swanson. Manchester: Manchester University Press, 1996.

Tsai, Tsung-Han. "The 'Appassionata' Sonata in *A Diary for Timothy*." In *Soundings: Documentary Film and the Listening Experience*, edited by Geoffrey Cox et al., 187–200. Huddersfield: University of Huddersfield Press, 2018.

Tsika, Noah. *Traumatic Imprints: Cinema, Military Psychiatry, and the Aftermath of War*. Berkeley: University of California Press, 2018.

Tunbridge, Laura. *Singing in the Age of Anxiety: Lieder Performances in New York and London Between the World Wars*. Chicago: University of Chicago Press, 2018.

Vaughan, Dai. *Portrait of an Invisible Man: The Working Life of Stewart McAllister, Film Editor*. London: BFI Publishing, 1983.

Webster, Wendy. *Englishness and Empire 1939–1965*. Oxford: Oxford University Press, 2005.

Webster, Wendy. "Mumbo-Jumbo, Magic and Modernity: Africa in British Cinema, 1946–65." In *Film and the End of Empire*, edited by Lee Grieveson and Colin MacCabe, 237–250. London: Palgrave Macmillan, 2011.

Weight, Richard. "'Building a New British Culture': The Arts Centre Movement, 1943–53." In *The Right to Belong: Citizenship and National Identity in Britain, 1930–1960*, edited by Richard Weight and Abigail Beach, 157–181. London: St. Martin's Press, 1998.

Weingärtner, Jörn. *The Arts as a Weapon of War: Britain and the Shaping of National Morale in World War II*. London: Tauris Academic Studies, 2006.

Western, Tom. "Securing the Aural Border: Fieldwork and Interference in Post-War BBC Audio Nationalism." *Sound Studies* 1 (2015): 77–97.

Whitesell, Lloyd. "Concerto Macabre." *The Musical Quarterly* 88 (2005): 167–203.

Wiebe, Heather. *Britten's Unquiet Pasts: Sound and Memory in Postwar Reconstruction*. Cambridge: Cambridge University Press, 2012.

Wiebe, Heather. "Music and the Good Life in Postwar Britain: The Phenomenon of Eileen Joyce." In *The Oxford Handbook of Music and the Middlebrow*, edited by Kate Guthrie and

Christopher Chowrimootoo. Online ed. Oxford Academic. December 19, 2022, https://doi.org/10.1093/oxfordhb/9780197523933.013.6, accessed June 30, 2023.

Williams, Gavin, ed. *Hearing the Crimean War: Wartime Sound and the Unmaking of Sense*. Oxford: Oxford University Press, 2019.

Williams, Tony. *Structures of Desire: British Cinema, 1939–1955*. Albany: State University of New York Press, 2000.

Wright, David. *The Associated Board of the Royal Schools of Music: A Social and Cultural History*. Woodbridge: Boydell, 2012.

Yudice, George. *The Expediency of Culture: Uses of Culture in the Global Era*. Durham, NC: Duke University Press, 2003.

Zachernuk, Philip S. "Who Needs a Witch Doctor? Refiguring British Colonial Cinema in the 1940s." In *Film and the End of Empire*, edited by Lee Grieveson and Colin MacCabe, 95–118. London: Palgrave Macmillan, 2011.

Zank, Stephen, and Richard Leppert. "The Concert and the Virtuoso." In *Piano Roles: A New History of the Piano*, edited by James Parakilas, 203–216. New Haven, CT: Yale University Press, 2002.

Index

For the benefit of digital users, indexed terms that span two pages (e.g., 52–53) may, on occasion, appear on only one of those pages.

Figures are indicated by an italic *f* following the page number.